volume 1

DOMINATRIX

candid interviews
with 20 lifestyle
dominatrixes

COMPILED & EDITED BY ROY TURNER

MAGNOLIA BOOKS

Contents

About the writer

Born in London in 1952, Roy Turner graduated from Middlesex University and Saint Martins School of Art. He studied sociology and anthropology and wrote several historical biographies based on his extensive travels around the world.

Roy Turner was best known as the founder and editor of the fetish magazine Domina. Earlier career re-incarnations included teaching, acting, painting and decorating, carpentry, window dressing and window cleaning. He also worked briefly in a Wild West Rodeo in Arizona and had a shot at bullfighting in Spain.
Sadly, Roy died in 2007 after a long battle with cancer, but his diligent research and unique insights into the sadomasochistic world live on. A sister volume 'Submissive' featuring interviews with 20 female submissives, also compiled and edited by Roy Turner, is also published for the first time in book format by Magnolia Books and a second volume of 'Dominatrix', will be published soon.

Introduction

'Dominatrix' (Volume 1), is an exploration into the largely hidden world of the sadomasochistic female, along with Volume 2, it offers the definitive and most broad-ranging international study of the subject ever undertaken. Conducted over a 10-year period, by the BDSM magazine publisher and writer, Roy Turner, these eBooks offer a full, frank and totally unique insight into the real world of the dominatrix, those who work within the 'sex industry', as well as those who live out the 'Fem/Dom' lifestyle in private.

Mistress Antoinette reveals her Spanish clients were into 're-ligious' punishments whereas in England the number of men here who have a 'knicker' fetish continually amazes her. Interestingly enough, black knickers seem to be the big turn-on with men in England, whereas in Catholic Spain it is nearly always virginal white knickers that perhaps unsurprisingly, are the most popular.

And, Mistress Brigitte of the Dutch SM-Studio Phoenix, who form a very happy extended S&M 'family' comprising of a married Mistress and Master together with their male and female slaves who live, work and play together. And even do the baby-sitting and the school-run!

For the dedicated fetishist, no trip to the German city of Munich would be complete without a stopover at the studio of Lady Claudette; otherwise rather aptly named 'Bizarradise'. The true connoisseur of outrageous eroticism will find everything on offer and even the more unusual tastes happily accommodated in this liberal, or rather less conservative, oasis of traditionally ultra right-wing Bavaria.

The no-nonsense, business like approach of Mistress Jacqueline, is typical of American dominants. Her autobiography, 'Whips and Kisses', as well as her many TV appearances, mail order company and lecture tours Jacqueline has established herself as quite a formidable force on the American fetish scene.

Tokyo born Mistress Midori is the daughter of a Japanese mother and German-American father. Both her parents are university professors. Following a varied and successful career in the United States Army and in commerce, see how she found herself a professional dominatrix in San Francisco.

As her name suggests, Miss Spiteful's interests definitely lean toward the hard-core end of the SM spectrum, including the nailing of foreskins to tables and the burning of swastika's into flesh with cigarettes. She is also a leading practitioner of the intricate art of Japanese rope bondage. Despite her predilections for the more extreme forms of game-playing, she strictly adheres to the limits of safety and consensuality, practicing her dungeon crafts in South London.

Plus, many other revealing interviews with professional and lifestyle mistresses including the Chinese Dominatrix, Mai-Ling. Mistresses; Adelle, Andria, Christine Deering, Cassandra Payne, Dominique, Eva, Hades, Rowena, Xena. Goddesses, Venus and Dianna Vesta, plus Lady Amber and Madam Karra.

Publisher's Note: This book contains explicit sexual content, graphic language, and situations that some readers may find objectionable. It is intended for an adult audience.

Chapter 1: Mistress Antoinette

Born of mixed Spanish and Danish parentage, Mistress Antoinette spent her childhood in both countries before finally settling down in the United Kingdom. She has been a professional dominatrix for five years and divides her time between her dungeon and her nutritional health business.

One of the first dominatrix I ever met was this woman in Spain who was actually a high court judge! She was working from a very plush apartment in Madrid, and had given up her career in law in favour of being a dominatrix. She was the only one I knew of in Madrid who really understood what she was doing. In Spain, there are a lot of women who 'say' they do domination, but don't really know what it's about. They actually think that men who want this kind of thing are total perverts and hate working with these people. They think it's wrong, but they'll do it anyway for the money. You have to look at the history of Spain, I think. Franco died in 1975, and about 1987 you first started seeing things like pornographic videos and sex shops opening up. I take that as a signal of things relaxing a bit more. But even today, you can still walk into a sex shop in Madrid or any other Spanish city and you'll see very little that caters for domination. It's still in its infancy there.

I got to this level because I'm naturally a very sexual person. As a child in Denmark, I was always reading contact adverts like: 'Well endowed male seeks…', and all this kind of stuff. In Copenhagen, pornography is around everywhere. When I was five or six years old,

I got sent to the kiosk to buy normal newspapers and magazines for my mother and some pornography for my father! It's quite normal there and seen as quite creative, in fact.

I was involved in the fetish scene while I was still living in Spain, but not on a professional level. By that, I mean an exchange of money being involved. I wanted to get to know more people, but I didn't want to compromise my relationship; so I decided that, if I put money between it, then no one is going to get the wrong idea. They won't think that it is the prelude for a relationship or whatever. I'd gone to Madrid originally just for a long weekend, and a friend of mine put an advert in a magazine advertising for submissives. He interviewed the people for me and sent them a questionnaire to find the kind I would be interested in. I found three or four suitable people from different parts of Spain. Whenever I was in town, I would meet them in a nice luxurious hotel room. It had a wonderful marbled bathroom that was great to play in and old fashioned furniture that was really good for bondage.

When I practiced my profession in Spain, I found people were quite into 'religious' punishments. Here in England, tastes are a little more, how shall I put it, 'traditional'. Overall, I would say there is far more demand for my services in this country. Also, the number of men here who have a 'knicker' fetish continually amazes me. As I am quite a lingerie addict myself, there's plenty of scope for fun and games in that particular area. Interestingly enough, black knickers seem to be the big turn-on with men in England, whereas in Spain it is nearly always virginal white knickers that are the most popular.

Going back further, I really discovered S&M by accident. I was playing with a friend of mine and he told me about some things with domination that he wanted done to himself, and I started thinking: "Well, we can do this and we can do that!". My imagination just got going on it! I thought that this was great and really interesting! When you meet someone you can do this with there is a development between the two of you. It's your skill plus the other person as the recipient as well; how he reacts and discovers new things about himself. It's fun too!

That first time is rather a long story. Let's just say that, during a rather heated exchange of opinions, I got rather aggressive and then saw the astonishing effect it had on him. It must be said though, that I've always had a dominant nature, even as a child. But I didn't realise, until this particular incident, that it could be used so positively! My experience developed when I got introduced to the subject of spanking. That is, with me being the subject! I was very lucky because it was with a person who was very experienced and very skilled. He was English and had been doing it for years. I was working for a company doing consultancy around 1990 or 91, and we contacted this person through an advert. He showed my partner different techniques and we became good friends. He's since become a millionaire (though not through spanking!) And has moved to the United States. My partner and I just wanted something to add a new dimension to our relationship that didn't involve actual sex with other people.

I wasn't thinking of myself as either dominant or submissive at this point, because spanking in itself isn't like discipline; it's very erotic exercise. For me, what was interesting was the sensation. Anyway, I don't think a person can be a proper dominatrix unless she knows what's going on from the receiving end. As far as a female can, I've tried out all my equipment on myself, often without anyone's help. I've experimented with everything from nipple clamps to electric's, so I then know how it feels and it helps me develop new ideas on how it can be used. For instance, the medical and sports equipment I use is not erotic in itself, but in the way it is used.

I never take anyone on who I don't find interesting. After doing this for some years now, I pretty much know within the first few seconds whether I'm interested in the person or not. It's a personality thing as well, whether you go together or not. A submissive wouldn't find everybody dominant to him in a way he or she could accept, so it's important on both sides. If not, it becomes more of a farce than a game! That's not to say that there isn't any laughter. Sometimes there's quite a lot. For example, I was doing something with pegs, and my slave didn't want any more pegs. He put a funny German accent and said: "Nein, Nein!". I didn't understand what he meant, so I just said okay and put nine more pegs on him!

I would also refuse anybody who wanted scenarios that I didn't enjoy myself. Lately, a lot of people are ringing up and asking if I do castrations or tooth pulling and things like that. How serious they are, I don't know. I never get that far with them to find out! People also ask for kidnappings or to be chained up in public, but I don't do that either because I don't want the attention it would draw. I don't fancy being 'set up' by some newspaper either! I don't think that would be very beneficial. The people who are interested in the things I want to do are not interested in pushing it in the face of the rest of the public. I'm certainly not, anyway. It's a private thing and I don't think anyone needs to stumble on somebody tied up to a lamp post or whatever. I don't think it's fair on people. If I had a secluded garden or something then that would be fine. It would just add a different dimension.

I'm very professional in what I do, and try to establish a good relationship with my slaves from the outset; that way there is mutual respect. It's also important that people realise I am sensitive to their requirements and will do my best to explore their fantasies with understanding and invention. Sometimes they come along with fairly complete fantasies in mind. However, I'll always try to add something of my own to the proceedings. I am never predictable!

It is important that people realise that this has nothing to do with sex or perversion. There is an obvious visual side to it, but many people fail to grasp the mental side. For example, many of the men I see have wives or partners who aren't interested in every aspect of their sexuality. They don't come to me looking for sex (which, I stress, is never on offer anyway), but for someone who understands domination and is willing and capable of taking control of their life for an hour or so. Usually, this control is established through role-play, along with a combination of punishment and subtle teasing.

I get couples and single females sometimes as well; though usually the female is part of a couple and the man will speak to me first. They want to sort out if I will be responsible with her. Then he will drop her off and leave her with me. Sometimes they want to watch, but not often. I will, of course, insist on talking to the female myself to find out if she really wants to do this herself. There's no point for me otherwise. If a person can't relax and trust me, then there's no session. I wouldn't get anything out of it, and neither would they. There's no point in doing a session with someone who is unwilling. When I go into a session I want to be totally there and completely on the line with what's happening with that person. When I practiced in Spain, it was not at all uncommon for women to visit me for domination. You must understand that people have become much more liberated there since Franco, and that includes the women! Nowadays, they're not afraid to buy porn videos or to seek alternative forms of sexual satisfaction. I think it's an interesting comment on the social pressures in this country that, despite the occasional call from submissive women, only a handful of them have ever made an appointment!

The couples I see are usually both submissive. I'm kind of a catalyst, really; a sort of third element that's safe for them. They're often interested in the use of my dungeon and my experience with things that maybe they haven't thought about doing together before. When you are a couple you often notice that you're too close together, so it's quite nice to watch each other in bondage and see each others reactions. Plus you can play the two against each other, which I think works very well. When you are partners with someone and you've been together a long time, it's quite difficult to keep the fun going in the relationship. That's really how couples get into things like domination, and then maybe they find that they naturally like it, either as a dominant or a submissive.

The kind of clients I see are all very intelligent and very 'on the go'. They are making decisions and are interested in all aspects of life. This is probably contrary to what people have a picture of; that is, someone who just sits there and reads perverted magazines all day long! They are absolutely not that kind of people. They're simply looking to expand their view of things on all levels, including the sexual side. They're exploring things about themselves and sex in general. It's a very good process on many levels.

I'm sometimes asked if I will teach other women how to be a dominatrix. My answer is always no, because I don't think you can. For me, at least, when I'm together with a slave it's a very special thing. Each session is so totally different, which is what I like. It appeals to my imagination and challenges me. It's not like a cooking recipe! Even with one client, their pain threshold and so on can be completely different from one session to another. My clients tell me that's what they like about coming to see me; that every time is different. And that's not because I sit down and think about it all the time or analyse it too much. It's because when the person is reacting in a certain way, I follow that route and it becomes an exploration for both the mistress and the slave. I dislike sessions where I don't have an imaginative input. I might as well be packing chocolates!

I enjoy role play very much. I have a large wardrobe, so I try to become the authority figure in their dreams. Schoolroom scenarios seem very popular in this country. I can be a strict headmistress, a punishing governess or a bossy head-girl. Then there is, of course, the typical dungeon mistress in PVC or leather. In addition, there are my medical uniforms such as doctor or nurse. Sometimes I will play the part of the hard-nosed businesswoman in a smart suit with 'power-padding' who punishes the office boy for slacking at work. There's no one role that is my favourite, though I must admit I do quite enjoy the policewoman's role. In fact, I've got a Spanish police woman's uniform from a friend back in Spain, and I've done a few interrogation scenes where I've been speaking Spanish. It's fun because you enter completely into the fantasy and shut out the real world. They will try and bribe me as a police officer and, of course, make it worse for themselves! One person in particular wanted to be dealt with as if he were a football hooligan who had been arrested abroad. So I put on my uniform, strung him up and gave him a good thrashing. I also conducted that whole session in Spanish. By the end of it he was so confused, I think he actually believed he was in Spain! It was very funny to see.

I do 'white room' therapy also. This is a tiled room with medical equipment where I do examinations and colonic hydrotherapy and electric's. I know a lot about the body through studying nutritional medicine, I'll never do anything that I'm not confident about or I feel is not safe. The medical room creates the same feeling of fear and anticipation as the dungeon. It brings back all those feelings of going to the hospital or the dentist. Discipline is a very interesting subject, too, because there is the challenge of not leaving marks. You have to be quite skilled to do that. The cane has got a very special pain with it. One or two of my clients just want to see how much pain they can endure, which can be quite interesting. I haven't got any particular passion, though. I enjoy a whole range of activities. After all, this is my hobby as well as my job. I'm genuinely interested in it. But it is a very expensive hobby!

I don't really go out of my way to see transvestites, as it's not a subject I'm particularly interested in. I do have some lingerie, but that's used more with humiliation. It's the same with 'adult babies'. I don't have anything against it, I'm just not that interested. Unless, of course, the person is interested in the same things as me and we can incorporate their fantasy with my games. But, if I have to enter completely into their game, then I'm not interested. For instance, if a TV wants discipline too, then that's okay. Does that make sense?

My other interest is nutrition and all aspects of bodily health, so I'm always happy to offer that service, too. The dungeon is quite separate, so there is no need for a 'normal' patient to be any the wiser. However, having said that, it's very strange how one thing can lead to another! I had a person come for a 'colonic' once, and he was a few minutes late. When I joked that I would have to punish him, I could tell straight away that he was interested in spanking. Now he comes regularly for domination sessions. So, you could say the clinic works well for me in all respects!

I don't go to fetish clubs or scene parties that much, because I don't like all that posing. Maybe I'm just boring! I get to do enough posing in front of a camera anyway, so I don't think I have to prove anything to anyone. But I'm always looking for things I can incorporate into my games. Even somewhere as 'normal' as a garden centre, you'll be thinking "that's an interesting bit of rope" or whatever. For instance, I once used a little paint brush to circle a woman's clitoris until she had an orgasm. I'll also look out for special stones on the beach that I can roll around the tip of the penis. For a man, it feels just like a blow-job! It's not just about pain, but about pure sensation. It's the whole spectrum of things. What is the most painful thing is when you have so much pleasure and can't get release.

I really do get a lot of personal pleasure out of my work. I wouldn't be doing this otherwise. And, if the number of my regular slaves is any indication, they're also fairly content. It's always nice when people come back to see me again and, of course, it is much easier to explore the limits of someone I know. Some of the people I see have been very surprised at our lifestyle and the fact that we are just normal, sane people! One American guy from New York who came here told us the last so-called 'mistress' he'd been to, had her boyfriend sitting at the kitchen table cleaning his nails with a flick knife! It's the sublime to the ridiculous in this business!

Chapter 2: Mistress Adelle

Mistress Adelle is a life-style dominatrix married to a master. Now both retired they continue to enjoy a dominant lifestyle with a variety of male and female submissive guests to their home.

I suppose we are slightly different to most of the people you've spoken to, in that we are both dominants. As neither of us are interested in being submissive, all our games are played with a third party. This can sometimes be together with a transvestite or a female. Usually, however, we play separately, though the other partner is usually around 'in the background' somewhere.

We discovered the 'scene' together soon after we got married. We have both been married before and have grown up children by our previous partners. Neither of us had any experience of sub-dom or SM before that. We initially started out in the swinging scene, but soon discovered that was not really for us. Although they are two very different scenes, some fetish people do cross-over into the swinging scene and vice versa.

I have always had quite an assertive personality. Consequently, I've found that I've always attracted rather weak and subservient male partners. Though I enjoy the dominant role in play, I hate weak people in 'real' life. Does that sound odd? It's two completely differ-ent worlds, really. In a relationship or marriage, all women (includ-ing dominatrixes!) like to feel protected by an even stronger male. No woman wants a wimp for a husband, that's why I married a master. My husband found his previous wives a bit too passive, as well. We are true equals in every sense of the word, and we have no need to try and dominate each other. Why should we? We've got plenty of willing submissives to fulfil that role for us. You do have to keep these things separated. The scene is for fun, it isn't real life! If you start getting the two worlds muddled up in your mind, then you're heading for big trouble! That way madness lies!

We've met people of all age groups and inclinations since we first got involved in the scene ten years ago. Having said that, we rarely meet people under thirty, and usually in their forties or over. As we present ourselves as a dominant couple we tend to meet a lot of other couples, as well as a lot of TV's. One of the most unusual and interesting were a couple in their early thirties who were both submissive. In a way, they were in a similar situation to ourselves, in that they needed outside stimulation in their play. Interestingly, apart from the first time they visited us to chat things over, they don't come here together. I think they both feel a little uneasy about being in a sub role in front of each other.

The wife is very much into 'school girl' fantasies and spanking, but only with a mature 'head master' type male. I played no part in those scenarios, but I think she felt safer knowing there was another female around. She would show up on the doorstep, dressed completely in school mode. She even had a satchel and a pencil case! Luckily, she is very petite and can get clothes straight from normal school outfitters. She had her school girl 'persona' all worked out and very fixed in her mind, as regards her character and 'age' within the scenario.

Her husband, who I took on as my slave, was into extreme verbal humiliation and female-worship. Obviously, on a fantasy level, their two worlds were incompatible. In all other respects, they were very happy and contented together. I'm telling you this as an example of how this scene can work to complement and enhance a relationship, rather than threaten it. Without these little interludes you would have had two miserable people on your hands. In the end, that gulf of sexual needs might well have grown out of all proportion and threatened their marriage. As it is, they can come here, or go to other dominants, and have their fantasy side fulfilled without any risk to their relationship. They then go home happier people and get on with the rest of their lives.

This is only a small part of most people's lives anyway. We don't strut around in leather and PVC all day long, and neither do the people we meet. As I said earlier, that way madness lies. Sometimes people dip into this for a short period in their lives, it's a stage they're going through if you like. You'll see them at all the clubs and private parties for a few years, and then they'll disappear from the scene altogether. That's fair enough, I've no problem with that. Their curiosity has been satisfied, I suppose. Or maybe they just had certain agendas that they needed to sort out, and that was that. Then you'll find others, mostly the older men, who've been doing this for years. Some will bore you with blow by blow accounts of sessions they've had with mistresses forty-odd years ago! But at least they know how to respect a mistress, and how to behave in her presence, which is more than a lot of the younger ones do! When that older generation of slaves dies out all you're going to be left with are the younger guys who come along and treat this as just another service. I don't deal with paying clients myself, but I know women who do, and this is what I've heard.

For me, and I suspect for many others too, SM and role-play is a wonderful way of exploring different parts of your own personality that maybe you wouldn't otherwise know were even there. It's lots of other things as well but, to me anyway, it's basically a 'grown up' version of Cowboys and Indians or Doctors and Nurses. When I've got a slave kneeling at my feet and submitting to me, it's such an incredible feeling of power. It's a real surge! And I know that it's the same for my submissive—only from the other angle. You have to remember that 'submissive' is not the same as 'passive'. I think this where a lot of people on the outside don't understand what's happening. Passive means 'inert', like a sack of potatoes. In my experience, submissives are rarely like that. In fact, a lot of them are real drama queens and out and out exhibitionists! Basically, it's a sex pantomime—and it looks much worse than it actually is! Really, you could say we are both actors in our own play—and our own audience, as well!

Actually, outside of this situation, I am quite good friends with my submissives. We might go to the theatre or whatever. People would think we were just normal people out together for the evening. And the truth is we are normal people, because we've left our respective 'roles' behind in the dungeon. We can pick them up anytime we want. That's the beauty of it. As I said earlier, very few people live this way all the time. You couldn't, really. It would drive me mad for a start, having my submissive ask me what he's allowed to eat in a restaurant or when he's allowed to go to the toilet. That kind of slave wouldn't last very long under my charge! You've got to be normal sometimes!

I always take into consideration who I'm playing with: the personality of the submissive and what their limits are and so on. I need to know what buttons I can push, and which I should leave alone. I love being able to walk through the door and have a slave drop his trousers and instantly go down on his knees before me, with just a click of my fingers! I love manipulating a man's obsessions. And I adore being the mean and unreasonable bitch of his dreams—or nightmares! Believe it or not, I'm actually quite a nice person away from the dungeon.

Sometimes, when the session is over, you feel a real bond with the submissive that quite defies description. It's because we have shared something very intimate, very special. At the basis of most dominant/submissive relationships there is actually a strong sense of equality and mutual respect. Although we are playing different roles, we're still equal partners. Does that make sense? A common misconception is that submission is the same as weakness. This completely underestimates the power and the strength of the 'sexual' submissive. In the kind of consensual relationship I'm talking about, the submissive doesn't give up his social or professional power, and he's not very likely to accept authority from anyone else but his dominant partner. You know, many subs have actually told me that when they surrender sexual power to me and fulfil all those taboo fantasies, it's a profoundly empowering experience for them. There's a tremendous sense of freedom in being a slave!

The ideal dominatrix has to control herself before she can think of controlling a slave. In a sense, you have to discipline yourself first. You have to constantly reassess yourself and what you're doing. Well, I do anyway. As far as I'm concerned, anyone who calls themselves a dominant and isn't willing to admit when they've made a mistake isn't worthy of the title—and probably isn't very good at the role anyway! There's a kind of humility in dominance. I found that one of the secrets to being a good dominatrix is knowing, and accepting, that you are not an infallible 'super woman'—even though your submissive is constantly reinforcing that image. That's a very important point to remember when you take up the responsibility of 'owning' someone who is prepared to give themselves to you. Remember, a slave isn't just for Christmas!

In the eyes of the so-called 'normal' world, sado-masochism is a pretty sordid business. They always think the dominant must be some sort of sex fiend who gets a perverted kick out of brutalising some equally freakish victim! The reality is that the exact opposite is true. An SM relationship is the most democratic in the world. Both partners have to work hard to achieve the kind of level trust that you need to share your deepest fantasies.

As long as it's creating pleasure for both parties, we can keep on exploring and expanding. We always set limits at the outset so that we have a frame work in which to play. But, of course, limits can change. By 'limits' I mean when it stops being fun, basically. I'm not doing this just so I can beat someone black and blue. That's not the point at all. The idea is to give and receive pleasure. When it stops being fun, we stop. I always watch my submissive's body, looking for signs and signals. I can always feel the energy flow back and forth between us. If I feel a blockage there, or a sudden change in that energy, I know that's a good place to take a breather and take stock of what we're doing and where we're at. This transfer of energy thing can be very subtle, but it's unmistakable if you're tuned into it.

Contrary to the common held belief that pain is a bad thing, it is a quite natural capacity. Pain is a system that warns of dangerous situations or of physical damage that needs attending to. Basically, it's a biological safety system. If it's given without consent, then it is negative and wrong. No dominatrix would argue with that. But, given with consent, between willing equals, it becomes a most incredible form of love. In our society, where people conceive of all love as being of the 'gentle and affectionate' variety, that might be hard to take on board. Try and look at it like this. Take fitness freaks who spend a large part of their time in the gym, for example. All that exercise hurts, doesn't it? No one would say there's anything particularly pleasurable about the actual exercises themselves, but what is nice is the end result. They do it because it makes them feel good about themselves when they're finished. People are so conditioned to traditionally 'affectionate' relationships that they can't conceive how anyone could get enjoyment from these activities. We're so conditioned into seeing all pain as being abusive and involuntary that we can't conceive it as a form of love. At the end of the day, SM is about hurting people. But it's about hurting them just right!

This gets back to what I was saying about the dominant being in control of herself and the situation, as well as the submissive. When I'm in control of a scene, I'm in control of the pain being inflicted on my submissive. I control how much pain, when and how it's inflicted. Unintentional pain or too much pain is 'bad' pain, and it means I've lost control and failed in my responsibilities towards my sub. In some ways, it's a lot harder for dominant women than for the submissives. We dominant women are in a weird sort of double-bind situation here. On the one hand, if a would-be dominatrix overcomes all her anxieties that being sexually assertive is unfeminine, then she has to deal with all the feminist stuff about playing up to men's sexual fantasies and all the rest of it. I can assure you I'm not pandering to anyone! As I'm not a professional dominatrix, and I'm not getting paid to do this, why should I? This is a two-way traffic in pleasure!

My favourite scenarios are the ones that are a bit risqué and a bit mad. I especially like open air scenes where there is a danger of being caught. We generally use woods or selected car parks where swingers and guys meet for sexual encounters. That's a whole sub-terranean world of it's own but, if you know where to go, it is great fun. The most memorable bit of out-door fun I can remember was when I replied to an ad from this American businessman which he'd placed in The Times newspaper. It was very unusual for me to reply to any advert, but his was so intriguing. It was very 'cloaked' with only the most subliminal references to what he actually wanted. Ap-parently, he'd had seventeen or eighteen replies, but I was the only one who'd 'got it' and understood the hidden agenda. He turned out to be a big, burly businessman who'd recently split up from his wife. He took me to a fantastic restaurant, so that was a good start. He had been to a professional dominatrix back in the United States a couple of times, which had really whetted his appetite. Unfortunately, he had made the serious blunder of confessing his desire to be submis-sive to his wife, who subsequently used it against him during their divorce and accused him of being a 'depraved and degenerate' per-son because of it.

We have some lovely old, disused windmills in the countryside near our home. I had always thought this would be a great place to play with a slave, so my husband and I took him up there late one night and tied him up to the machinery with his trousers down round his ankles. However, unbeknown to him, we had secretly ar-ranged with a dominatrix friend of ours and her husband to be out walking their dog at this spot at the appointed time. I made some excuse that I had to go back to the car to fetch something and, while I was gone, these friends and their little dog 'just happened by'! She kind of sidled up to him and started talking to him, asking him what he was doing there all tied up with his trousers down and his cock exposed. They then left him and I came back. The poor man was absolutely petrified. I then proceeded to punish him for not having trust in me and thinking I would abandon him. My idea was to teach him to trust me and to put his complete faith in his mistress. Later, we all met up in a pub and he realised it was just an elaborate joke. He explained to me that he had really believed his ex-wife back in the States had set us all up as Mafia 'hit-men' to murder him! That was why he had freaked out so much.

We have been known to take one of our regular male slaves out for a drive in the boot of our car or tied to the roof rack with some tarpaulin over him. We got pulled up by the police once when they spotted his foot sticking out and must have thought they had a dead body on their hands! They were quite befuddled when they found out what we were doing—and a bit embarrassed too, I suspect, as they were quite young officers. In the end they let us go, apparently they haven't got a law against transporting a willing slave around on your roof rack! He was securely tied 'luggage' after all, so there was no danger anyway!

I tend to meet a lot of transvestites. Maybe that's because they like a more mature woman. Some of the guys, especially the younger ones, would be shy of being 'feminised' by a young girl who was closer to their own age. Somehow the 'mother-figure' is safer for them, I suppose. The youngest I've had was around twenty and looked quite stunning made up. If they are particularly convincing as a girl, I won't mind taking them out for a drive or for coffee somewhere. I don't take them into pubs, not even at lunch time, because that's a bit too dangerous and is asking for trouble.

People have suggested to me that I get myself a TV maid as a proper housekeeper, but they don't understand the mind-set of most maids or TV's in general, for that matter. What they're after is the 'trappings' of being female: that is, all the glamorous and 'girlie' bits. The last thing they want is the hum-drum reality! Think about it, you never see many transvestites hanging around Mothercare, do you? And that goes for maids, too. They're not at all interested in actually doing any real house work. They just want to flounce about for a while with a feather duster in their hands, most of them. Even if they did do any genuine housework, you'd have to be forever behind them telling them off for not doing things properly. They'd even drop your crockery or ruin your carpet on purpose in order to be punished. So, as well as being time consuming, you wouldn't even get the job done! And you'd probably have your home ruined into the bargain! No, it's best to keep fantasy and reality apart.

The nearest I've come to having that kind of scenario is with my 'butler', who I've dubbed Jeeves. He's not really a servant, as such, and certainly doesn't do any housework. At nearly eighty, he's not really up for doing much physical work. But he loves the role of being my manservant and, I must say, I really can get into that one myself. There's nothing really happens, it's just wonderful to be treated like royalty for a day. He'll act as my chauffeur and run me around on trips up to town whenever I want. He likes all the bowing and saluting and opening doors for me. It's delightfully old fashioned. He's even got himself a proper chauffeur's cap and driving gloves. As he's quite well off and drives a Rolls, we really do look the part. It's an absolutely wonderful game to play, and I do love turning heads when we go out for a drive! As I say, Jeeves doesn't do much work as such, apart from carrying the odd bit of shopping—if it's not too heavy! But at his age, I wouldn't ask him anyway and, besides, the whole scenario is so much fun, it doesn't really matter. Jeeves has been around for years, and was one of the first people we ever met on the scene. Nowadays he's more of a friend than anything else, and he's such a dear old soul.

The strangest slave I ever had was this Spanish bank manager who stayed with us for three days—and couldn't speak a word of English! He'd replied to one of our adverts somehow, and we invited him to stay over for a weekend session. He turned out to be a very 'dapper' little man who was totally obsessed with these Spanish erotic cartoon books he'd brought with him. I must say I thought they were ghastly, with all these pictures of women in medieval times having very brutal and horrendous things done to them. Pregnant women being beaten and thrown into wells, and all sorts of disgusting images done in an almost child-like and fairy tale way. They were extremely strange. Anyway, his ideal was to be one of these abused women! He wanted to be dressed up in medieval sack cloth and ashes and be completely degraded. He refused to sleep in the guest room we'd provided for him. Instead, he insisted on sleeping in a tiny corner of the attic. It was a little hidey-hole no more than a foot high, but that was where he wanted to be! I cottoned on to what he wanted (despite the language barrier) and tore up some dirty old sheets that we used for decorating and made a little nest for him, and he was as happy as could be!

Apart from the sessions themselves, we usually treat our slaves as normal guests in our home, but he would have none of it! He wanted to be treated like the scum of the earth all the time! He loved to eat the scraps off our table out of a dog bowl on the floor with his hands tied behind his back. He also loved to clean the kitchen floor in the same manner, on all fours with a filthy cloth in his mouth. Oh, and he liked to be called 'Begonia' too, for some reason!

We had a party while he was here with all of our 'scene' friends invited. Begonia didn't want to socialise in a normal way, even though there was a Spanish dominatrix present for him to talk to. All he wanted was to be dressed up like a medieval court jester and have everyone push him around and make fun of him! Even the other slaves thought he was stupid! A fact he delighted in, of course! The more everyone (including slaves) treated him like dirt, the better he liked it.

The most amazing thing about it all was that, by the end of the weekend, I noticed that his penis had shrunk completely! What had started out as quite a respectable sized cock was now like a tiny button mushroom! Obviously, our Spanish bank manager was over-joyed at this metamorphosis! The more we laughed at his little prick, the more he loved it! That weekend was about the strangest I've ever experienced. Normally, when we slaves here, I know what they want, but he really baffled us. Maybe we were too nice for him, and not as depraved as he would have liked. He seemed to have enjoyed himself though, and was very grateful for everything we'd done for him— and to him!

Obviously, I do tend to get more people to play with than my husband does. That just seems to be the nature of the game, I'm afraid. It's very one-sided, but there's very little one can do about it. The reality is that male slaves are very easy to come by, whereas the female equivalent is notoriously thin on the ground. As a couple we tend to have a bit better luck than a single master would in attracting the little darlings out of the wood work, but it's still not easy. I know they're out there, but how one gets hold of them in any quantity, I don't know. And neither does anyone else on the scene, as far as I can tell. One can find lots of 'masters in waiting', but never any slaves girls. Apart from the submissive couple, I mentioned before, we've seen no more than half a dozen sub-females.

One couple we knew in north London had a very bad experience with a 'supposedly' submissive female who answered an advert of theirs in a contact magazine. They were advertising for a live-in slave girl, and this young woman answered. Apparently, she was very convincing when she came round for her 'interview' and was very wised up on the scene and everything. They were completely taken in by her. Anyway, ten minutes after she left their house, they got a call from a public phone box down the road. It was this girl saying that she had to inform them that she was from one of the Sunday 'tabloids' and that they would be in the next one! Sure enough, they were. Complete with their names and address and everything! As it happened, they didn't really care that much. He was retired and, being Danish, didn't have any relatives in this country to worry about. She was a little embarrassed when her family and neighbours read about it. Even so, the point is that, if he'd have been a young guy with a family and a career, that could have ruined his life. We know of one teacher who was sacked because he held a private fetish party in his home that was infiltrated by the press! His headmaster was very broad-minded and was very good about it, consigning the newspaper in question to the litter bin where it belonged. Unfortunately, the parents weren't so tolerant! They didn't want their precious children taught by this 'monster'! The school had to let him go in the end, and that was the end of his teaching career!

The laws in this country are disgraceful and should be changed to come in line with the sort of invasion of privacy laws they have in France. These newspapers are destroying people's lives just for the sake of a five minute read and a bit of a cheap thrill on a Sunday morning! And for what? What harm have they done? Who cares if someone wants to dress up in PVC and have his bum smacked or whatever! It's not exactly the crime of the century, is it? It's not as if they're a threat to national security or anything like that. We're all adult people, and we're not forcing any of this onto anyone who doesn't want it. We're just enjoying an alternative lifestyle, that's all.

The truth is that fetish people don't pose a threat to western civilisation or have any intention of corrupting your children or abusing your household pets! Neither do they practice wife beating, blood drinking, human sacrifice or whatever the latest wild imaginings of the gutter press may be! In fact, all the ones we've met are a disarmingly well adjusted lot who lead surprisingly normal lives away from the dungeon. Who knows, your readers may even have one living next door!

Chapter 3: Mistress Andria

Andria is a 29 year old, full-time transvestite dominatrix who specialises in married men seeking something that extra something special!. Originally from Birmingham, she now lives and works in the South Coast resort of Brighton.

I started working as a dominatrix seven years ago and it was really from a theatrical angle. I regard myself as a fantasy figure in that 'Andria' doesn't actually exist. And I think that's where some of the excitement for both me and my clients comes from. I use the persona of Andria to create a situation that excites somebody. It's all theatrical illusion, really. When you're a transvestite dominatrix you create a character that's unique and , to a certain degree, you are guaranteed to be successful because they won't find that character anywhere else. And the better you do it, the happier you'll be and the happier the guys will be.

Before I became 'Andria', I was in sales. I was selling holidays in Tenerife, and also doing exhibition work. I travelled all around the country doing exhibitions. I would be in a different city each week. That was how I first came to visit Brighton, when I did an exhibition in Hove. I used to run along the sea front every morning and I realised what a nice town this is. Even further back I was in Engineering, which is pretty tragic thing to be in, if you want the truth. But there's really not an awful lot to say about my past, there really isn't.

Andria came into being in a very round about way. When I first came to Brighton, I started out on the gay scene. One older gay guy introduced me to simple things like caning and spanking. I used to visit him three or four times a week as a guy. He told me his first experience of being caned was by his local vicar when he was a boy. I was very green then, I didn't know about any of that stuff. Later, I used to advertise in the phone boxes as a headmaster called Mr Cummings!

I started doing domination as The Headmaster, but I didn't have very much equipment. So I used to mix it in my head with fantasy clothing and with girls clothes. I went out and bought Doc Martens and leather shorts, which was the male gay side. The next item I bought was a pair of thigh high leather boots with six inch heels. But when I started mixing the male and female gear, the gay guys didn't like it at all. They wanted a man, not someone like me who was completely shaven and wearing female clothes. Gay guys don't like transvestites or transsexuals. In fact, some of them are very hostile towards us.

My gay clients started drifting away. That was when Andria was born. Most of my guys are straight. They certainly wouldn't want to go near another guy if he was hairy or looked like a guy. They wouldn't want to know. So, you've got to represent what they want; which is a girl with extra bits! They want a girl with a cock, basically. An ordinary girl they can find on any street corner but, occasionally, they want something different. If you can supply that something different and you're very well endowed as I am, then you'll go down a storm in Brighton! But they're definitely not gay. They're straight and nearly all married. They might just be bored with their wives.

I do get approached by couples but we never get round to setting it up because I'm not really interested in girls. What happens is that the guys will try and persuade their wives or girlfriends to come along and see me. When a couple phone, I'll always ask if I can speak to the girl when he's out of the room. Two things I always check is their ages, because I don't see anyone under the age of thirty. And, if it's a female I'll ask her if he's been pressurising her into doing this. The answer to that is usually yes. I'll ask her to pop him back on the phone and then I'll discretely tell him that I don't think it's going to work because we might clash, and leave it at that really. I'll make some excuse for not seeing them without him thinking that she's put me off. I'll even continue the conversation with the two of them for a bit and cool it down naturally. But one way or another they probably won't be coming to see me. It's just not something that particularly interests me.

Concentrate on the married guys and keep it simple, that's my motto!. The simpler you can keep things, the better. As soon as you begin to complicate it, it starts to fall to pieces. That's why I concentrate on the married guys. Hopefully, they're sensible. They're less likely to carry any diseases. They don't want any embarrassing things to crop up. And they're very, very discrete. So there's lots of positive aspects. Besides, I like married guys. They treat you good.

I see guys between the ages of thirty and eighty. Everyone has to have their standards and rules. In this game you've got to create your own rules and then stick to them. That's why I won't see guys younger than thirty. That way it's safe, sensible and secure. There's no need to see anyone younger than that. My oldest guy has got to be in his eighties because he used to drive tanks in the war. He comes for a combination of cock and ball torture, domination and restraint. Maybe a little bit of water sports, too. The majority are in their forties and fifties.

I do everything from domination, humiliation, water sports, bondage, seduction; all those kinds of things. And, of course, all the personal services to go with them. I wish now that I'd specialised solely in domination when I started. But I do like to enjoy myself. I've had a great deal of fun. When you're a transvestite it's restrictive in your lifestyle.

You've got to have a good figure for this and a good smile! A good smile will always win through. Plus an understanding of what's required. I used to have different routines. One routine I used when the guys arrived was that I was always wearing a micro mini skirt and I'd make sure one of my switches was turned off; either my television or CD player. I'd sit the guy down, take his coat and fix him a drink. Then say: "Oh gosh, this isn't working". And then, of course,

I'd notice the plug and bend down and every single guy would grunt and groan when I did that. So you know you're okay then. It sounds a bit simple, but you have to have that assurance that the guy is approachable. The guys are great, but you have to be sure.

A time when that routine was a real asset was when I had a lot of army guys come to see me. It was during that period when the army were talking about homosexuals in the armed forces and I was getting a lot of quite high ranking officers coming along. I think a lot of the guys who had to make decisions on it wanted to experience it for themselves. Whether they were actually ordered to come along and see someone like me, I don't know. But I did quite a few and some of them were very hard. This goes back to what I was saying before about having to be sure. Even though the guy is sitting on my settee, I've got to know I'm okay to approach him. I'll always keep my distance and have a bit of a chat and make him a drink. Then I'll offer him a massage.

I always remember one guy who was really hard. You know, these army guys are really tough. I ended up giving him a massage and I think he was determined that nothing was going to work in that department. I think I gave him hand relief or whatever. Afterwards, he admitted that he didn't think that would happen. I just smiled sweetly and said: "But it did, didn't it, Sweetheart?" I think he went away quite changed in his attitudes towards things. To be blunt about it he was stiff as a board!

It's the facts of life. If you're not taught the facts of life when you're a kid, you've got to learn them at some point during your life. For some people that could be quite late. Some of my guys might be in their seventies and they say: "Andria, I've always wanted to do this". I based one of my adverts on that. I put: 'For gentlemen who've always wanted to, but never have'. It was very successful. They don't feel alone then because there are lots of other guys who want to try.

A lot of the guys who call me are very shy. They're just phoning to see what's going on, but deep down they really want to come and see me. So, I never write the phone calls off. It's my life line, after all. Even with the Internet, the phone is still the best way of getting business. The only time I get a lot of hits on the Internet is when my contract is due for renewal and it's the company themselves calling up and pretending to be clients. What will really change the 'hooker scene' is when they have phones with vision. You will actually see the person you're booking the appointment with. So, if you're not up to scratch, you'll be out on a limb. There won't be any hiding place. The world is changing and you've got to change with it or you won't be as successful as you should have been. A photograph is worth a thousand words, as they say. A guy will fall in love with a photograph. He won't fall in love with words, unless he's a philosopher and I don't get many of them!

People don't realise the huge amount of preparation you have to do as a transvestite. It's a lot different to any other scene, even the gay scene. A girl's a girl, and a guy's a guy. A transvestite creates an image, which could take you between an hour and an hour and a half every day. You have to have a full body shave, do your hair and your nails. If you're like me, you might have spent an hour in the gym in the morning to keep your figure in trim. And then there's hygiene and cleanliness if your offering personal services. So, just to become your creation, you've spent a lot of time and effort. Then, if that creation you've made isn't really accepted by society because, basically, they will always see you as a guy in a skirt, then you really are a prisoner in your own dungeon! You've created your own little world and you have to live in it. You can't even pop down to the shops for a newspaper or go out for a cup of coffee. That's why you need to have a lot of advertising out there to make sure you're busy and don't get bored. It's not easy. When you're transvestite, it's very restrictive on your life style.

A transvestite mistress has a shot at about one guy in every hundred. If a hundred straight guys are visiting town and you take away the ones who are just looking for girls, you'll end up with five or ten guys who might consider visiting you, if you're lucky. So, you've only got about a tenth of the hit rate a girl has got. At the moment, for instance, we've got the Labour Party Conference coming up in Brighton. That's my busiest week of the year. The town expects about twenty thousand people coming here that week. Another changing face of this scene is simply that more of those people are going to be women. Equality has done nothing for me! A lot more of the people involved in these conferences now are female and their not out there looking for sex. Not only are they not out there on the street looking for sex, the males at the conference will spend a lot of their time chasing them. So, they're taking the business away from all the working girls and people like me. Sex is more available for them away from home if the conference is split fifty-fifty between men and women.

I think if you're only doing domination it's probably better to isolate yourself away from somewhere like Brighton. I've enjoyed Brighton and I've had a great time here but, looking back on it with my experience, you are better off moving out somewhere to a bigger premises and just do domination. The clients will travel for a good mistress. In Brighton, there are just too many people offering these services, so you've got to be very good. You're only as good as your next appointment with the client you've got at the time. I'm always thinking about the next appointment and making sure the guy wants to come back.

I've been asked to do most everything over the years. I had one guy who wanted to sit in the bath while I did some water sports. Then he'd bring out his shaving brush and shaving foam and he'd want me to fill his eyes full of soap, because he wanted me to be a very wicked mistress with him. Another guy asked if he could bring a banana to eat out of my bottom. When he arrived he had a whole bunch under his arm! Even after he'd left I was still passing bananas every time I went to the toilet! They do want all kinds of weird things.

If you're doing bondage scenes, you've got to be very careful that they're not on poppers or drugs. You've got to have eyes in your bottom. And they all think they can hang upside down for hours on end. All these things are in their heads. You just don't do anything dangerous, you direct the scenario another way. I've had at least eight guys faint on me. It's not a very nice experience having some-one pass out on you. It's very frightening. I've been a hairs breadth from phoning an ambulance on two occasions.

Some of the guys want extreme scenes. They've seen things in videos and that's what they want to do. But if you're in control, which you should be, you direct it another way. And, to be blunt about it, I don't get paid the kind of money for me to do the absolute bizarre stuff. If you're specialising in bizarre scenes, then you want the money for doing it. If the guys haven't got the money in their pocket or aren't willing to pay, then I don't do them. It's as simple as that. I won't open my dungeon door unless I get the rate I want.

I don't understand how anyone could be submissive professionally. If you're being subservient all week, your body is going to end up being bashed and battered. You'd have to be on hundreds of pounds for doing it, and you'd only be able to see about one client a week. I used to have an opera singer come down from London to spank me, but I always had to make sure he didn't hit me too hard because I didn't want to be bruised. You experience all these things, but you soon learn that being sub is not a good idea as a profession. You can't control the guys if you're being submissive. Once you show you're submissive, you're in trouble, aren't you? You've got to be in control all the time. You can't hand over the controls to the client. It gets too dangerous.

Everyone in this business should work with somebody like a maid around, especially the girls. Even a dominatrix needs someone there for security. I have thought about working with a female dominatrix, but the problem is that if you get two dominatrix in the same room, they're going to collide. There's inevitably going to be a clash of egos. Unless you've got your own separate premises or a big enough place that you can split down the middle and just come together for certain scenes, it's going to be very awkward to get your personalities to mix.

I knew a guy who had a dungeon who rang me out of desperation because he was looking for a girl who could come and work for him. He'd got his dungeon but couldn't find the girls who could do the business. It's not as simple as you think. A lot of people can't do it. They can't be violent. They can't spank or use a paddle or a whip.

It's just not in them. This guy had employed two girls, but they would just stand around and giggle. They were finding it comical. If he'd just had one good dominatrix, it would probably have been fine. But his mistake was having two girls working together in that situation. They just saw it as a comedy.

I wouldn't describe myself as a lifestyle mistress. A lifestyle mistress is a very serious woman and a very serious dominant. Some mistresses just are the way they are. They believe they are that persona. You wouldn't cross them, otherwise they'd automatically expect you to be on your knees to them. They wouldn't doubt you were going to do it, either! If they've got a husband, he probably panders to them as well. If you think about it the best mistresses' around are in the Royal Family, aren't they? The Queen Mother has been worshipped and looked after by servants for a hundred years. If that's not a top class dominatrix, I don't know what is!

Chapter 4: Mistress Brigitte

While promoting my magazine at an Erotic Fair in Valkenburg, Holland, I had the greatest pleasure in meeting the colleagues of the Dutch SM-Studio Phoenix. I say 'colleagues', though this is hardly the right word, for they in fact form a very happy extended S&M 'family' comprising of a married Mistress and Master together with their male and female slaves who live, work and play together. And even do the baby-sitting and the school-run! I was immediately drawn to these people, seeing in them something special I had never encountered before on the fetish scene. Here was a professional 'scene' couple who didn't simply put their whips away at the end of a session and say 'see you next week', these people actually had the courage and commitment to live out their chosen lifestyle to the full.

To most people our story will seem quite unreal, as it's the perfect S&M story of a dominant couple living together with their slaves. How did this happen? Well, I think someone who really wants to live like this can pick up the right signals and find matching partners. Although there is the danger that if you crave it too much, it'll stay out of reach.

Let me start by introducing myself and my partner. Gerald is a tall, well-built, blonde dominant. I am Brigitte. I'm also tall, slim and grey-blonde. We've been living happily together for over ten years now. During that time we've tried everything, especially things that had to do with S&M. After eight years of marriage and lots of experimenting privately, we started the SM studio 'Le Bateau' in Breda. The studio was, in fact, a dungeon on a great boat; a 100 square metre space filled with every possible torture and pleasure equipment. We worked together. I received the slaves in my floating dungeon, while Gerald took care of the rest of the business. It was during my time on the boat that I really grew into a professional mistress. I achieved a lot with my slaves and was even able to treat the real 'enfant terribles' in the Dutch SM community!

Unfortunately, this wasn't to last for long. In January 1994, a big fire destroyed our floating home completely. A disaster for our team and for our guests, who didn't know where to turn. Immediately, we started looking for another location, which we eventually found in Roosendaal; a town between Rotterdam and Antwerp and about one hour drive from Brussels and Amsterdam. Hence, the name of Phoenix, as in 'rising from the ashes'!

It was while we were still on the boat that I got pregnant with our first child, but things didn't really change for me at that time. I was perfectly happy, having the opportunity to play a large variety of scenes with my guest slaves. My altering physical state didn't bother me at all. Most of my slaves didn't even notice that I was bearing a child. On the contrary, I felt more and more secure of my capacities as a dominatrix as my experience increased with every scene. Unfortunately, my beloved Gerald didn't have as many opportunities to act out his S&M feelings, and certainly not his fantasies. We decided to put an ad in the newspaper for a submissive girl for him to play with, and to assist me on the boat. A couple of days later I received a telephone call from Pauline. We made an appointment to meet that coming Friday on our boat.

At one o'clock prompt, I opened the door to find a little girl about five feet tall with dark hair and impudent eyes standing there. I invited her in and we talked for a few minutes. The rest of that afternoon I was so busy with my slaves that I hardly got another chance to speak to her. In the meantime, however, Gerald did a good job with her! I was pleasantly surprised to find that she was still there in the evening. So, I finally got a chance to meet under less strenuous circumstances.

A few months later and my little baby girl arrived. And, with that, there was suddenly so much to do around the house and studio that Pauline ended up staying at our place more than her own home. A year later and she had moved in with us on a permanent basis. And then the strangest thing happened! Pauline, who had initially been Gerald's slave, had become more and more my personal slave-girl. So much so, in fact, that Gerald began thinking of acquiring another slave-girl. Several young ladies volunteered, but he didn't find the one he was looking for. Then one day, when he was visiting a friend who was renovating a store, he met the owner and her boy-friend. Her name was Anita. Whether this was fate or coincidence, we'll never know. What we do know is that three weeks later she moved in with us. Complete with her little daughter, but minus the boyfriend!

There's one more story to tell: my male slave, Bad-boy. The first time I saw him was at an Erotic Fair. I was buying some toys for my dungeon and this slave was assisting me. His manner was very sophisticated and elegant. Normally, I don't pay much attention to male slaves, but it occurred to me that this one was different. Any-way, a few months later we met again at a 'couples night', where he had come with his mistress. At least, that's what I presumed. So I didn't pay any attention to him, but that didn't keep me from ob-serving him throughout the evening. A few weeks later I told him that, as far as I was concerned, he could be my slave. So, that's how I adopted Bad-boy!

One of my favourite things is bondage, especially the Japanese style, because it looks very good on a slave and has a great effect. When I have a submissive tied up the way I like it, it is impossible for him to move, as he'll be totally immobilised. I enjoy teasing my slaves when they are in such a helpless state. Wet games, or 'golden showers', is another of my specialities. It's not just that you piss on somebody, it's more the way you do it that gives the thrill. It can

be a very exciting act, even to me, but I can also do it in a very humiliating manner. I seldom visit the bathroom in the studio these
days! In fact, my capacity has become famous in Holland, because
I've never disappointed anyone who wanted a wet game. One slave
even compared me to Niagara Falls, though that was going a bit over
the top! I have to admit that I love my slaves to 'swim' in my juices.
Actually, it's one of my favourite recipes in an SM scene, because it's
dominant, erotic and intimate all at the same time.

As we manufacture most of our equipment ourselves, I possess
a large variety of whips. Each has its own character and individual
purpose. There are whips that caress, whips that punish, whips that
threaten and whips that tickle. For me, discipline is one of the major
principles of SM. It belongs to the basics that one has to learn when
becoming my submissive. Rules have no meaning if there's no sanction on disobedience. A slave that doesn't behave according to my
rules will be punished! I always make myself very clear to my slaves.
I talk slowly and articulate very well, so there can be no misunderstanding between the two of us. If a slave doesn't listen to the things
I tell him, he will inevitably be punished, either by physical pain or
by humiliation. I can be very severe if I'm disobeyed. I think listening well is what marks a good slave. One's reaction makes my action.
For example, when I tell a slave not to move and then I hear him
move behind my back, he will be confronted by my power and has
to take the consequences of his behaviour. Therefore, discipline is in
my opinion one of the basics of real dominance.

So what do I mean by 'basics' in SM? Well, when a slave first
comes into my studio, I will have an honest conversation with him.
I'll try to find out what kind of mood he's in. Not every slave is the
same, they all have their specific passions and limits. It is important
for me to know what he really dislikes, because that leaves the rest
up to me. I need room for my fantasy, too. I don't like to be dictated
to in a scenario. My games are spontaneous, impulsive and full of
surprises! As a professional dominatrix, though, I realise that my
guests pay a lot of money to spend time with me. So, I will always
respect their feelings, keep in touch with their emotions and never

push them beyond their limits. In return for my total dedication, I want them to put their faith in me, trust me and let me be responsible for my actions as a woman of art.

It seems to me that nowadays a lot of slaves dictate their favourite treatment to a mistress, who then fulfils their desires like a puppet. I'm nobody's 'puppet'! I always act upon my own observations. The kind of game where the dominant follows blindly the wishes of the sub has got nothing to do with SM as an erotic play of power and submission. If you want to be my submissive, take your chance , and let me guide through the labyrinth of fantasy. That's what I have to offer as a dominatrix, and so far my slaves seem to like my way of treating them. At least, they keep coming back for more!

I can be a very severe mistress if necessary. I can be very tough to deal with, especially in the psychological way. Bargaining is not possible with me. Often new slaves are surprised to discover my attitude. Though I'm only severe when it's needed, I'm always strict. When someone is under my supervision, he has to listen very carefully. If not, he will be punished for not paying attention. Sometimes the 'threat' can be worse than the actual punishment. For slaves who can take it, the treatment can be physically very hard, and in ways they don't always expect! Remember, discipline is one of my favourite games and it has many faces.

People ask me for my definition of a 'good slave'. It's a difficult question because there are so many different kinds of submissives. So many men, so many ways of expressing themselves. I think the most important quality is respect, and by that I mean 'mutual' respect. I love the very obedient, dedicated kind, but I also very much enjoy playing with the naughty ones who will grab every opportunity to disobey—even when they know the sanctions I have laid down. They may even try to manipulate me and, as long as I consider it fair play, I will eagerly pick up the gauntlet. However, let me give a warning to future playmates of mine who may be reading this: never challenge me in my role as dominatrix when you can't take the consequences!

So what does Studio Phoenix have to offer? In the apartment

we have created three playrooms, each with a style of its own. The moment you walk through the door you enter a totally different world filled with a large variety of professional equipment which can be used. There is no bar, no video show and no stage acts. What we offer is pure SM for those dedicated to this thrilling kind of eroticism. Don't expect standard games or forms to fill in. We prefer a personal approach in dealing with guests visiting our studio for a private session or for our special monthly evenings.

I believe Phoenix is for anyone who likes, participates in or is simply just curious about SM. Men, women, couples, whether heterosexual, homo-sexual, bisexual, active or passive, single or in a group, we will make your fantasies come true! And not just SM fantasies. All sorts of secret wishes or erotic adventures are a challenge to our team! Above all, however, SM is our greatest passion. We want to share our passion with as many people as possible. For example, have you and your partner ever taken an interest in, or have already been experimenting with SM and are looking for new challenges and possibilities? Then you could try our unique, free-play couples nights. You can play as much as you like, experiment in all kinds of ways or enjoy watching others play. This all happens in a relaxing atmosphere. We are always willing to explain our special, often self-developed, equipment. If you feel like it, you can invite one of us to join your play for assistance or to create an extra dimension. And don't think it's too expensive. We only charge 125 guilders. For this you can play, eat and drink as much as you like at no extra cost. The high standards we set for SM, incidentally, also apply to our catering service, so we recommend not to dine before joining the party. Our couples nights are meant for all kinds of couples, no matter what their composition, as everything's possible. You can even bring your personal house-slave with you as a couple, if you wish.

If the idea of playing in public is too big a step for you, we can offer the opportunity of renting one of our rooms in which to experiment in private with your partner. Nobody will be watching you, and you'll find lots of new toys to use, and without restrictions! Of course, you can also have your first experiences as a couple in a private room under the guidance of a master or mistress. Or even live out your dominant fantasies with one of our well-trained slave-girls, who will most certainly enjoy a 'triangular' game! On the other hand, if you are a submissive male with exhibitionist tendencies. In other words, if you like being watched, where would you go? Here you can get in touch with others who share your submissive feelings. Every second Tuesday of the month we have an open play-night. This special 'slave education' night has been organised with the intention of giving every slave present proper treatment. On your first visit you may choose to just watch the mistress play with other visitors. Though, I should add, the general rule is that on this night you are 'victim' as well as 'spectator'. The success of our formula has proved itself over the years. Witness the still-growing attendance and enthusiasm of those who regularly attend. These evenings provide an excellent introduction to SM, as well as to our studio.

Where do you go when you love SM, but have no one to share your fantasies? During opening hours you can visit the studio to experience all kinds of SM: from soft-erotic to extreme hard or bizarre-perverted. The first informative conversation is very important; that is the key to your fantasy world. As long as it stays within the borders of discretion and hygiene, we can fulfil all your wishes, the choice is yours! We offer every variation with mistress or slave-girl. Both together, with a master, together with a slave or with two slaves or two dominatrixes. If you want to know about SM, this is the place! So, that's my story. So far, that is! You don't have to believe it, but just remember it could happen to you!

Chapter 5: Mistress Cassandra Payne

A one-time leading light on the Canadian fetish scene, Mistress Cassandra was based in Vancouver, British Columbia. Since this interview was conducted, however, and following some bad experiences at the hands of her manipulative Number One Boy, she has now quit the fetish scene altogether and moved back to Toronto, where she has resumed her former career as a beautician.

I'm originally from Toronto, and have been involved in the fetish scene there for about twelve years. Sadly, the scene there has gone the same way as most serious scenes in recent years; that is, a victim of repressive government policies, opportunistic retailers and a sudden influx of self-styled 'experts' in the fetish world who feel the need to 'educate'. Government policies can be fought (albeit slowly) and money-grabbing hucksters can, and should, be avoided like the plague. Unfortunately, well meaning, but ill-prepared, pendants do more harm than good to a thriving fetish scene and, short of some discipline around the head with a blunt instrument, are almost impossible to stop!

I learned to be a dominatrix by starting out with an assertive nature, asking a lot of questions of dominants whose skills I admired, and taking a thousand baby steps on my own towards achieving the technical expertise I knew I needed. The psychological acumen a dominatrix requires is gained only through experience. I have led a dominant lifestyle for the last fourteen years and have performed almost six and a half thousand sessions, and yet not a day goes by that I don't gain some new insight into the dominant/submissive dynamic. It boggles the mind that there are people out there with, at most, three years experience, actually teaching courses on how to be a 'professional dominatrix'! It's bad enough that 'kink' is being turned into some odd form of 'pop psychology', with discussion seminars and support groups, but to some poorly trained dominant 'wannabe' committing untold unpleasantries on potentially valuable slaves is at best frustrating and, at worst, downright dangerous! We need more good slaves, not more bad dominatrixes! There are, at most, five people in the world actually qualified to teach 'kink', in my opinion. Sadly, only one of them is doing it. Kudos to the excellent Cleo DuBois! I will now get down off my soap-box!

I like attention to detail at Payne Manor, but only within the bounds of good taste. I began offering my dungeon as a bed and breakfast several months ago, advertising through word of mouth and in 'select' fetish magazines. The response has been enthusiastic, to say the least! Vancouver is a splendid tourist destination, located as it is between the mountains and the sea, and Payne Manor is a convenient fifteen minutes drive from almost everything. Kinky couples staying here have access to golf, boating, shopping and night life, while residing in relative luxury in a state of the art dungeon. I get to meet the nicest people, too!

I've been thinking a lot about house slaves recently, as I am in the process of interviewing candidates for some vacancies on my staff. However, after two solid weeks of 'auditions', I've sadly concluded that 99.9% of the submissives who covet a semi-permanent position don't have the faintest clue as to what this entails, or even know what's required of a successive candidate. Admittedly, a good house slave is a rare commodity, but from my experiences over the past fortnight, it would seem that this years crop of candidates is the poorest quality ever! I have kept slaves for fourteen years and am always on the lookout for quality stock, but I'm totally at a loss for an explanation to the present lack of talent. Perhaps the current glut of 'nouveau dominas' has resulted in a lowering of standards, or maybe the polarisation of sub-dom culture worldwide has diluted the slave pool with dabblers and hangers-on? While not all mistresses will agree with my opinions or standards, I feel that any house slave candidate who adopts what I suggest will be well on his way to achieving his goal. In any case, the situation warrants a comment or two, at the very least. So, indulge me here, while I get this off my chest!

Firstly, when I advertise for house slaves, I am not looking for a sexual partner! You should not try and impress me with your genital endowment or tales of oral abilities! I want someone to serve me, not service me! While the scene has a highly charged sexual aura surrounding it, the fact is that sex in itself is actually nothing more than one tool out of many available to a capable dominatrix. I can't stress enough that it is a dirty, largely communicable world out there. Aids, and the various strains of Hepatitis are only the tip of the iceberg. I plan to grow to a ripe old age, and have no intention of risking my health in the pursuit of house slaves!

I follow my usual screening process when examining each days postal applications from would-be slaves. Obviously, if there is no self addressed envelope or token, the letter is immediately consigned to the trash without even being read! If, on the other hand, the letter is sincere, genuine and captures my attention, it gets placed in a document folder for my further consideration come bedtime. I prefer to do my correspondence at night when distractions are minimised. It's interesting to note that fully 80% of the letters I receive are scrapped; a statistic matched by most of my mistress friends. I think there's a lesson here for all aspiring slaves!

I have no interest in listening to a long list of what you would like me to do to you. I have professional clients who pay me lots of money for the privilege of having me consider such requests. Being a house slave is about you doing things that I want done, not the other way around! In the context of rewards and punishments associated with your training, I am more than capable of deciding what, where, when and why, without your assistance!

Being a house slave is, to quote my Number One Boy: "not a gig for the faint of heart". The hours are long and the tasks, shall we say, 'challenging'. I once had a candidate who neglected to inform me of his diabetic condition. While I appreciated his enthusiasm and dedication, his succumbing to insulin shock whilst doing the windows was a terrifying experience for both of us! Luckily, we both survived the experience and remain good friends to this day, but he would be the first to admit that he wasn't up to the task at hand.

If there is any qualification which I would deem most important for a slave, it would have to be 'honesty'. I don't care if you have a wife, but if there is a chance I might encounter her, I'd better be aware of her existence. And I don't care if you've got millions (though it would be nice), just don't make claims or promises that you can't deliver. You'll never be able to make up a story that would impress me more than an honest, heartfelt admission of your devotion and submission.

There's no such thing as a free lunch! Remember that phrase? When you apply to be a house slave, you enter into the 'real world' of domination and submission. It's not like you imagine, not even close. Contrary to popular belief, a dominatrix doesn't not roll out of bed in the morning wearing skin-tight leather catsuits, six-inch heels and full theatrical make-up. I won't be standing over you wielding a riding crop while you wash the floor, either. Nor will you receive a fully involved two hour session just for showing up on time!

I have a busy, active life, which is one of the reasons I need slaves. My whole household is busy and active, too. We actually have a lot of fun and, yes, there is a definite 'kink' to the ambiance of each and every day! The successful house slave candidate is an active part of such a household, part of a team of skilled, dedicated slaves whose main reason to be is to serve to the needs of a worthy dominatrix. Yes, there are parties, but there are also dirty dishes and filthy toilets. It is the real world, little man. And, if you remember that, you'll not be disappointed.

Your job is do 'things'. So make sure you know how to do things! Like carpentry, leatherwork, horticulture and fabric care. Washing windows and knowing which end of the vacuum cleaner sucks is not enough anymore. You must have skills and you must be prepared to use them. And don't lie about what you can do, either. I'll be really pissed off and, if that happens, you won't enjoy the experience!

I can't bear stupid slaves; or stupid people in general, for that matter! This isn't the same as being smart. This is a warning not to screw up! Accidentally or on purpose. If I give instructions, follow them to the letter. Take notes if you have to, but get the job done. And get it done on time, and to specification. I'm a reasonable person and I won't make outrageous demands. I remember I once sent a slave out to pay some bills. He got on the bus and then got lost. And I mean really lost! He didn't even have the sense to ask someone for directions or call me for an update. He stayed lost for five and a half hours and my bills didn't get paid. He didn't know enough ways to apologise for his colossal cock-up. Needless to say, he was fired on the spot. I will tolerate the occasional error, if it's an honest mistake. And, naturally, you will be punished for it. But, if you intentionally err, in an attempt to goad me into disciplining you, I will know it and, as I said earlier, you won't enjoy the experience!

A dominatrix is just like any other girl; she likes to get gifts. Flowers, clothing, automobiles! Don't spend outside your budget, but don't be cheap either. I once had a slave who brought me a used broom and dustpan as a present! This man was a highly placed politician with an investment portfolio worth millions and, I'm not joking, a collection of antique automobiles! Don't get the impression that I'm greedy, but I viewed his so-called gift as insulting, pure and simple. That display of disrespect earned him a curt invitation to depart.

As I learn about your abilities, you should learn about my needs. Anticipate them, and act accordingly. There's a definite hierarchy among the slaves of an extended household, with everyone jockeying for Number One Boy status. Friendly competition makes for a vibrant stable, and the most versatile, indispensable slave does enjoy privileges as befits his rank.

My current Number One Boy, Kris, has held that position for three years now, and the lengths he's gone to in order to maintain that exalted state are almost comical! Once, while I was in the process of auditioning equipment 'techies', Kris took it upon himself to build me a St. Andrew's Cross and a vaulting horse (both quite attractive and functional, I have to say). But he then decided to use only his Swiss Army knife and a house brick to complete the task! It took him two days, during which time he also managed to handle 60% of the domestic duties as well! His hands looked like hamburgers when he was done, but he had proved himself to me.

I've had Kris for five years now. Originally, I took him from another mistress and, right from the start of my ownership of him, I had subjected him to the most intense training and conditioning in order to bring his natural submissiveness to full fruition. He's now my most reliable slave, and serves me as my executive assistant, aide de camp, general lackey and convenient whipping boy! He's also the only slave I've ever seen fit to have branded with my personal initials as a life long symbol of his servitude to me. Today, he wears my insignia proudly on his left shoulder. He took the branding very well, staring off into space and muttering his pain mantra under his breath. He never flinched once as the branding iron struck, burning the stylised CP motif into his flesh. A year after coming into my service, he quit his successful rock band to accompany me across the country from Toronto in order to attend to all my needs as I established myself in this wonderful city.

I cherish all my slaves, especially the ones I've trained to my standards. In return, I know my slaves cherish me. The hardest slave to train is the one who has bounced around from one mistress to the next, staying only a few months with each, picking up bits and pieces of training, but never completely committing. I'm usually hesitant to accept such a slave, since he has so many bad habits to break; not to mention questionable loyalty! If you're lucky enough to be accepted by a mistress, commit for at least a one year contract and immerse yourself totally in her world. You'll find your patience rewarded many times over, I can assure you.

The camaraderie between slaves that inevitably develops 'below stairs' can often lead, amazingly enough, to strong friendships. I know of at least one successful rock band whose members met in the stable of a well-known mistress! The role of the house slave is definitely a fulfilling one for the true submissive who is aware of the demands of the position, and is prepared to put the time and the energy into serving his mistress with subtlety, precision and humour.

Obviously, these points only touch on the broad issues a house slave candidate should consider. Each mistress will undoubtedly place a different emphasis on these requirements. But, if you take what I've said on board, you're definitely going to be prepared, mentally, for the job. Believe me, it's well worth the effort because a fully developed mistress/house slave relationship is as rich and as full as any relationship you'll ever experience.

Chapter 6: Lady Claudette

For the dedicated fetishist, no trip to the German city of Munich would be complete without a stopover at the studio of Lady Claudette; otherwise rather aptly named 'Bizarradise'. The true connoisseur of outrageous eroticism will find everything on offer and even the more unusual tastes happily accommodated in this liberal, or rather less conservative, oasis of traditionally ultra right-wing Bavaria. Lady Claudette herself is a petite, deceptively soft-spoken brunette who originally started out in the cosmetics industry as a representative for a large company. Like many before her, she originally encountered the SM scene through a relationship.

I had a friend who had masochistic tendencies. I didn't know anything about SM then. This friend introduced me to it on an intimate level. The relationship broke up, but I knew that with my next boyfriend it would have to be the same. Above all, I was curious to know everything I could about it. Back in the early days, I didn't know any of the private circles. I didn't even know such things existed. And I certainly didn't go into sex shops to buy literature on the subject. However, I did get hold of one of those contact magazines, but it was all full of adverts from professional ladies. So I made a decision then to take some unpaid leave and use the time to look around and simply find out what there was to know. Besides, I thought, at least it would give me the opportunity to meet the kind of men who would suit my interests!

I did a little round trip, first through Stuttgart; but up there I found no demand for a dominatrix. I could have worked as a maid, but that was completely out of the question, naturally! I found out from a friend that there was a vacancy here in Munich. That was here in my present studio. I learnt a lot from this mistress but, looking back, I don't think she had what it takes. Not many clients came and eventually she couldn't pay the rent and had to leave. The proprietor came to me and asked if I would like to take over. I had to make a decision then and there. Because I had already enjoyed myself enormously during the short time I had worked there, I said to myself: "Yes, sure. Before I go back to my old job, why not make my hobby into a profession?" That was back in 1991.

Getting a studio here in Munich is very difficult. Because of the 'No-Go' district, it is restricted to a very small area. The walls in this type of studio have to be quite high, so the cost would increase by about 70%. And then, if you just mention your trade to a potential landlord, he'd rather not let his property at all than rent it to you! Munich is tremendously conservative, as you probably know.

The studio now consists of four main rooms. The first, known as The Leather Room or sometimes, more provocatively as The Cuddle-Up Room, has a bed with four chains where one can tie somebody down really well with arms and legs apart. There's a pulley which can be used to hoist a client up to any height you want above the bed. We've also got a full wardrobe with everything from rubber knickers to cat-suits and even rubber suspension suits. Everything is included in the price and all the clothes are in extra large size. I feel that, even though the outfit might be a little loose on a really small person, the main thing is actually the feel of rubber against the skin.

Next comes The Marble Room, complete with metal bar for tying up slaves. There are two columns with tying up devices. One of these has a leather harness which tightly fixes a client to the column. Also, there's a rack with metal candle holders. Various play gadgets and some fifteen different masks hang from the wall. The Marble Room gets its feel, as the name suggests, from the flooring made from finest Italian marble, as well as its marble columns.

Besides this, there is The Torture Chamber with a pillory, a punishment horse, cross and a solid wrought iron cage. The whole ambiance is decidedly medieval! Next, we come to The White Room, more commonly known as The Clinic, for doctor/nurse games. This room is divided into two areas. The first, The Treatment Room, has a gynaecological chair, couch and all the medical equipment necessary to offer the patient an unforgettable stay of classic luxury. There's also our Wet Room for lovers of toilet games, with a single toilet and a shower for each guest and lots of space to lay out a client. To ensure absolute hygiene, the floors and walls of both rooms are finished with tiles. Outside there is The Open Space where we have at our disposal a playing field of over 150 square metres surrounded by a three metre high wooden fence to ensure absolute privacy from the prying eyes of the 'normal folk'!

I currently employ four females slaves and three mistresses. The degree to which a client can 'go' with a hired slave depends on the individual girl. Some girls can't take very much, admittedly, and tend to work more as maids. For others, even a good hard lashing that results in whelts would be quite acceptable. Above all, I can assure you, all my slave-girls really enjoy it! This is an important factor for me. I make absolutely sure that they have just the right predisposition for the job; which means they love it! Two of my slave-girls, in particular, are able to take a considerable degree of harsh treatment. They couldn't do it for money alone. Imagine if you were tied up and required to take fifty lashes on your backside. Maybe you could stand it for half an hour or so. But if it went on for another hour, then either your psyche has had it or you are really into it yourself. There has to be a tendency towards it. I know that's how it was for me.

I'm not suggesting a girl will reach an orgasm with every client, because obviously empathy and chemistry play an important part in any scenario. But it can happen that a client, who at first seems unappealing, does the training so well that the sparks really do fly! Sometimes a woman will come out of the room and tell me how fantastic it was!

My slave-girls are all very well experienced in their chosen field and, no matter how excited they may be getting, never let things get out of control. If a client doesn't know how to use the whip properly and goes for the thighs or the spine with too much force, we use a code word to stop the action and the girl will explain to him what she can endure. If they still can't manage to come to some agreement, we'll give the client his money back and suggest he come to a demonstration evening. These evenings are a unique part of the life of the Studio, in which clients new to the scene can learn and understand all its aspects with a particular emphasis on safety. I have noticed that, unfortunately, there are some people who have no idea what SM is all about. They probably think the slave is like a piece of meat they can just hit as hard as they like. I started these demonstrations to show that the whole thing is something more than that!

These Community Education evenings are not for small talk or hesitation. You go for it! All those present are educated according to their disposition, and I will expect you to dress strictly fetish. The classes take place every two weeks, and always with a particular theme. Sometimes there are 'slave only' evenings where slave-girls from our house, as well as private guests, are demonstrated on, either by a mistress or by their own masters. Other evenings might be mixed and include both male and female slaves and are designed to show the various ways a whip can be used. For example, how to gradually increase the force instead of hitting too hard right from the start.

My team and I will also explain how to deal with weights; how many one should use and how to proceed with care. Sometimes there are evenings where they demonstrate The Clinic. Here the 'patient' will get examined by a male or female 'doctor'. Various areas of expertise covered here are catheter or bladder cleaning. I, myself, have gained a proficient level of medical expertise to enable me to carry this out competently and safely. I have acquired all my knowledge from 'real' doctors. My acquaintances taught me everything; particularly when I first began. There was always a doctor at my side, an emergency surgeon who also took part in the demonstration evenings.

Generally, I'll limit the number of people present at any one of these evenings to twenty. The demonstration will take place in the middle of the room and the people stand around the sides. Sometimes the visitors are involved as well. They help with the tying up or are even allowed to caress the slave. But there is strictly no sex-play. The absolute beginner or committed voyeur has also the chance to experience SM live as a spectator during the weekday evenings. Education from soft to hard! The show features mostly female slaves, but male slaves are rigorously handled too! No dress code is required for these display evenings. There are also regular fetish nights here which offer a relaxed atmosphere, whatever your sex or sexual orientation. Naturally, strict fetish clothing is compulsory for these theme parties which are arranged in co-operation with a local private SM club called Aktives Munchen.

There is a strict procedure to follow if one wants to attend a personal session at this studio. First, the prospective client makes a telephone appointment. When he or she arrives (the studio also receives visits from couples and, very occasionally, a visit from a lone woman) we will talk briefly about their wishes, with particular regard to their pain threshold. I consider everything else totally superfluous. We don't need to make a detailed plan of action. I find it important that the girls are able to do their job well and that they have enough fantasy skills and the necessary sensitivity. If someone gives us an exact description of what they want then, of course, we'll do it. We also cater for TV training and have a wide range of clothes, shoes, wigs, make-up and silicon breasts for that purpose.

I'm also very clear with clients concerning where the borderline is involving sexual intimacy. Sex is not part of the agenda with any of the mistresses, of course. We keep it strictly separate. A woman takes either the part of a dominatrix or a devotee. There is a limit to how much a mistress will allow herself to be caressed. My absolute borderlines are my thighs. However, we do have mistresses here who will allow a licking to go much further. It depends entirely on their own preferences. Sexual intercourse with a dominatrix is, as I said earlier, an absolute taboo here. But a different rule applies for slaves. After all, that's why they're slaves! Within reason, they have to be game for anything. They must be prepared to kneel down and lick feet or anything else the client may desire.

My slaves work two days, then have four days off to recuperate. When a girl comes back she'll be in good form and looking forward to the next session. It would be too much to do this five days a week. She just wouldn't be able to give her best and the whole act would become mechanical. I'm afraid clients expecting a session with me personally will be likely to be disappointed. I don't do training very often these days, but I do stand in if necessary. My main work is taking care of the organisation and staff. It's important to me that every one of my guests leaves here completely satisfied, and that's only possible if I keep an overall picture of what's going on. It's a pity in some ways, because we used to be smaller and things were easier to manage. But the clients are happy; more women means more variety, after all.

Chapter 7: Goddess Dianna Vesta

Dianna Vesta is both a life-style and professional dominatrix, as well as highly successful businesswoman. Residing in South Florida, she publishes the monthly fetish magazine 'Attitude', and runs a worldwide organisation called The Fetish Network.

In 1968, when I was ten years old, it was apparent to everyone around me that there was something very different about me! My strong persona extended way beyond what might be called aggressive. 'Stubborn' was my middle name! That's what my mother used to call me, anyway. Although I tended to cause a lot of trouble, my parents seemed to recognise my creative ability to manipulate circumstances to my advantage. At this age, I told my father I would no longer be going to Catholic Mass with them. I felt instinctively that my life had a different destiny. Luckily, he didn't press the issue. He did, however, continue to invite me each and every Sunday.

It was at this young age that I began to realise our world and our God was all male! I didn't like the roles women were forced to play. I read the Bible and the books required at school. I also borrowed books from the library. Hour after hour I would day dream about a world I created. I remember crying sometimes because I thought something was wrong with me. I was totally out of sync with the rest of the world and everyone around me.

I played a lot of challenging sports with boys at the time, and particularly enjoyed tackle football. Once I jumped to tackle this boy. I flew at him and knocked him to the ground. He was older than I was, and no one expected a boy to whimper. Holding back his tears, he removed himself from the game. I still remember the sensations I had over that experience. It was sheer power-surge! My heart raced with excitement. I felt a drawing and pulling sensation crawl up the inside of my thighs, and my head became very light. His total defeat excited me beyond anything I could understand at the time!

Through the years I kept most of my religious and personal philosophies to myself. I enjoyed Greek mythology. Unfortunately, at that time, there were very few books that focused on matriarchal attitudes, so I developed my own little world and practiced my own solitary religion. Over the years I cultivated a special energy. I've been asked many times if this energy (that is my 'dominance'), is a reaction to a negative experience in my childhood. Maybe. This goes back to how I viewed our world as being so male and about the devaluation of women, as I saw it. Women seemed to hold it altogether and, to me anyway, were far more spiritually, emotionally and physically complex. Birth and procreation seemed more god-like, more of a miracle than man's god-like image. I believe all women have been exposed to some of the animal instincts of masculine energy. Some survive and some don't. All women have been violated to some degree and it's socially accepted. I knew I wasn't going to accept this as my destiny! However, I needed a way to balance this extreme energy. I had to find a truth that I would recognise.

My cultivated powers of persuasion helped me move very fast in the world. I dated some highly intelligent and successful men, and always found it challenging to take their power! I absorbed their knowledge and penetrated internal areas where no one had ever been; certainly no woman. Ultimately, I would break their hearts. I have always felt far superior to any of them. Even to this day these men are in love with me and they hate it. Their words are usually something like: "Why do you exist to torment me?"

I then married a boy ten years younger than myself. I owned my own company by this time, and was very successful. I taught him and showed him how to be the man I wanted. This man moved elegantly in social circles, yet this boy crawled to me at home. With this impressionable young boy I explored a sexuality that was considered very forbidden in the circles we frequented. For the most part, he stayed home doing everything a woman is normally expected to do for her husband. This role-reversal was unknown to many in my 'other' business world. I travelled a lot, and in every city I seemed to be able to find some man to do my bidding. Sometimes an eager bell-boy, sometimes an executive at 'happy hour', or sometimes both! Let's just say, I found many ways to entertain myself! My husband and I explored cross-dressing, anal play, bondage, servitude and very intense levels of humiliation. I would have him serve me and a couple of my most trusted girlfriends. After a few years, though, I began to neglect him and he took off.

I dated both men and women during this period. Women were submissive to me in a different kind of way. Their submission seemed to me more like an earned prize, whereas I just expected it from men. At this time, the words and the 'theatrics' of domination were not present yet. My female lovers felt uncomfortable with my dominance over men and tried very hard to replace my need for them, but were unsuccessful. I enjoyed dominant sex with men too much, and I liked having them at my service.

In 1988, a friend of mine called me a 'dominatrix'. I didn't know what the hell he was talking about! It was the first time I had ever heard the word. He told me about the clubs he went to in New York and some of the professional dominatrixes he knew there. By this time, I was tired of the double life I was leading and wanted to know more about this world. One day he brought over a bunch of films and magazines. For the next two days, I scrolled through their pages and watched some of the more bizarre forms of sexual expression. To be honest, a lot of it didn't appeal to me. It seemed kind of 'lower end' of the market and didn't seem like anything I was doing myself.

At the time I didn't do anything about it. However, it didn't leave my mind either. I thought a lot about the women in the magazine and I analysed their behaviour and the behaviour of the men involved. It didn't catch my attention at first, but later on it occurred to me that these magazines, much like ordinary pornography, were written and published by men! I examined them more carefully and decided to test the waters myself. Having had a lot of experience with advertising and promotions, I began placing a couple of ads in the classifieds and in some of the contact magazines. The ad read: 'Aggressive woman seeks passive man in high heels'.

The letters flocked to my post office box. It was time consuming and tiring to go through them all, and it didn't take a rocket scientist to figure out that a lot of these guys purposefully exploited the game. I made an attempt to become a professional dominatrix and charged high fees to wear leather costumes and use some stupid implements that some of these men brought to me. But, I already knew that the most important implement in my arsenal was my mind and that I already had that power. At times, I felt more like a common prostitute catering to their bizarre fantasies, while dressed in some kind of Barbie Doll fetish attire! I soon realised this was not for me. It wasn't difficult finding the clientele and the money was most definitely overwhelming. Most of the men were white collar businessmen in high stressed jobs or very shy, quiet types. Some of them became friends and I still see them.

Yet, I still wanted a way to expose myself to the 'scene' proper. After writing for some of the S&M tabloids, I soon became very well known. I went to New York and rented an apartment there, travelling back and forth to Florida. Eventually, I was able to give up my previous career and could focus on building up a network where people could openly learn about creative play. Having been a victim of misunderstanding myself, I realised that there were a lot of other people out there experiencing the same things I had.

I also realised that there was an awareness that was changing the consciousness of both men and women. Men were forced into roles they couldn't always live up to. They would constantly have to harness their insecurity and their fear of defeat. As women have become more independent over the years, it has only served to intensify their insecurities. The whole sexual arena began to take on a new form. I've studied and analysed these behaviours and read a lot of research from Erikson and Freud to Jung. My Jungian research provided me with more real recognisable truths than the others. My sessions, regardless of their nature, provided many of these men with a therapy they couldn't receive from 'normal' psychology. The simple fact that I cared enough about human destiny and was willing to extend my knowledge into these esoteric levels of human expression did, in fact, qualify me to help these people explore new aspects of themselves.

I believe that role-play and self exploration are holistic form of self-discovery. Sometimes a good dose of 'counterbalance' is all a busy executive needs to alleviate high levels of stress. Sometimes we need that other world, because we feel it's a very real part of us. The trick is to 'integrate' it into an already existing lifestyle, and not allow any one part of you to become obsessive. In a world with Aids and a total disregard for sexual intimacy, I feel that role-play and S&M 'alternatives' are a futuristic approach to exploring each other. I envisage psychology eventually becoming obsolete in many areas as human awareness excels. I can also see violent crimes diminishing as forms of role-play and self expression become socially acceptable and taught as an integral part of human interaction.

Imagine the frustration someone might feel when they are confused about an emotional aspect of life and told they are 'sick'. They enter into therapy only to find, after years of sessions, that there isn't really a cure for what they are feeling! Think how that person, who has harboured fantasies that do not fall into so-called 'normal' behaviour, is emotionally forced into believing themselves to be strange and unacceptable. It doesn't surprise me that their psyche would rebel. It also wouldn't surprise me if it constantly created interruptions throughout their entire lives, causing limited growth.

I enjoy Female Domination. I enjoy watching a male shake at the sight of me because he realises that I have power over him. He is prepared to relinquish his power to me and surrender his will. He is willing to do whatever it takes to please me. I look at this man on his knees and in absolute fear, and yet with the strength of a king, ready to accept any challenge his queen bestows upon him for the sake of her happiness. I look at this man as being superior to other men because of his submission to me! I accept his offering as a prize far more valuable than anything else he could offer. These men are my allies. My trusted confidants and assistants in my journey to know myself. This man understands female priorities, and I would consider only these men to be my equal!

I suppose I have a passive side, too. Sometimes I feel like a little girl, and my attitude might become very playful or melancholy. However, I think my nature is definitely dominant. I can't share intimacy unless I have respect for someone. My dominant expression will often test those who pursue me until they have proven themselves worthy to enter this world I've spent a lifetime to create and nurture. I'm willing to sacrifice whatever it takes and to wait patiently, sometimes for years, just to experience the erotic heights I encounter from the perfect fusion of dominance and submission. Highs that are so high that almost anything can take place, providing that person has succeeded in reaching the inner core of my being.

While waiting for these moments, I want to teach other people and set a positive example. I want to teach women not to be afraid of their power, even if their power lies in their submissive nature. I think they haven't been given a chance to really know their options, especially when it comes to sexuality. Women don't usually want to entertain themselves with the 'lower ends' of sexual expression. They prefer a much more imaginative approach, which is why you often find that women read much more than men. Often they feel guilty about some of their fantasies and therefore they don't share them. If a woman is given 'free rein' to exercise her own imagination, without influence from a demanding partner, she will eventually pass the erotic heights of her lover. Unfortunately, this is not easy in the world we live in today and, until the priorities of women are really accepted, they will not take this 'free rein'.

Chapter 8: Mistress Dominique

Ex-librarian turned lifestyle, then professional mistress who famously suffered at the even crueller hands of Britain's notorious 'gutter' press! Mistress Dominique now lives in quiet, rural seclusion in Sussex on the South Coast of England with her two transvestite personal maids.

My late husband was fascinated by the SM scene, and we used to visit the clubs in London quite regularly. After he died, I drifted out of the scene for a while. Then, when I remarried, my second husband shared my interest in S&M and we used to go to some very heavy parties and private events. In those early days, before AIDS, there used to be blood all over the place. But never any sex. Nowadays, I don't really know what goes on.

About five years ago, my husband became very ill. I needed to work from home to be able to look after him and, if you live in a very small village miles from anywhere, there aren't too many types of work you can do at home, so I decided to turn my main hobby into a profession. I wasn't sure at first whether I'd be successful as a professional. All the professional ladies I'd met at clubs and parties seemed to be more into the verbal humiliation and boot licking type of scenarios, whereas I was primarily into bondage and mental control. At first, I just advertised in Axis, my favourite contact magazine, but I was lucky because everyone I met initially I got on with. In fact, the very first slave I ever saw still visits me now, despite the big change of location.

Jayne, for instance, who's now one of my live-in transvestite maids, was originally a guest of mine. I always think of people as 'guests', by the way, never clients. They're guests in my home. Anyway, Jayne's wife had died a few months previously, so she was brand new to the scene. And I really didn't know what I was doing either! It really is a whole different ball-game, being amateur to professional. We decided to do an outdoor session with a cross in the garden. It was my very first session outside and it was the unintentional bits that were the best; like me trying to use a dressage whip while the cat was sitting on the other end!

As I said, I don't deal with verbal domination; all that shouting and screaming that they are 'pathetic worms who should be grovelling at my boots' etc. It all seems a bit false and simply doesn't work for me. The idea of pretending to be cross with every single person who comes in leaves me cold. I just like having fun.

I love bondage, especially rubber! And, as you can see, I'm fairly TV friendly! My ultimate favourite is electric's. They're marvellous! I first got interested in electric's when I worked as a librarian in a health library. I adore making people helpless and playing with them. A lot of people, for instance, don't like corporal punishment. It's either the wrong sort of pain, that is, too intense, or there are problems with marks. There are also people I know who'd literally wear my arm out and they'd still not get the endorphin 'high' they need from caning. However, electric's are so accurately targeted (and I only use safe boxes, most of them have got medical applications anyway) it's an incredible, erotic pain/pleasure sensation. Nothing to do with the old idea of banging something into the mains and putting a couple of bulldog clips on. At the top end of the boxes, I can get a 'mercy' out of anybody, particularly with the electric catheters which are seriously lethal, nasty, painful little things. But at the bottom end of the scale, you've got pleasure all the way along the line. It's gorgeous! It's like turning a radio down. It's starts off low and builds up. I can tease and torment. Everything from a mild tingle to excruciating pain with just a switch of the dial. The reason I've got about ten, twelve boxes and counting, is that I need the different sensations. I'd get bored with just one or two. I get bored very easily. Plus, like every mistress, I'm frightened of one day burning out. There are so many different things you can do with electric's. They're very versatile.

In fact, one of my fondest memories of Julie, my TV housekeeper, is of finding her, one blindingly hot summers day, head to foot in rubber, gas mask on and doing the ironing with a tell-tale little lead from her apron pocket to another part of her anatomy. She had actually wired herself up to the electric's while she was doing the ironing! That's how non-painful they are. You can actually walk around with them in. If I think Julie's falling asleep when she's supposed to be on duty, I'll twitch the dial a little bit. That usually wakes her up!

I remember an hilarious conversation with my accountant about electric's. At first he thought I was re-wiring the house! When I explained, he said: "Let me get this right. You mean people actually pay you to electrocute them? And you even need different ways of doing it!" The conversation sounded like that Bob Newhart sketch Introducing Tobacco to Civilization.

What can I tell you about the transvestite side of things? Well, I don't do 'dress for the day', as I just don't have the time or the facilities. I feel that if you're going to do that you've got to have a massive wardrobe. What we do have is the skills to transform someone into maids uniform or perhaps little tarty stuff, that sort of thing. I find it's a total switch for people. It makes them far more vulnerable. I love TV's for their soft side. I think they get a very raw deal in society anyway. I can't understand why there's so much resentment against them. They're also afraid of being ridiculed themselves. But, to me, it's a chance to wear nice materials and to have a complete change from the outside world. Loads of people are latent TV's but, either don't have the courage or the opportunity, to do anything about it.

The important thing is that when people visit us they can see straight away that we are genuine and this is our lifestyle. It's not a case of them walking in and finding that the mistress really doesn't like TV's, and all she's got is a few 'glad rags' and that's it. We live this way all of the time, and very happily so. Then they'll come out of themselves and admit that they'd quite like to try it themselves. They know we're not going to turn round and think they're a weirdo. For us, it's our normal way of life. I remember one person commented that he was surprised this wasn't sordid, but was really rather cosy. Of course, it's not sordid! This is my working environment, as well as my home! One of the reasons for moving down to this area is that it is so TV friendly. In the Midlands, if Julie or Jayne had gone out dressed, they'd have been stoned! We'd already had dead animals thrown into the garden. Down here, even my hairdresser knows what I do for a living!

Not many TV's are into SM, actually. They're mostly into the fetish side and the verbal humiliation and so on. When Jayne first came to see me I was advertising as a headmistress. I got this long letter from her asking if I gave 'correct' lessons and did they include Latin? I thought I must have a nut-case here! She wanted to be 'correctly' dressed for each occasion. I'm sitting there trying to work out what is the 'correct' dress for a dungeon, and what is the 'correct' dress for outdoors, and…oh God, the list went on and on! I think transvestism is a kind of uniform fetish as much as anything else.

What I'm curious about is what I can show on the Web, and what I can't show. I'm interested in doing things like 'live-cams'. I'm certainly going to do a recorded video clip of the dungeon, so that people can see what I've got to offer. I've heard so many times of people who go to a mistress and she'll say things like: "Oh, that's on order" or "The electric's aren't working today" or "No, I didn't say the room was mirrored" or "You should have told me you were a size twenty". So if I do a video, people can link in on the Internet, have a look around the dungeon, and see it's real. Okay, I'm not exactly photogenic but, this is me, it's not a studio shot and I am the person who will be seeing them. People will go and see a mistress and she's nothing like the illustration! Maybe they'll find that they haven't even spoken to the person who's there on the day. That seems so unfair. I think the Internet is going to be the way to go, but how much will they let me show? Will they let me show a live session; bearing in mind that, after the Spanner Case, it's still technically illegal here?

When the national newspapers exposed me, it was devastating. I was immediately homeless. I had to move right out of the area and was unable to find work for several months while I relocated; which was financially devastating. A lot of ladies have contacted me and asked me how the newspaper decided on me. Was it a tip off? How can they avoid being exposed? The answer is that, in this profession, there is no way you can avoid exposure indefinitely. It's all down to pure luck, I'm afraid. In my case, they never even entered my dungeon! They just took photos from the outside, including one of me in a summer dress! So even the ladies who wear wigs and masks aren't safe. They will just take a normal 'snap' as well, if they can. It's something you just have to live with. Down here, I doubt very much if anyone would be bothered if I was featured again.

My local newspaper thought it was all marvellous at first! The previous week their front page had been about double parking in the town centre, and now there was this 'sex den' on their doorstep that they didn't know about. They were knocking on our door at all hours for weeks on end. Then they tried to break into the house. They even contacted the local police and said, basically: "Hey, look at this! There's a vice den here. What are you going to do about it?' And the police told them that they had known I was there for years. Their attitude was that I wasn't doing anything illegal. I was advertising in a private magazine and there had been no complaints whatsoever. One very unhappy reporter! He was the bane of my life for months, that guy. They were very upset in the end that it had been going on under their noses and they hadn't a clue, and that a national newspaper had taken, what they considered, their story.

On the day the paper came out, we had something like fifty-odd people camped outside, trying to take pictures. But, because we knew it was going to happen, I was already house-hunting down here, so I wasn't even there! In a situation like that you certainly get to find out who your friends are, too. All the people who used to come round once a week and borrow books, have a drink or whatever, didn't want to know. One or two people stuck by us. But the amount of people who said: "Oh, I don't really know the lady", and I'd known them three or four years and thought they were friends! It's an abrupt way to find out who your friends are! It was a nightmare. I don't think anyone I've spoken to has had as many problems. But I do know three or four mistresses who've retired because they've realised these people don't need a reason. In my case, they printed my address and everything! I think they've got a file on all of us and, if there's nothing else, they'll use it. A mistress friend of mine was done recently, and she wasn't even working at the time! It's a very gray area. What they should do, of course, is legalise it all and run decent safety checks. They should come in to check for things like basic hygiene and safety, particularly. If someone is upside down and you've got 'wonky' suspension, you're in big trouble! It would be better for everybody all round.

We were very naive when we started out. We used to lend books and clothes to people. The amount of underwear I lost in the first year! We had so many things that never came back that you harden up in the end! I think every mistress goes through it. I once caught someone walking out, quite openly, with a pair of nipple clamps! He said he thought he'd just take a souvenir! I was so dumb founded I didn't even tear his head off! This is the side of things that people don't see. Like the stalkers, like the newspapers, like the people who ring at two and three in the morning. I've actually been physically attacked half a dozen times in the dungeon! That's why a lot of ladies give up. But they won't change the law and let us work together for self protection. As the law stands that would be considered a brothel and be illegal.

People see what they think is an idyllic lifestyle of the mistress and her bevy of slaves, but don't realise the pressures; especially if the mistress is renting a property. If your landlord knows what you're doing, he'll probably charge you four or five times as much rent for the privilege. If he doesn't know and does a spot inspection, as he's entitled to do, you may well get evicted with very short notice. Then have a battle on your hands afterwards to get the deposit back! And you learn very quickly that you can't have an awful lot of friends in this business, either. If you're too friendly with people, the next thing is: "Can I pop in for a cup of tea?" Well, no, because we do strict one-on-one sessions here, and privacy is a luxury for both me and the guests. People come to me because they don't want to see someone else sitting in a waiting room like in the massage parlours. They know that the only people who might be here will be Julie or Jayne.

When a guest arrives, he is probably met by my TV maid or housekeeper, who'll give them a brief questionnaire to fill in and then bring them down to me in the dungeon. It saves me having to stand there and ask them about fifty different questions. If I've already spoken to them at length on the phone, I'll say: "Look, take a little bit of time out. Write down the things you love and the things you loathe. Put me inside your head". The first session is always about building up trust, more than anything else. Especially with people who've had horrendous experiences. Perhaps they've gone to a 'so-called' mistress and, no matter what they asked for, they've just got straight CP. They're in and out in twenty minutes. What we call the 'whip and wank' brigade! The thing to remember is that there are bad apples in every profession. People just have to keep ringing round, keep asking questions. If a mistress won't talk to you on the phone and there's not a lot of information on hand, then she's not going to take the time to listen to you during the session and try to get it right.

When we first came down here one of the things I needed to know was the quality of the mistresses in the area and what sort of competition I'd got. It's quite amusing that mistresses will actually send their own slaves round for a session to check each other out! It's really just to see what the competition is like. It's happened to us dozens of times and we've done the same thing. Sometimes they will admit at the end of the session: "Well, actually, I've been sent by Mistress Whoever. I'm her live-in slave". Or a mistress will phone up and ask if they can send their slave over to get some information on electric's in exchange for something else. That's okay, it's not a problem.

It's lovely to talk to other mistress's, because then you don't feel so isolated. We have a very good relationship with each other. I regularly go out to dinner and socialise with other local mistress friends. Sometimes we find we share the same clients! A few weeks ago I was chatting with one friend, Mistress Diane, and realised we had, had a client who had booked with me at one o'clock, with her at three, and I bet he'd booked with Mistress Antoinette at five! What happens is that someone will be having a meeting and not be sure when it's going to end, so they book three different appointments to make sure they get one session in!

We have a good relationship with our neighbours, too. From their point of view we're quiet, conservative people. We never go out dressed. If this place were let to a group of students, there would probably be parties every night. The only risk now in this business is the gangs of kids who might find out what you're doing though the Internet. And, of course, all the kids are on the Internet these days. But, if a very young voice phoned up asking for details, we wouldn't accept the call anyway.

One of the problems with this job is the adrenalin surge in the morning. I look in the diary and see I've got four people booked; which is fully booked for me. Everybody confirms between nine and eleven o'clock. You think, this is going to be a great day! Right, how much money can I spend? Where are the catalogues? And a little voice in the background is saying 'overdraft'! Then, perhaps, the first one doesn't turn up and we're thinking that maybe he's got lost? Or we're standing here and see him going to the wrong house across the road, despite our very explicit directions! That's heart attack time!

Like any other mistress, I've had my fair share of, shall we say, the more 'unusual' requests. There was the 'parcel tape' man, for instance. We actually discouraged him in the end. What he wanted was to be wrapped up from head to foot in Post Office brown parcel tape. It was a fantasy he'd had for years, and he'd even brought his own tape along with him! I took one look at it and pointed out that it would take all his hair off if we did what he wanted, so we switched him to tight rubber-wrap, instead. He hadn't worked out the results of tearing it off, you see. We often say to people: "Yes, it's a very nice fantasy, but you've got to think it through'. From the sketches he showed us I could also see that he hadn't left himself any breathing holes. I know it might have been a trivial thing to him, but I'm the one who would have had to dispose of the body! Then there was the guy who wanted to ironed and then put in the oven and baked! I turned him down, too. I couldn't get my head round that one, to be honest. Another man wanted me to stand on his tongue. Another wanted to be hanged, and I won't do asphyxiation. Another wanted to be beaten senseless and raped. They've got this picture of their fantasy in their minds, but it just won't work or is too dangerous to do in real life.

Some of them are so amusing though. We had one guy, back in the very early days, who said on the telephone that he wanted to be interrogated. Now, I love interrogation scenarios. I told him to just think of a story line; with an address or a telephone number that I can drag out of him gradually. He assured me he was quite tough. He even brought me a little note saying that marks weren't a problem. We took him upstairs and he took one look at the room (which, by our standards today, was really quite basic) and his jaw dropped! I went straight into the scenario and bellowed: "Right, you're go-ing to tell me how you got my name and phone number!". And he mumbled: "From a contact magazine, Mistress". No, no, I thought, this really isn't how you play this game. So I tried again: "I don't believe you! I don't advertise anywhere like that. How did you get my address?". Again he blubbers: "I just went to the phone box and you gave me your address and I think I've changed my mind and I want to go home now!" We had to sit the poor chap down, give him a cup of tea and suggest that we started all over again. It was like that Monty Python sketch where the chap pays to have an argument!

Another one arrived and handed me two envelopes. What's this all about, I thought? Anyway, I ordered him to undress and put him on the frame and I could see he was petrified. He was standing there in the most beautiful metal chastity belt and shaking like a leaf. One envelope contained my 'gift' and in the other was the key to the belt and a brief note from his mistress telling me that if he performs properly I could release him, if not I was to send him home. What am I going to do here? Oh, I thought, you poor little love! I just gave him a little hug in the end.

I do the same with the female submissives who are occasionally brought to me. They walk in and they're petrified. I tell them to calm down and assure them that I'm not going to hurt them. And, if they're afraid their male partners are going to hurt them, I remind them that women rule supreme in this house and I'd tie him up and beat the living daylights out of him! I'm not bisexual, so I really don't know what to do with the little darlings anyway! It can happen the other way round, too. I've had couples where the male is submissive and he wants me to teach his wife how to dominate him. Well, it's hard because you're either into this or you're not. Sure, I can show them a few basic techniques, but I can't make them enjoy it! I'll see couples very rarely. It's not something I encourage.

There's one lovely old gentleman of eighty five who comes to see me most Sunday evenings. He always has to have his little joke, whereby he'll 'hide' my gift in something unusual. Once he handed me a piggy bank sealed with superglue! Another time it was in a coffee jar with a chain and a combination lock! Or it might be a sweet jar with 'bomb' written on it! Oh, and there was the tiny hippo that took me ten minutes with a pair of tweezers to extract my gift from. He must spend hours thinking of all these novel ideas and, not only does it amuse me, I really appreciate the effort he puts into it. He goes to so much trouble, and he's always making me little things for the dungeon.

Then there was another one who'd come along for maid-training, so I set him to work cleaning my kitchen. Now, I'm used to having to go in and telling the maid that they haven't done this or that properly as an excuse for punishment but, in this case, I walked in and the kitchen was spotless and he was looking round for other things to do. Instead of punishing him, I found myself saying: "Oh, you must be exhausted. Sit down and I'll make you a cup of tea!" We've also had power cuts in the middle of intricate bondage sessions and all sorts of things. Luckily, there are always plenty of candles lying around in a dungeon!

You have to have a sense of humour in this or you'd just go mad. You also have to laugh when things don't go quite right, or even totally wrong. One of my submissives, Steve, who has been with me from the very early days, and who I treasure greatly, tells me he always knows when the session is going right because I radiate peace. He's more concerned that I, as the mistress, enjoy myself rather than just go through some set routine. The last time he came, I'd just seen a picture on the Internet that was quite intricate bondage, and I was playing around with this and it wasn't going right. He assured me not to worry about it. I got there in the end, and he said that he could feel me relax as the scenario was starting to go well. That's the kind of empathy you can build up with a submissive.

I always invite people to write to me after the session and critique it. Yes, I know a mistress is supposed to be perfect, and never gets things; you know, the goddess image! But, in actual fact, I like to know how the session went from the other persons viewpoint. The feedback's terrific, and I've learnt a lot like that. I want people to let me know if something didn't work for them. I also keep notes with the questionnaires and the critiques. When they come back in six months I look up my notes. I'll know their likes, dislikes, clothes sizes, everything. People are hurt if they phone up and you don't remember who they are. Steve never fails to write after every single session. These critiques have been invaluable to me over the years in enabling me to see the sessions through the slaves eyes and to learn from that and enhance my skills. He has helped me evolve and I appreciate that. We have what we call our 'Lottery List'; which means, if we won the Lottery, what submissives would we continue to see for free? Steve would be right there at the top. He's kept a pictorial record of every dungeon I've ever had and is the only person, apart Julie and Jayne, to have seen me evolve as a mistress. He has suffered (or enjoyed!) my every passion and enthusiasm, and I always experiment with all my new toys on him.

Another favourite, and the only person I've ever done a 'hotel visit' for, is my 'little corset girl' in the Midlands. She's in her eighties now and adores tight corseting and CP. It was 'her' birthday recently and I went back to the Midlands, stayed overnight and she visited me at the hotel. She's written or telephoned me every week for five years; that's loyalty! As I said, when we left the Midlands so abruptly we found out very quickly who our real friends were. We desperately needed references so we could rent somewhere to live, and we were desperately hurt by the people we thought were close friends and then totally disowned us. My 'little corset girl' did everything she possibly could to help us. I was very grateful and I have a very long memory.

Most of all, I like the lovely people who bring me new ideas to try, and the ones who don't care if I wear similar clothes each time (having a 46" bust makes trying to find new clothes in PVC or leather a nightmare), people who appreciate what I do and are enthusiastic and I can have fun with! What I don't like are the time wasters and the people who try to play psychological 'games' with the mistress. I'm very explicit about what I do and what I don't. Most people can get a first appointment, but even at that stage I'm still weeding out the time wasters, and people have been known to be asked to leave. One 'gentleman' turned up, refused to fill in the questionnaire, took one look at the equipment and said: "Yeah, fancy decorations. Now what do you charge for sex?" He proceeded to pull out about one thousand pounds in fifty pound notes from his wallet. I promptly informed him I don't 'do' sex under any circumstances, and further suggested he put the notes into a particular orifice and I would light them for him! However, after we had sorted out this little difference of opinion, he became a devoted slave, and I still him occasionally. Apparently, this was a little 'test' of his to see if the mistress is a real dominatrix or just a prostitute posing as one. I did ask him once which ladies had passed the test and who had failed; but he's very discrete, and so am I!

There are a lot of people I wouldn't want to see again, yet there are also a lot I would. I wondered at first, when I turned professional, whether it would spoil it for me. But you get more and more involved, and it's fun! Everyone who walks in here is like a jig-saw puzzle that you have to put together. They're all so different, and looking for such totally different things. That's why I encourage people to send me fantasies and feedback.

Often there is no logical end to a particular fantasy or, as I've said, you make the fantasy real and they find they don't like it. One unexpected problem I've encountered is when someone has brought me a fantasy, and I've done it for them, and they've said: "Yes, but that's my fantasy, and you've done it! What do I do now?" I got an e-mail from someone recently, saying: "Thank you very much, but I don't know where to go from here! I'll be in touch when I've thought of a new fantasy!" What happens often is that they will go to a mistress and they'll get a 'little bit' of their fantasy, perhaps. What we do is enhance that. We do the fantasy exactly as they want it the first time, then try and make it more and more realistic.

A good example is one gentleman who's come to see me half a dozen times for a 'prison warder' scenario. It was quite detailed. When he came to the front door, Jayne was dressed, as near as we could get it, in a trustees uniform with leg irons on. I'd blanked out my old librarian's security badge and written 'prison warden'. We'd got files with his name on and details of his offenses. We enhance the fantasy each time.

Jayne and Julie will get involved in sessions only if they are specifically invited by the guest to join in. It is useful to have an extra pair of hands with the more complicated bondage; particularly the cling-film, as we use very large rolls which are too heavy for me to handle on my own. But they would never enter the dungeon without being specifically invited. In a dire emergency they would slip a note under the door, and we do have a subtle alarm system that the guest isn't aware of.

Julie, in particular, loves to join in rubber bondage sessions as she's an ardent rubberist. She's probably responsible for my love of rubber, and she makes all my rubber clothes as I can rarely get anything in my size. Our main problem is finding a strong rubber adhesive, I tend to put rather a strain on the seams as I love rubber skin tight! Julie's always busy and, if she isn't making clothes for me, she's repairing things like hoods, making maids dresses, sorting out my Internet site, doing the accounts; not to mention all the housework!

As I said earlier, I don't consider that corporal punishment is an essential part of every session. Some people simply don't enjoy that type of sensation, and many are worried about marks; though only an inept or careless mistress leaves telltale signs on a guest's body. That's not to say that I can't cane extremely accurately! I've had plenty of practice, particularly with Jayne (who is also a wicked schoolgirl called 'Jennifer'). Not only can she be unsuitably flippant at times, she just happens to enjoy being caned in front of people, too! It's very often well deserved and, at the end of each caning, she always kneels, kisses my hand and thanks me for her punishment. She's only forgotten once in five years, but the resulting extra strokes ensured that, oddly enough, she has never forgotten again! And I broke my favourite cane in the process that time!

When we go away, we usually stay at a gay hotel so that the 'girls' can dress if they like. It's very funny sometimes, because people can never quite work out what's going on! We'd come down together and one minute the girls would be dressed and the next they'd be straight. For a start, there are three of us, which is an odd combination. They'd be thinking: "What is this woman doing with these people?" They always assume that anyone TV has got to be gay, so it totally confuses the life out of them!

An awful lot of people who come to see me are very stressed out businessmen. If they've done competitive sports, particularly, they're used to an adrenaline surge or an endomorphic high, and the body can't replace that. They really do have difficulty coming to terms with the fact that they need to visit someone like me, especially if they are genuinely happily married. But their bodies are going crazy. They need some sort of deep relaxation, and that's what a good SM session should give. They need to be divorced from the outside world. The sessions will usually end on the long bench with the slave bound tight with either latex or rubber; which gives unbearable erotic tension, followed by ejaculation and, finally, relief! Then I'll let people relax and unwind for a few minutes before I slowly remove all the bondage and they gradually come back to the real world from the 'twilight' world. I think it's a much nicer and friendlier way of bringing proceedings to a close. I know some mistresses who will simply bang on the light and their jerked back to reality. We'll chat for a while and it's amazing the things you talk about. Like their guilt, for instance. I'll explain that really this is true stress therapy, in the same way their wives may go out and get a new hairdo or even have aroma therapy! She doesn't feel guilty, does she? I don't break up marriages. They're still faithful to their wives, but they go home happier and more relaxed. Men don't leave their wives for this kind of mistress. Being totally 'out of control' from daily life and its responsibilities is the main thing. Being able to trust somebody enough to hand yourself over to them and empower them, that's my thrill! It's a total power kick for me, having that finger-tip control over somebody. That's the beauty of this job, and I get to wear my favourite clothes, too!

As long as you remind yourself that there is a real world out there. On the other side of these walls there are cars going by and people walking about. This is the fantasy world, the twilight world. Step through that door and bang, it's reality again. There are mistresses who've come to believe in their own 'immortality', if you like. That's silly. I saw one mistress at the Fetish Market once who had her slave trailing around behind her, bare footed! Now, come on, this is the real world! There's broken glass on the floor at events like that. He's going to get stamped on. To me, this isn't about having a slave who'll do whatever I want. This is saying: "I'm an idiot and I've got one with me to prove it!" There was nothing dominant about that. It was a screaming health risk and a total disregard for the well being of the slave. One of the main responsibilities of the mistress is the slave's welfare.

I've always maintained that anyone can inflict pain, but not many can make it erotic and fulfilling. Building it up sensually is a very different matter. If it weren't, there would be an awful lot of ladies doing this because it is very lucrative. I certainly couldn't be earning this in the library service, unless they've drastically changed the rates of pay! It's easy to beat someone into submission, but I wouldn't find that fulfilling and it would ultimately bore me. What I do is to combine erotic stimulation with pain until people want to submit! And I always make sure I give people 100% in the dungeon. If I'm not feeling my best, or I'm not sure about a particular scenario, I'd rather not do it than give less than my best.

This may surprise some people but, outside of my role as a dominatrix, I'm not a particularly assertive person. I'm even quite shy. I like a peaceful life with a good book to read and I'm not terribly sociable. I think that's probably why I can't get into all the 'shouting' aspect that some other mistresses are very good at. We know one mistress who is absolutely brilliant at it. She'd worked in a care home and she'd got two kids! She was used to arguing with people and being assertive all the time in real life, and this came across brilliantly in her maid-training.

I couldn't stop doing this now. It's like a drug. Look at it from the mistress's point of view; I've got people who, in normal life, would pass me in the street or in a night club without a second glance and they're coming here, kneeling at my feet, licking my boots and telling me I'm a goddess! And you think I could give that up? No thank you!

Chapter 9: Mistress Eva

From her exclusive London apartment, this blonde former dancer and performance artist reigns supreme over her harem of 'little slave boys' in her self created world of dominant delights.

My first experience of domination for pleasure was when I was in my late teens. Because I'm six foot one tall, I found when I started dating guys that the kind of men I attracted were secretly subservient. I also had a tendency to want to be bossy sexually anyway, so it kind of evolved from there. I just got into it more and more and more. I'm thirty three now, so it's been over a period of about fifteen years.

I went to live in Miami for a while, so I didn't know about the scene in London. I started going to fetish clubs there and, to be honest, the first one I went to was a bit of a shambles, really. It was kind of like a high school dance! There were lots of people with bits of PVC on just standing around and not really doing anything. And I was there ready to kick everybody's head in! I'd even brought my own collar and lead with me ready to drag some slave around the floor! People were looking at me a bit strange, I can tell you!

Then I came back to London. The scene was very underground then. I started going out and meeting people on the scene. I'd stopped dancing professionally at this point, so I thought what shall I do for a living now? Why not do something I really enjoy and get the most fun out of? So that's how I became a professional dominatrix.

Because I live on the premises, I've redesigned the whole place with a sort of gothic, semi-liveable, semi-dungeon feel. That means I don't have to restrict the play to the dungeon itself. I can have a slave as a foot stool in my living room while I'm watching a movie or something and it's still got the right atmosphere. It's not like going from a dungeon to Laura Ashley, which is not my kind of thing, and not the slave's either, I'm sure.

I do a whole spectrum of scenarios from erotic dancing and tie and tease, to quite heavy-handed violent scenes involving fisting, face slapping and flagellation. Because of my size, I can do a good line in beatings! That's top of my list of favourite activities. But I do know just how far to go, so everything I do is safe. My other top favourite is using my strap-on dildo. I find that at least 85% of submissive men like that, they just won't admit it! I have to talk them into it sometimes. I get quite a range of requests for heavy bondage and body bag scenarios but, to be honest, I can't be asked to do anything that I don't enjoy. It's too time consuming and I'd start getting bored. The reason I do this work in the first place is because I enjoy it. It genuinely gives me a thrill to work with slaves. They tell me they can feel that I'm actually enjoying it myself, and that I'm not just doing this as a job. Then it would be mundane and I'd do something else to get me out of the house. I really enjoy 'cuffing' someone or having them on their knees staring up at me for hours. I love it! It gives me goose bumps!

You get some mistresses who will just go 'tap-tap-tap' and tell them what a naughty boy they are. You get the impression that they're just doing it for the money and don't really enjoy it at all. I earned enough through dancing for ten years so that I don't have to do this for the money. I do it because I love it. The beauty of having the dungeon in my own apartment is that I don't have to work ten to seven, Monday to Friday. I work seven days a week, but I'll have a day off whenever I feel like it. If I don't want to work for a few days, I won't. I don't work regular hours either. I might see someone at nine o'clock in the morning or one o'clock at night. I think that works better because not everyone can come and see a mistress between ten and seven o'clock. It's also very useful when I get overnight kidnappings and stuff. What I usually do is keep them in the cage and I'll sleep in the bed next to it. They have to stay awake, of course, till I fall asleep. And they have to make sure they're awake before I am in order to greet me correctly and prepare my breakfast!

I have some great people I kidnap on a regular basis. I've got one client I always kidnap at Toddington Services on the M1 motorway. It's the first service station you get to leaving London going north. I see him once a month. I won't say his name, but he knows who he is! It's always the same rigmarole; I drive up in the car and buy myself chicken and chips or something. Then, as I'm driving out again to come back to London, there he is waiting at the entrance to the motorway with his thumb out hitch hiking. I love it so much my heart starts beating away with excitement as I stop! I'll get out of the car and ask if he's okay. He'll tell me he doesn't know where he is or where he lives because he's lost his memory. And I'll say: "Oh, I'll take you to the nearest police station, you poor thing". Then I'll blindfold him, open the boot, shove him in and bring him back here and lock him up for two days. He'll be beating on the inside of the boot all the way back and I'll be swinging the car from side to side as I drive along. He's my absolute favourite. Mr Motorway, I call him. It's the most fun, even though it's the same scenario every month, and in exactly the same place. He's probably parked his car there or maybe his house is behind the bushes, I don't know. I've never asked him. I think the monotony has actually become part of the excitement for me! I vary the 'verbals' sometimes, depending on what kind of day I've had. If I've had a good day, I'll be all sympathetic or, if I've had a bad day, I'll give him a good smack as I bundle him in.

Then there's The Milkman. I call him that because he spends half an hour acting like a pussycat. I'll give him the cat bowl and he'll lick me and I'll stroke his head like a pet. I've got The Slapper, too. He likes having his face slapped for hours on end. They're my favourites. Sometimes it can get a bit mundane. When I do a sensory deprivation scenario with blindfolds and earplugs, for instance, I'll be sitting on top of the cage with a cup of coffee and my newspaper or doing some paperwork. It's quite comical really, and the slaves see the funny side of it too.

I'm very much into costumes and role playing. I like the scenarios where I'm wearing a police woman's uniform or Gestapo outfit, and I get to shove a lamp in their faces and that kind of thing.
I'm supposed to have caught them and have to interrogate them. I
also enjoy 'secretary' ones where the client is my male secretary and
they've done something wrong or their sales figures aren't up this
month. Basically, I'll rape them and fuck them up the arse! I'll have
the strap-on under my skirt. I'll whip it and pound it into them. I
enjoy those ones a lot, actually. They're fun to do. Well, I wouldn't be
doing it otherwise, would I? And I shall continue to do it for a long
time yet!

Scenarios that I won't consider doing are things like 'hard
sports'; just the thought of it makes me feel sick! And I won't have
any conversation in the session to do animals or children. If they
want to dress up as little boys, that's okay. But if they're using con-
notations of a paedophile nature, then they're straight out the door!
There are things that I don't personally like, but I will do them if
the client requests it. Mostly, I mean the kind of things I mentioned
earlier that I find a bit tedious, or things that I think are a little extreme. For instance, some harder forms of cock and ball torture is
just not good for you and can be very damaging for the future. I've
seen someone at clubs actually dangling fire extinguishers from their
testicles! That person is going to suffer so much in the future. Even
if he's confident in his technique, that technique could fail one night
and his balls will be gone! It's up to the individual to do it or receive
it, though. I'm not trying to put anyone off it but, personally, I won't
go beyond a certain point.

I won't doing piercings, either. That's for professional people to
do. Branding is okay. In fact, I branded my ex-husband! He'll have
to carry that on his back for the rest of his life! Scarification I won't
do, because that's very dangerous, too. Also, the submissive is caught
up within the moment so much that, under the spell of the mistress,
they really feel they want to be scared. But when the session's over
and they go back to their other life, I know they'll regret it. I think

that's taking advantage of my position and my power. They're only doing it because they really are under the power of the mistress! I've studied the medical side for each job I do, because there are certain things I need to know. I am also a qualified first-aider, so I know what to do should a situation arise.

Generally, I love all the fun stuff! Tease and please and bring you to your knees kind of stuff! I love watersports, too. And I absolutely insist on body worship, because that always gets the session moving. Remember, a lot of times the clients are very nervous, especially if they're first timers. They're always scared walking into the dungeon for the first time. They think they're going to be thrown down on the floor and beaten unmercifully, but that's really not the way it is. Maybe they've had bad experiences with a mistress who just didn't listen. I'll normally bring them into the lounge if they're first timers, and sit them down and have a chat. I'll give them my 'safe word' and ask them for a list of things that they really don't like. Things that really scare them, that's a good place to start. We'll exchange contributions and then go in and do it. I like the fun of working them into it slowly, and getting them into the dungeon scene that way. I'll put a favourite song on and I'll do a full strip and tease them while they're tied up. I love getting up so close they can almost kiss me, then I'll pull back! I love all the teasing and caressing and whispering and taunting them. That's what I like the best because I am a real exhibitionist when I'm doing it. I'm really a quiet little pussy cat inside, but don't tell anybody that!

A lot of domination is theatre, if you think about it. And I'm a born actress! I'll change my hairstyle and clothes to match the scenario; whether it's school mistress or secretary with my hair in a bun and severe glasses, or long flowing red-head vamp. It gives me a great opportunity to dress up in corsets or rubber cat woman outfits and wonder bras. That's what I love about the job the most. I still do some dancing and television work, but out of all the jobs I've had, this is my favourite. I'll carry on for about another ten years professionally, though I know that'll be a big disappointment to all my little boys! I'll still keep a dungeon in my house, but that will be just for pleasure. I love all my naughty boys who come into my life and make Mistress Eva's comical world of dominant delights spin and spin!

It is a wonderful lifestyle, as I keep saying. If I decide to go away for three weeks, I will. I'll just shut down and put on the answering machine and tell them I'll be back on such and such a day. My regular clients, I'll refer to other mistresses who I know I can trust. Rather than let the poor puppies go without, I'll ask them if they can look after a few of my boys for me. I know that the other mistress will take care of their needs, and that they're not going to be mistreated or poached. We don't do things like that. There's enough to go round for everybody.

I've only had to turn away two clients in my life. One because he was so filthy, and I was actually cruel enough to tell him so! And the other because he came in very drunk and was very obnoxious towards me. He wasn't violent, so I wasn't threatened by him, but he was saying things like: "What are you going to do to me then?" And I said: "I'll tell you what I'm going to do to you, love. I'm going to throw you out the fucking door". I grabbed hold of him and threw him into the street! But that was the only two occasions. Generally, I find the submissive male immaculately clean and well behaved. Because they've come to submit to me, they're very compliant and polite. Even if I've almost drawn blood from giving them a beating, they still want to bring me chocolates or flowers, which I think is really sweet. I don't have to buy flowers ever again. Sometimes the dungeon looks like a funeral parlour!

As I said, I do have a fully equipped dungeon here, complete with leather bed built on a metal cage and all sorts of bit and bobs. But it's not always the equipment that counts, it's what the mistress does with it! You can dominate someone with one hand and with no dungeon at all! If you're that good and that strong, mentally and physically, you can do it. For instance, if any of my slaves tell me they're allergic to my pet cat, I'll put the cat in the cage with them just to torture them a little bit more! If they've misbehaved, I'll rub them a little bit with the cat. It completely freaks them out!

This is a complete lifestyle for me. Even if I go out to a 'vanilla' club, I'll always wear six inch patent heels with rubber trousers; something of a fetish nature anyway. It separates the boys from the toys, as it were! If they see me and they've got submissive tendencies, they'll know what's going on. That's how I attract my personal slaves who I'll bring them back to my little harem. That's what I'd like to have really, a harem full of hunky male slaves! They can pamper me all day and serve me and carry me everywhere. I could have them all on leads like little puppies. I can quite see myself as Cruella de Ville!"

Chapter 10: Mistress Hades

Well known and much respected on the British fetish scene as the power behind the London Fetish Fair (the capitals monthly 'scene' market), 28 year old Mistress Hades is also an accomplished dominatrix in her own right. Though American-born, she was educated in Britain and now lives and works in North London.

I would call myself a life-style mistress because I could never see myself not being kinky or into kinky sex or not being into games of dominance and servitude and all that. Running The Fetish Fair, for example, I'll sometimes see a mistress who wants to give up her dungeon and she'll come and take a stand and sell all her stuff. I couldn't do that! I'm too emotionally attached to my equipment. I'd be remembering what good times I'd had with that flesh-grabber! Happy days! I couldn't get rid of that! I've had too much fun with it!

You also get a certain amount of psychological freedom from doing this work. I mean, I've done a lot of jobs before I decided to become a mistress where I'd have to wear a skirt and a blouse or some crap like that and I hated it! And they hated the way I thought and the way I wanted to dress. It's like if you were an extra in a film and they wanted a bunch of punks, they'd hire some real punks because they'd look comfortable in those clothes. Whereas I just wasn't comfortable not being dressed up in some gothic fetish clothes; and it showed when I wasn't dressed that way.

I became aware of a fetish side to my character at about thirteen when I started collecting whips. I had no intention of doing anything kinky with them, and that's the God's honest truth! I had seven or eight bullwhips, and on Sundays I would practice hitting things. I just wanted them and it interested me. But I didn't know that was kinky and I didn't think that I'd like to hit someone with them. I just knew I wanted to use them. Maybe things come out slowly that way. I've got a picture of me at nineteen at sixth-form college dressed up on Vicars & Tarts Day and I'm holding a whip and dressed up in rubber! So there must have been some inkling there of the shape of things to come! I started buying rubber and latex and stuff at about seventeen and I went into the scene at twenty three. So, if you take that into account, I was a fetishist for a good ten years before I actually got into the scene.

So these things tend to develop. It's not like I had some awful experience and became a mistress to get back at all the men in the world! Some mistresses do have that attitude, they definitely do. And I'm not anti-mistresses, I'm very pro-mistresses. I think they all have their beauty and their own talents and abilities. It's great when they have the presence of mind to empower themselves and be interested in sex and get everything they can out of it. But then, sometimes you get this little undertone that they hate men and they want to make them pay for all the ills in the world. At the end of the day one man is totally different to another. You can't make one pay for the mistakes another one's made. It's just stupid. They want to beat them to make themselves feel better, and that just perpetuates and feeds a sort of monster or hatred thing that has no place in fetishism or SM.

I don't want to be negative, but their motivations are dubious. There's everything from: "I want to prove that I'm the hardest Dom in the world, therefore I'm going to slice you up"; which I've seen and which made me really sick. Somebody came to see me and he'd left his mistress because she'd carved a swastika into his backside with a razor blade. I was absolutely livid. I couldn't believe how irresponsible and stupid that was. And, on top of that, I couldn't see him again because I couldn't look at that. I said: "You've just got to go away and heal yourself up and we'll talk again, but I can't look at this". I don't use razor blades or needles. I've got no axe to grind. I haven't got to prove that I'm the hardest Dom in the business. Who cares?

I spend a lot of time mistressing because I like men. I like being around them in a fantasy capacity. The only ones I have put a little aggression into my swing over have been ones that needed to be taken back down to earth because of their shitty attitudes towards others. I'm not angry at men. I love them, really. I like the idea that I live in the fantasy side of their world and that's it. Beyond their fantasies and that part of their mind, I really don't know them at all. And that suits me fine, actually, because that's the part that interest me. Ironically, if I were to know too much about them, they wouldn't be able to tell me every filthy, sordid, slutty fantasy and then I'd be upset! We're just in a microcosm of sexual fantasy and nothing else, and that's what I'm there for. That's my profession. It's never boring, I'll tell you that much!

If you're a mistress, it can go either way. You can see so much of men that you want to be with women just to have a change in your sexual experiences or a degree of intimacy; and some mistresses are gay and go home to their girlfriends. Or, if you have so many sexual experiences with men on a professional SM nature, you get more heterosexual! Basically, you just turn into a dirty old man in the body of a woman!

There are so many different attitudes of people who go into the scene, as well. Some people are like: "Right, I'm leaving behind my old life and I'm taking on my life as a 'perv' for ever more now, and my whole life will be changed". And yet it doesn't change. You're still you. You can never get away from who you are and what you are. It's like they think they're joining a nunnery, only it's a 'rubber nunnery'! And that does happen. There's different motivations, but it's nice when people are just relaxed and they're enjoying it and there's no guilt and it's just a facet of their lives.

It's like, if you get a live-in maid, what happens when the 'maid' wants to go and see Arsenal verses Tottenham at football? No, you can't go because you've got to stay here and clean the bloody dishes or whatever. It can't work on a twenty four/seven basis. Though people will probably read this and say: "Yes, it does work. It works for me!" But as much as you've got a dominant nature or as much as you've got a submissive nature, you've also got a lot of other sides (or should have), to feed and grow and all that hippified stuff!

I do know one mistress who's got a live-in slave who does everything. She's got this guy at her feet all the time; doing the washing up and the laundry and he just lives in her house. But what about when she wants to do things that are non-SM related? It's one thing if you dive into the SM scene for three hours a week, it's quite another when you live it day in and day out. You've got to have a certain amount of time to actually come back down to earth. If you don't, then before you know it you'll be trying to tie up the guy at the local shop because he's given you the wrong change or something! I mean, you've got to get a perspective if you don't want to turn into a loony. And I've met some real loony people on the scene! They started out okay and then slowly lost their marbles over the years. They ended up needing a check-up from the neck up! And I'm not keen to do that.

I've always been into foot worship scenarios; high heels, thigh high boots and all that. I always think of my toes as being five little cocks that need a blow-job! I've one friend who is a slave (though he's not my slave, he's just a mate), and he told me his mistress said to him that thigh high boots only exist in male fantasies, they're not something that women like. Which is bollocks! We do like our thigh high boots. We like all the clothes. I like all the dressing up side very much.

Above all, I like playing games with intelligent, open minded people. Bondage scenarios, ownership scenarios, humiliation scenes. Public exhibitionism to an extent, but not where there are any children around or people who are going to be really offended by it. I respect other people's life-styles as much as maybe they should respect mine, so I don't impose my life style out in public to that extent. It's better to do something discrete and maybe let someone in on the game if you think they might be cool enough to appreciate it. But, other than that, I don't want anyone to know because they might be really upset by it. And I won't allow it on any of our own doorsteps, either.

Having said that, I've had quite a lot of fun with public exhibitionism. I love going to restaurants with long table cloths so you can kick the slave from underneath. I'll make them tip double to the waitress, if they've been stuck up or rude. Or I'll make them tell the waitress embarrassing home truths. I'm more likely to do a public scene with someone who needs mental correction. I'll order horrible things for them that nobody would want to eat! I'll put too much salt and pepper on their food and then just sit there and watch them try to muddle through this horrible meal. In that vein, I'll concoct little 'witchey-poo' type drinks for them. I've gone to their cupboard and I've picked out everything I can and mixed it all up in a big blender, then sat there and watched them drink it just for fun.

As for humiliation, that's just whatever makes me laugh at them, I'm up for really. Whatever is degrading or whatever is amusing. I understand the mind well enough to know when you're overstepping the boundary, and when you're starting to 'physically' hurt the mind. Like it or not, there are boundaries to what the mind can take before it starts to get damaged and hurt. You have to be careful to build people up to it. They will be able to do more as they go along. However, a lot of them just want to go straight into some heavy scenario that they mentally can't handle. As a mistress, you're either serious about it or you're not.

As I say, I like games where they're going to be degraded or demoralised, and have to do things that make me openly want to laugh at them. The last one that I really liked was getting someone to openly give oral sex to a rubber teddy bear with a big rubber strap-on dildo on it. That was incredibly humiliating for him because it looked so ridiculous. So there's those kinds of levels of humiliation you can do. You know you've done something mad and something humiliating, but there's no repercussions afterwards.

Another kind of humiliation that interests me is where the person has had a really negative sexual experience in their life. It's possible for a mistress to 'graft' new memories onto it, by reliving that and putting it into an S&M scenario. Say, if something awful has happened to you in your life, and you want to play that out again (only do it in an ultra kinky, sexual way!), then you can actually 'graft' new memories onto it and new associations. It really does work and can be quite healing for a lot of people.

For example, you could re-live the day you're girlfriend dumped you. Except I could play the role of that girlfriend and can make you feel degraded, but turned on at the same time. Does that make sense? And then, every time you think about that, the mind flips forward to thinking about when the mistress did the same thing, but used you and abused you in a sexual way. Therefore, the motivations and the reasons are more, well, slutty! And a bit more fun, as well! It can be very therapeutic for you to work through that. You can't help thinking about one without thinking about the other. I don't know how many people are thinking about it in that way, but they should be! That's what humiliation is all about for me.

I didn't understand humiliation before I went into the scene, but I understand it now. Before I used to think I wouldn't like that; that it wouldn't be me and I wouldn't want to do that. But now I realise that people into humiliation do have a certain amount of mental freedom, actually, because it doesn't matter what they do; because they're free from their own personal insecurities. They're actually quite strong people. They interest me very much and I'm always happy to see them!

I also love role-play a lot. Things like 'ownership' scenes, where this person is my property and is going to do whatever I ask of them! I like slaves to be thinking about me, as opposed to just thinking about themselves. And they really do feel as though I own them. Sometimes I've had slaves phone me up years later and tell me that they never felt like anyone owned them more than I did! I remember being young and thinking that I really did want to own people. And that was outside of SM. I just felt that possessive of people at times that I wanted them as my property. I guess that's why I like that kind of role-play so much.

However, you can only really achieve this level of play with on-going slaves over periods of time. With a one-off visit there's just no point. All you can really do for one-off visits is a 'smorgasbord' of different types of SM that they can try. Because ultimately, if they're a novice (or they say they're a novice, which is what they usually do) I try to do two or three things that are completely different from each other , so that the slave can find out what it is that he likes. Because they don't know themselves half of the time. If they've come straight from the world of 'vanilla' sex to rubber, leather and barbed wire, then it's: "Do something kinky, but I don't know what!". The concept of licking somebody's high heels or being trussed up like a calf at a rodeo, or being made to bark and drink from a dog bowl are all very different things, and you wouldn't understand at first why it would be fun to be naked and have this kind of stuff done to you. But then it opens up a part of your mind that you didn't even know you had. In fact, they're usually quite high after a session and have to sit down for ten minutes just get back down to earth. They're not just high on endorphins from being spanked or whatever, it's the fact that it's popped open a part of their mind they didn't even know was there!

That's the good thing about really intimate one-on-one sessions. I know it's probably more lucrative to have six guys in different rooms, and you go from room to room giving them a whack and telling them they're naughty or whatever, but that doesn't really appeal to me. I like the more intense psychological one-on-one sessions. I've been a professional dominatrix for five years, and I don't think I would have lasted this long if I didn't have that sort of rewarding intensity that keeps me interested. And five years is a long time in this business when you consider that a lot of mistresses last about two years nowadays. They go in, they set up, they're on the scene, they're in the clubs, they're in the dungeons, and then they're gone! Usually, they're renting a dungeon from somebody which can be astronomical. I don't know why they rent dungeons, because it would be cheaper to just rent a place and put dungeon equipment in it.

Whatever the scenario, I like them to be 'non' run-of-the-mill. No two are ever the same, just as every slave or submissive is different. I like slaves that are genuinely pleased to serve me as my property. I love it when they have the presence of mind to bring me a bunch of flowers. Then you know that they really do want to please you. Also, I'll always leave plenty of time between sessions to sterilise all the equipment. I don't care how long it takes. If it were me, I'd want that kind of security. Maybe I don't make as much because I have that high standard, but that's the only way it's going to happen.

It's very difficult, at first, to get used to being a mistress. It's very nerve-wracking. I think I must have broken about three pictures or something by accident during my first few sessions. I was dropping glasses all over the place, because I was such an absolute nervous wreck. I really didn't know what was going to happen. All I knew was that I had to be in control at the end of the day. Now I'm very relaxed and easy with it because I do it my own way. If I did it any other way, I wouldn't be doing it at all. It's sad, actually, that it becomes so nerve wracking and so stressful for some mistresses, mainly because they don't think they can do whatever the hell they want. They think they have to please the client. And, to an extent, pleasing yourself is pleasing the client. At the end of the day a good submissive should be out to serve you, after all. But maybe mistresses have done things that they didn't enjoy and that would put anyone off immediately. They may feel pressurised into doing watersports or body worship or something else they don't like. Of course, it rubs up against your personality and who you are! And then mistresses will disappear off the scene; which is a shame because a lot of them are real stars and are very talented.

Suppose some slave is phoning up demanding toilet training, then she should very simply say that she's not going to do that because she doesn't enjoy it, and that's it. But she might feel: "Well, I'm a mistress now so I have to do all of these things". Consequently, she does do it and she's totally upset for days afterwards. Who's benefited from that? Nobody. Especially her. So it's very important to maintain a level of individualism that makes her happy to be a mistress. And every mistress is different. I doubt if you'll ever find two mistresses alike, in the same way that no two submissives are alike. Maybe the scenario is similar. But the 'take' on it is different every single time.

This is a crazy world where you'll never walk down the street again, thinking that all these people are straight and I'm the only one who's kinky! You'll walk down the street knowing that a good percentage of them have at some point in their lives tried something out of the ordinary. I was at a 'normal' party with a girlfriend recently, and this guy kind of sidled up in front of us both. Okay, we were dressed in black, but we weren't dressed up as mistresses; yet he was visibly shaking! He was actually hanging onto the table as he got closer to us! Now he must have got some 'vibe' from us. But, then again, a mistress sits differently, she speaks differently and she walks differently. There's infinitely more confidence there. The more skilled you become at S&M, the less vulnerable you are. You don't have a problem with walking down the street in the middle of the night because you know you've the skills to not be messed with now. That doesn't mean I'm totally invulnerable. But it does mean that, because I'm constantly breaking the barriers with people I don't know at all and just going straight at them, I don't have that same level of personal space that other people have that they feel can be invaded. Does that make sense? It's a psychological vibe I give off that says: "Don't fuck with me".

It's difficult, though. Mistresses are not completely invulnerable, just because we've got a house full of torture equipment and the skills to asphyxiate someone in fifteen seconds if we need to. We've got the skills, but if someone was determined that they were going to do something, then there's nothing you could do. Having said that, I've never felt threatened myself while working. That's because my clients have all been strongly 'vetted'. I would rather take the time to talk to them on the phone and find out what they want and where they're coming from and give myself the opportunity to say no. But I rarely have to. Most people who have the guts to phone up a mistress are going through their own problems as it is. Anyway, you'd have to be off your nut, really, to go and see a mistress with the intention of harming her, when mistresses spend all their days calculating how to turn almost any item into a weapon! Everything from the bloody spaghetti fork to a plastic bag is a weapon to a mistress! A good mistress doesn't really need any equipment at all to do what she does. An old slipper and a teddy bear could keep a slave amused for hours, if she wanted it that way!

I keep phone calls very concise and to the point because, for one reason, people are notorious for booking a session and then never showing up. That's usually because they've just gone away and totally jacked off on the idea that they've been speaking to a mistress! One guy even put on a woman's voice and called me three times. He must have thought I wasn't going to remember his voice. If they're really impolite, I'll phone them back during the daytime and say: "Why were you so rude to me at midnight last night when you were pissed out of your mind? I don't believe that's right". Generally, I don't have to do that. That happens about once a year. They are usually very polite, very genuine and I have very few problems. Because my web-site is very well laid out, people know just what to expect. I don't hide any details about what to expect when they come to see me. Sometimes I will even book an appointment over the Internet, depending on how well written the application is.

Every mistress is taking a risk at the end of the day. But if you're intelligent enough you won't be taking that much of a risk. Most of them have got it sussed out enough that they know when someone is just a total wacko. It usually has a lot to do with where you advertise, as well. There are so many contributing factors. Some mistresses are taking a much bigger risk than me. They've got card boys out putting adverts in phone booths and taking anyone off the street. And It could be anybody. Any idiot could pick up a card in a phone box. They might be pissed out of their mind and think: "Oh, I think I'll go and see this mistress and maybe I can fuck her." The only way people can come and see me is through my mobile at fifty pence a minute or whatever it is. So unless someone is really serious they're not going to phone me at all. They'll phone one of the local numbers and jerk off there. But, to be honest with you, most of them are really good. They're a nice bunch and I'm friends with a lot of them and I like them. I've also got a good group of clients I've had for five years who I see regularly, maybe once a month. Once a month is enough. It gives them a chance to go away and heal. Over five years, that's a long time and many sessions indeed!

During that time, you become very good friends and the sessions themselves can really go off into 'outer space', because you've built up such a rapport and understanding. If they let you get into their mind, that is. Some people have got a deliberate wall and they want you to break through it, as if to prove that you're intelligent enough to do it in the first place! It's a lot easier if they just put in a bit of trust and give themselves over and let it all happen. The mistress can then get on with what she wants to do. It becomes difficult when they want to play psychological games to the extent that they want you to break through their will. Which doesn't take me long anyway!

Usually, we'll sit down for five minutes, have a cup of coffee and discuss what fantasies have been running through their mind. Things play on your mind, you know. Sexual fantasies can play themselves over and over until you get them out of your system. So I find out what they are. They know they can tell me absolutely anything they want, and I'm not going to bat an eyelid. Then, once the session begins, they are my property and that's it. They don't say do this or do that. They don't need to. I've never used 'safe words' once in any of my sessions, either. I never felt I had to. I think they're ridiculous. To me, 'safe words' mean that the mistress isn't safe in the first place! Sure, I'd have bloody 'safe words' if I had somebody with needles and hot knives and razor blades at the ready! My 'safe word' would be: "Can I leave now, please?". I've heard some real horror stories, like the swastika on the buttocks, poppers up the nose, scary stuff. It's one thing to give yourself to a mistress utterly, but it's also nice to find out just who you're giving yourself to!

Having said that, I've got a lot of respect for many of the mistresses in the scene. But a mistress isn't the same thing as an escort. They fulfil a different need. I saw something in a Chinese film about escorts working in a bordello where there was this line about a prostitute being 'a wife to many men'. I thought that was pretty much 'on the money', because they do a lot of things for men. And, to an extent, a mistress is doing a similar type of thing. She's fulfilling a lot of their sexual fantasies. I kind of like the idea of that. So I have a lot of respect for the mistresses who know what the hell they're doing and are devoted and dedicated enough to get to the bottom of things.

However, I find it difficult when slaves are willing to give themselves to just anybody, and then have a horrible experience and ask why? It doesn't have to be that complicated. It just needs to be thought out carefully to begin with. In a way, the slave must be as selective about his mistress as the mistress should be about her slaves. He doesn't want to end up with his face all cut up or something awful like that, does he?. I don't think it happens that much, but they're taking a risk as much we mistresses are. It's a 'hitchhiker syndrome', in that the driver might think the hitchhiker could be dangerous and he might get mugged. But that driver is picking up that one hitch hiker and is in danger once, while the hitch hiker is getting ten or eleven lifts. He could be in danger from all those drivers. So, who's really taking the risk?

Many of the scenes I've done have been unforgettable and sometimes very funny, but I won't be able to go into detail for privacy reasons. A favourite was a scene with a man in his late forties. He wanted to be treated like a cheap little whore. I dressed him up in some slutty lingerie and stockings and high heels and sat him (or I should say, her!) on my sofa with her legs crossed high, pretending to be a bordello girl waiting to pick up her next client. I came in, dressed in a suit and corset, asked how much and what she would do for that. We negotiated as if she were a very cheap whore indeed. Then I took her into my dungeon area and made her do as many degrading sexual poses and acts for me as I wanted. I still get turned on thinking about that one!

The furthest I've travelled for a session has been to New York from London. I had a slave there who had such a wonderful vision of romantic idealism about SM. He wanted us to have the best of everything for our private dungeon, with an army of fetish costumes and a life of total kinky sex! It was to be an exclusive relationship. I was going to be free to wear fetish wear all day while I got on with things

I was interested in, like running my Fetish Fair business. It was all going to be leather corsets studded with semi-precious stones, heavily themed rooms for gothic scenes that go on late into the night, shiny thigh boots and spurs and totally over-the-top trips to the opera, wearing boned latex dresses. We were going to go for the whole lifestyle thing. To hear a man have such commitment to the quality of his sex life was quite exhilarating. But things didn't work out. One day he just started feeling guilty about the way he was and nothing solid ever came to pass.

As a lifestyle mistress, I have accepted slaves in the past who were not that financially well off, but I wouldn't do it again. I had issues with respecting what they were doing with their lives. Also that they just wanted to live with (and usually off!) a mistress. Those types are such losers and I can't be bothered with them. I prefer work hard, play hard types. I only once had a sex slave only who lived with me, but I am very selective about things like that. It wouldn't be likely to happen again. A lot of those types of slaves drain you like a vampire. So needy and self concerned.

I haven't had that many really weird scenarios. The people who want to be buried alive and stuff have been carefully told to go and jump in the lake or to go bury themselves alive! I had the phone slammed down on me once because I refused flatly to pull someone's teeth out. I thought that was hilarious, but he was deadly serious. I think those types have left their fantasies for so long that they're just getting too extreme. I will do extreme fantasy, but I refuse to damage.

Another guy wanted me to put him into bondage, along with his false leg; which I did. Then there was this other guy who wanted to rush off at the end of the session. So I said okay and got him out of his bonds and said: "Oh, have you got a meeting to go to or something?" And he said: "No, I've got to go to my brother's funeral". Okay, fine. Obviously, he must have been so stressed that the only way to get away from it for a while was to come and see a mistress. It wasn't really funny, but it was thought invoking about people's motivations. Sex and death do go together. They go hand in hand. Death is sexy! You can't really say it the other way around, it would just sound too wacky!

Nothing's ever been too 'off the wall', because I've been careful. But it's been very interesting sometimes! My own personal fetishes are always more wacky than the stuff I do in the scenes, anyway! Like zebra-girl and pony-carting. Next week, for instance, I'll be going to a pony-carting picnic and there'll be predominantly girls there. There'll probably be the odd Benny Hill-esque running off into the woods for a spanking type of thing going on, I'm sure. With these club meets, rather than anything serious, there tends to be a lot more laughs than anything else. I've been someone's birthday cake, all covered in fruit and chocolate, stuff like that. Then a food fight ensued. How could that be serious? That was just hilarious. Followed by domination sessions on Hampstead Heath in the middle of the night! This kind of stuff is supposed to be fun, after all, and you should feel a bit exhilarated afterward.

Sometimes there is a place for that kind of hardcore dominance and serious mistress-ing, and all that. I think it is important. But, if the mistress doesn't have a sense of humour, she'll always be open to ridicule for taking herself so seriously. You know, I've talked in depth to lots of submissives to try and get some background on this, and they say they've sometimes come away from a session giggling their heads off over that kind of mistress!

I think a lot of men really fantasise about being seen as a sex object and as a slut and everything. I don't think they get enough of that. They spend so much of their time being a husband and a provider, they just don't get the time to be the little cheap tramps that they are at heart! And I think they are little hussy's at heart till they day they die! This is the great thing about working in the sex industry; that you can pretty much define to a fine point the difference between a slut, a tart, a slapper and a hussy. They've got distinct meanings between them. I think the sluts pride themselves on being the lowest in the chain of command. They know they're at the low end of the rung and they like it that way. You know you can always go to them for anything and they'll do it, because they're just sluts, after all!

The scene is fun. I think it's difficult for people on the outside to appreciate that. I'm still the same ravingly kinky person I was at the beginning; it just gets worse every year! I think it's a little like rock musicians. You get the ones who produce one good album and then all the rest are crap, because they only had that one good album in them. Or you get the others, like Bowie or the Stones, who just get better. So you can chose one path or the other. You can either do your thing and get better at it or just get out.

The beauty of being a mistress is that you don't even have to be young and cute. I like that. I like the fact that you can see someone in their fifties out at scene parties, dressed elegantly in a leather corset or a neck collar or something, and they look excellent and they look elegant at the same time. I look at them and think that's where I want to be at that age! They still have the elements of sexuality that count and you can still relate to them on a sexual level. I guess it depends how important sex is to you in your life; to me it's practically everything!

It's the same for men; they can look elegant too. In my eyes, as long as they stick to leather and velvet, they can't go far wrong. But the rubber T-shirt brigade had better watch out, really. It just doesn't work. It's not about their shape, it's about the way they carry themselves. If you want to be a real body fascist, join the gay scene. Once you're no longer thirty and don't have a perfect physique, they don't want to know. But it's not really like that in this scene. A lot of the guys just buy clothes that will get them past the guy on the door at the fetish club, and they don't think beyond that. Anyway, I think the rubber and the PVC is more of a 'girl-thing', really. It's a shame, too, because back in the seventeenth century the men were the dressed-up peacocks and much more flamboyant. Outside of the fetish world, it's absolutely appalling nowadays!

I like to wear lots of kinky clothes to be sexual. More is definitely better and, the more fetish clothes you put on, the kinkier you become. Mistresses who go around with their breasts uncovered are not really being mistresses in my eyes. She's baring something personal in front of someone who is supposed to be her servant and who isn't really worthy. I know that sounds awful, but it's true. If a mistress is naked, then exactly what is she doing that makes her a mistress? She's making herself vulnerable to someone who is beneath her. We've got sluts to do all that 'vulnerability' stuff.

Also, I don't honestly think that men like sex as much as they say, or think, they do. I've seen this time and time again with beautiful, gorgeous, young, eligible kinky girls I know. When they meet a man and they offer all forms of degrading pervery to them, the men go completely off their heads. They just can't cope with the concept of getting what they want. They feel threatened. And they just lose it, they can't perform. So be careful what you wish for, because you might just get it!

It's easier, especially in England, to be the kind of girl who wears white knickers and feels guilty about every naughty little thing she does. Then the male can be the one who is perverting the course of justice for her. He can then feel guilty because he's made her do degrading things, and he can get off that way. That's actually a lot easier. This is what separates the fetishists and pervs and the kinky people from the mainstream. Here they're on equal ground where the women are as openly kinky as the men. That can be quite difficult for some people to get their heads round. The guilt aspect gets moved around quite a bit and becomes just another tool for fun.

What I do like about the fetish scene (apart from the lack of ageism, or sexism and racism) is the fact that games begin, are played and they end. The psychological games don't stem outside of the sexual relationship. They're always sexual games, and then that's it. You don't play emotional blackmail games outside of your sexual relationships because there's no need for it. You get a degree of honesty that I've never seen anywhere else. Most people who have been in the scene a while are very honest in this respect; they don't have to hold back what they're thinking or dress it up.

At the end of the day, my submissives are not 'committing adultery' when they come and see me for domination. Maybe their wives don't like SM, and don't want to know. But they still have homes and families that they don't particularly want to break up just because they like being tied up or subjugated every now and again. Once you look at it there becomes degrees of tolerance. To think I have submissives who are 'maids' with me and are only ever 'females' with me or slaves and things like that, then they go home and they're the husband and the father and all these other things once more. Yet they haven't broken up their home over something like being a 'maid' for a certain amount of time every month or so. People don't find themselves in their sexual mode till their thirties; although it's getting younger every year, thank God. But by then they might have been married ten years, so what the hell are they supposed to do?

I've known people who've shown a hard-core SM video to their wives and said: "This is what I'm into", and the wife has promptly divorced them and given them no access or rights to their children; which is horrendous for them and their kids! So, which is the lesser of the two evils? Those people have screwed up their own lives over something that is important, but not that important that it's worth ruining your home life for. It's different for me, because I'm kinky in my spare time as well. It's a lifestyle thing; which means I never have relationships with people who aren't kinky. There are things, like water sports, that I'll do with my partners, but I don't do with my slaves or professionally, so it's all kept balanced and it works. But then, I don't have to answer to any lawyers or anything.

I still have a lot of old friends who are non-scene and who know I'm a mistress and accept me. We don't go into details because I wouldn't want to do anything that made them feel uncomfortable. Anyway, it doesn't need to be in their face. Most people in the fetish scene have got other facets and other interests. It's very rare that I talk about SM with anyone outside of the SM scene, because they're simply not interested. I'm not going to bore them with SM techniques and politics, anymore than I would want them to tell me about the finer points of stamp collecting or airplane spotting or something. I'd be asleep in seconds!

The scene is a good community, but it's still very misunderstood. Which is a shame because people are missing out on so much. Those people in the main stream of society are turning a blind eye to their own sexual fantasies. Or even finding out what those fantasies are! Or just doing things and thinking about them afterwards. If you can't think of anything, just do some stuff and think about it later. I didn't have that many fantasies when I started as a mistress. I just used to do things. Eventually I got an idea of what I wanted. It's like any muscle, you have to build it up! Fantasy is a part of your brain that has to be built up. It's easier to develop it by doing it first and thinking about it afterward, and then you will be able to fantasise. Most people who are into SM don't actually fantasise at all because they don't know where to begin, and there's nothing wrong with that. It's a very under used part of the brain.

Frequently, it's the case where one partner in a marriage, usually the male, is into pervery and the other isn't. Only once, at an SM Pride event, did I meet a woman who told me she was really into all this but her husband wasn't, so she was there on her own. And I really felt for her because I had been in that same situation myself. I 'came out' at the age of twenty three to my straight twenty one year old boyfriend on his birthday, and he near enough had a nervous breakdown! He freaked out completely. In fact, he promptly burst into tears, stating that he didn't want to lose anymore innocence than he already had! I said: "What the hell are you on about?" We broke up eventually, of course. But not without me saying to him: "I want you to remember when you're an old man in an old age home that you had this opportunity of a twenty three year old girl dressed head to toe in latex and high heels and you didn't take it!" So I really felt for that woman. She didn't want to beat her husband up and throw him into a ditch or something. She probably just wanted to dress up and play with her dark side a bit. Where's the harm in that? I was trying to spank or beat up boyfriends from the moment I met them. And it wasn't because I was mad at them. I just wanted to do it. It's an inherent part of people who are kinky. It just runs in their blood. It's not that they had a bad experience when they were a child and it messed them up and now they're into all this unhealthy sex stuff. It's nothing like that at all. And it's not like they got too many gamma-rays, like in a 1950's sci-fi movie, and it turned them into raving latex pervs, either!

My attitude is that I'm here! I won't be here forever, and I am one of the most skilled mistresses in London! I have spent many a day with other Doms, be it on the fetish scene, the gay scene or whatever; and I've learned how to do each type of kink that interests me to an expert standard. So, although I am eccentric, I would want someone to treat a session with me as if it were going to change their lives and act accordingly. Once I get going, it's hell's teeth! under the power of the mistress! I've studied the medical side for each job I do, because there are certain things I need to know. I am also a qualified first-aider, so I know what to do should a situation arise.

Generally, I love all the fun stuff! Tease and please and bring you to your knees kind of stuff! I love watersports, too. And I absolutely insist on body worship, because that always gets the session moving. Remember, a lot of times the clients are very nervous, especially if they're first timers. They're always scared walking into the dungeon for the first time. They think they're going to be thrown down on the floor and beaten unmercifully, but that's really not the way it is. Maybe they've had bad experiences with a mistress who just didn't listen. I'll normally bring them into the lounge if they're first timers, and sit them down and have a chat. I'll give them my 'safe word' and ask them for a list of things that they really don't like. Things that really scare them, that's a good place to start. We'll exchange contributions and then go in and do it. I like the fun of working them into it slowly, and getting them into the dungeon scene that way. I'll put a favourite song on and I'll do a full strip and tease them while they're tied up. I love getting up so close they can almost kiss me, then I'll pull back! I love all the teasing and caressing and whispering and taunting them. That's what I like the best because I am a real exhibitionist when I'm doing it. I'm really a quiet little pussy cat inside, but don't tell anybody that!

A lot of domination is theatre, if you think about it. And I'm a born actress! I'll change my hairstyle and clothes to match the scenario; whether it's school mistress or secretary with my hair in a bun and severe glasses, or long flowing red-head vamp. It gives me a great opportunity to dress up in corsets or rubber cat woman outfits and wonder bras. That's what I love about the job the most. I still do some dancing and television work, but out of all the jobs I've had, this is my favourite. I'll carry on for about another ten years professionally, though I know that'll be a big disappointment to all my little boys! I'll still keep a dungeon in my house, but that will be just for pleasure. I love all my naughty boys who come into my life and make Mistress Eva's comical world of dominant delights spin and spin!

It is a wonderful lifestyle, as I keep saying. If I decide to go away for three weeks, I will. I'll just shut down and put on the answering machine and tell them I'll be back on such and such a day. My regular clients, I'll refer to other mistresses who I know I can trust. Rather than let the poor puppies go without, I'll ask them if they can look after a few of my boys for me. I know that the other mistress will take care of their needs, and that they're not going to be mistreated or poached. We don't do things like that. There's enough to go round for everybody.

I've only had to turn away two clients in my life. One because he was so filthy, and I was actually cruel enough to tell him so! And the other because he came in very drunk and was very obnoxious towards me. He wasn't violent, so I wasn't threatened by him, but he was saying things like: "What are you going to do to me then?" And I said: "I'll tell you what I'm going to do to you, love. I'm going to throw you out the fucking door". I grabbed hold of him and threw him into the street! But that was the only two occasions. Generally, I find the submissive male immaculately clean and well behaved. Because they've come to submit to me, they're very compliant and polite. Even if I've almost drawn blood from giving them a beating, they still want to bring me chocolates or flowers, which I think is really sweet. I don't have to buy flowers ever again. Sometimes the dungeon looks like a funeral parlour!

As I said, I do have a fully equipped dungeon here, complete with leather bed built on a metal cage and all sorts of bit and bobs. But it's not always the equipment that counts, it's what the mistress does with it! You can dominate someone with one hand and with no dungeon at all! If you're that good and that strong, mentally and physically, you can do it. For instance, if any of my slaves tell me they're allergic to my pet cat, I'll put the cat in the cage with them just to torture them a little bit more! If they've misbehaved, I'll rub them a little bit with the cat. It completely freaks them out!

This is a complete lifestyle for me. Even if I go out to a 'vanilla' club, I'll always wear six inch patent heels with rubber trousers; something of a fetish nature anyway. It separates the boys from the toys, as it were! If they see me and they've got submissive tendencies, they'll know what's going on. That's how I attract my personal slaves who I'll bring them back to my little harem. That's what I'd like to have really, a harem full of hunky male slaves! They can pamper me all day and serve me and carry me everywhere. I could have them all on leads like little puppies. I can quite see myself as Cruella de Ville!"

Chapter 11: Mistress Jacqueline

With the publication of her autobiography, 'Whips and Kisses', as well as her many TV appearances, mail order company and lecture tours Jacqueline has established herself as quite a formidable force on the American fetish scene. Formally based in Los Angeles, California, she has now relocated to the San Francisco Bay Area. This interview is a good example of the no-nonsense, business like approach so typical of American dominants.

I've been a practicing dominatrix for over eleven years now. And they've been very successful years full of fun and growth. I've met thousands of wonderful people. I'm very active and involved in the SM lifestyle, and I have a full stable of slaves who serve my every need. The 'scene' is my life and my life is the 'scene'! In fact, to mark my tenth anniversary in the scene last year I launched my own magazine which records highlights from my career. I'm very excited about this project. I know that anyone who has followed my career and even your people over there in Europe, who don't know that much about me yet, will get a lot out of it.

I've had SM fantasies ever since I was a young girl. My sexual proclivities always included pain and pleasure. I played SM type games with my boyfriends without even understanding the meaning of my actions. I've always been a naturally commanding type of woman. Boys and men have been doing my bidding ever since I can remember. After I divorced my first husband, I went all out on

a sexual exploration. When I finally had the guts to answer an SM
ad in a local sex newspaper, I knew that I'd come home. I took to the
scene like a duck takes to water. The rest, as they say, is history.

I've been on so many TV 'talk shows' that I really can't list
them all; particularly when my book was published. I did a national
tour that included every radio station in the whole country! Plus, I
appeared on major TV shows like Donahue, Joan Rivers, Sonya Live
and Montell Williams. I actually decided to go on shows way before
the book came out. I wanted to do these shows because I knew how
healing it was for me when I first came out of the closet and admitted
my SM side. I hoped I would be able to reach others like me. Judging from the mail response, I feel that I accomplished this. However,
studio audiences have traditionally given me a hard time It seems
that the nature of the game is to badger and provoke. Talk shows are,
by their nature, very exploitative. I'm still glad that I did them, but
I think there are better ways to reach people. Since then I've turned
down Geraldo, Maury Povitch and Jane Whitney. I'm no longer willing to go on shows with slaves in hoods and be treated like a freak or
cartoon character. I have better things to do! Did you know I didn't
even get paid.?

The book is my own personal autobiography. It's mostly about
how I got into the scene, and the struggles within myself, and how
I've overcome a lot of the crap I've had to deal with, both in my family and in society. Again, I wrote the book because I truly felt my story could help others like myself. As a leader and spokesperson in the
scene, I've found it very satisfying to have the opportunity to educate
the public and let them know of our existence. I'm a firm believer
that most people have sexual fantasies that could be considered 'out
of the norm'. Because we live in a sexually repressed society, most
men and women choose to suppress their feelings, and only admit to
what they perceive as 'mainstream' sexuality. Those of us in the SM
world should hold our heads high as we have taken the risk of admit-
ting that there is more to sex than tits, ass or a conventional 'roll in
the hay'! I have a great deal of respect for all of us who have come out
of the closet and made a decision to be who we are. As an educator, I

plan to dedicate my public image to help all men and women better understand the interplay of fantasy and human sexuality.

And I would consider myself fairly well qualified for the job, too. As well as being a professional dominatrix, I'm also a licensed psychotherapist. I have a Master's Degree in Clinical Psychology and I have my Marriage, Family and Child Therapist (MFCT) designation, as authorised by the State of California. I disclose this not to impress people, but to give your readers an insight into my own orientation toward the scene. I believe that bondage play and fantasy fulfilment are healthy, creative outlets to explore the feelings we have deep inside ourselves.

Recently, for example, I had the pleasure of running two support groups on a weekly basis for men and women. One group was for people into dominant/submissive relationships. Everyone involved in these groups learned a great deal about themselves. They found it healing to meet with other like-minded people, and to have a place to talk about the kind of things that they wouldn't even dare mention to their friends or colleagues. Lasting friendships were formed and participants left with the feeling that they weren't so very different after all! Because of the success of these groups, I then did a series of one-day seminars across the country.

On a personal level, I'm also currently involved in the best relationship of my life. I've waited a long time for this, so it's very special to me. What makes this so good is that we are true equals and love each other unconditionally. Of course, it's not a 'straight' relationship, you're talking to Jacqueline here! However, even though we do live stage performances together, our personal play is done in the bedroom only, and what we do there is intimate and private. Because my slaves are never my lovers, my private relationship does not intrude on my mistress/slave activities.

In my SM play I'm very versatile. Depending, of course, on who I'm playing with, I really enjoy almost everything in the SM spectrum. The most important thing is involvement. I love passion and excitement. When there is true commitment to a scene, no matter what it is, I find it personally very exciting. Mood, music, creativ-

ity, good costuming and theatrics all lend themselves to the drama
I crave.

I'm certainly a great spanking enthusiast, for example. I'm very
much a part of the spanking community and will always be. I think
spanking is something that is very separate from SM. The people and
the 'mindset' behind it are completely different. In addition to the
D/S support group I mentioned earlier, I also run a second group in
Los Angeles specifically for men and women who are into spanking.
I've separated the spanking group from the SM group because the
issues are not the same. Incidentally, I've done seminars on spanking in various locations throughout the country, too. These one day
workshops are called 'Spanking: The Definitive Seminar', and not
only provide important information, but also allow spanking enthu-
siasts to gather and meet others in their area. The workshops cover a
variety of topics, including how to place advertisements in the 'per-
sonals', how to meet others and how to overcome any shame and
guilt associated with being part of an 'alternative' sexual lifestyle. It's
another project I'm really excited about. And It's lots of fun, too!

Unfortunately, because I'm so busy these days, I hardly ever
have time to do private sessions myself anymore. However, I'll still
see very 'special' slaves for sessions in my own fully equipped dungeon from time to time. I'm very selective, naturally, but I can generally tell how honest and sincere someone is by the way they write
to me. I always feel that anything of value and quality is worth the
pursuit, and I'm confident that my slaves will all testify to the fact
that I'm definitely 'top-notch'!

I'm extremely versatile and fluent in all aspects of SM, fetishism, slave training and corporal punishment. Since I love spanking
so much personally, I give a particularly good discipline session and
absolutely love to role play! Though my favoured 'look' is leather/
rock, I can easily turn myself into a governess or school teacher and
administer sound, firm discipline. My dungeon lends itself to all
kinds of scenes. I have great bondage hardware, as well as facilities
for cross dressing scenes. My wardrobe is, basically, leather, leather
and yet more leather! I love it all! SM fashion will never go out of

style, as far as I'm concerned!

In addition to my male slaves, I do have female slaves who serve me as well. However, I must say add, the females in my stable always have priority over the men. That's just my personal way of doing things. You could say I'm a real believer in Female Supremacy! Whatever the sex, though, I'm always very selective in the type of people I associate with. Only those who prove themselves worthy get to come near me. Honesty, sincerity, loyalty and trustworthiness are attributes that come to mind. My slaves dedicate themselves to me in mind, body and soul. To me, slavery is the highest form of commitment! Consequently, the mistress/slave relationship is never one that should be entered into lightly. Before I accept anyone into my stable as a real slave, they must undergo rigorous training. As the saying goes: 'Only the strong survive!'

You'll notice I make a strong distinction between 'slaves' and the type of person I see as a professional dominatrix. However, even as a professional, I don't see just anyone. As my time is very valuable, I see only those who are truly into the SM or fetish scene. And let me just say this: I don't think slavery is for everybody! For the right person, I think that it's very healthy to play out fantasies in a safe, sane environment. A session with me in my dungeon is a very therapeutic experience. Many of the people I see are very powerful, influential people. Their lives are very stressful. When they come for a session, they lose their status. In my dungeon what I say goes! I help these people balance out. They release tensions and leave feeling totally relaxed.

Though, as I said before, I enjoy all aspects of the SM and fetish scene, I must say that my personal favourite is corporal punishment. To that end, I have a wide assortment of paddles, hairbrushes and straps. I get very aroused when I administer a severe whipping. Flogging on the back is one of my favourite activities. Believe me, I can flog a submissive for hours without ever getting tired!

I'm also well known for my 'transformations'. Everybody knows that Mistress Jacqueline turns naughty boys into very nasty girls! I absolutely love playing with transvestites. I have a great deal of respect for this population. Our society plays up on the 'macho' image so much, I think it takes a lot of guts for a guy to come out of the closet and explore his feminine side. My TV sessions are always lots of fun!

Although my dungeon and business is based in Los Angeles, I do travel whenever I can. I love the scene in New York. I also recently took my first trip abroad. I was most impressed with Club Doma in the Netherlands. I attended the Friday night show and it was very well done. I also have a wonderful slave in Australia whom I visit frequently. The SM scene is very strong 'Down Under'. I've had the pleasure of befriending Mistress Amanda of Salon Kitty. She and her establishment are truly first-rate.

At least there's some kind of scene in L.A! And that's better than most parts of this country! My favourite scene place here, as I said before, has got to be New York. In fact, NYC is my favourite place, anyway. Maybe that's because it's my hometown! I like the New York scene because it's wide open and always happening. Whenever I go there I'm always at The Vault or at Paddles. I love the freedom these clubs exude! The scene in L.A. is reflective of this city; and that's very 'showy'. It's pretty underground and it gets more uptight every year. However, I'm very lucky in that I have my circle of friends to party with and get plenty of activity. The local club, Threshold, is very active but, for whatever reasons, they have gotten so rule-oriented and have so many regulations when it comes to parties, that I've become very inactive. I'm a true anarchist and it's important for me to always to be able to do as I please.

But don't get me wrong. In my play I work within strict limits. I totally believe in safe, sane SM play. As long as a fantasy is between two or more consenting adults it's perfectly okay in my book. I wish more people understood that it's not only okay to explore fantasies, but it's also healthy and healing. Like dreams, SM play reveals a great deal about one's inner psyche. It's a great outlet with which to express hidden parts of our personality within a non-judgmental environment.

I'm also busy with a number of very exciting projects at the moment. My magazine Power X Change is published bi-monthly. Each issue gives an in-depth profile of several real life domina's as well as interesting scene places to visit; well written fantasy stories, letters to the editor, beautiful photos and lots more. The layout and design is top-notch. I'm very proud of it.

I'm also producing my own line of videos and CD-ROMS. But, let me tell your British readers that I never send videos out of the United States. However, there are plenty of items for foreign customers. In addition to the Power X Change, I have three other 'speciality' magazines, including Mistress Jacqueline Magazine, which everyone who knows me, or wants to know me, simply must have! This magazine is unlike any other scene-type magazine in the United States. Like your own Domina Magazine, which I may say is fantastic, I've made it very classy, sophisticated and intelligent in the way it approaches the scene. And, of course, my book Whips and Kisses. I also have a complete line of leather bondage toys, as well as other goodies.

Though I've been selling items through the mail for many years, I'm now revamping my entire mail order business. I know that everyone will be very pleased with the results. Most exciting, I have a fantastic line of leather items for sale at incredibly affordable prices. These items are specially made for me by my Slave Anton in Australia. He is a skilled leatherworker and has designed a complete range of bondage equipment especially for me. My catalogue includes hoods made from quality kangaroo leather, plus leather restraints and collars which can be personalised; a one-of-a-kind Koala blindfold made completely of fur, novelty key chains and other unique items. My fetish phone lines are also owned and operated by me and me alone. The mistresses who man the lines for one-on-one conversation were all personally trained by me, too. Maybe your readers should call and find out just how good my training really is!

Chapter 12: Lady Amber

Originally from Glasgow, 28 year old Amber is an enterprising business woman, as well as professional dominatrix, who now divides her time between the dungeon and her own successful fetish shop in London.

I've been a professional dominatrix for about five years now. I had an incredibly badly paid job in a hospital laboratory at the time. After I initially learned how to do the job, it became boring. This is what I tend to find with jobs. Once I've learned how to do it, I'm bored and I have to move on because I start becoming destructive! Fortunately, I've stumbled across, quite possibly, the perfect occupation for my-self where I can be destructive and get paid for it! Plus I'm naturally a bossy person anyway. I think, linguistically, my Scottish accent goes quite well with the image, too; Miss Jean Brodie or something.

I've had personal relationships that took in some aspects of S&M, though I wasn't consciously aware that we were playing games. Little bits of bondage games and anal penetration for him, which he used to love. It was basic 'tie me up and hold me down and fuck me like a dirty little slut' sort of scenarios, Obviously, I don't take sex into the dungeon. There's no need for that, and that's not my bag at all. But that's where the awareness came from. When I did my first trial as a dominatrix I found I took to it like a duck to water. None of it shocked me. I started doing it part time, and very quickly came to the realisation that I was allowing myself to spend eight hours a day being bored in the hospital when I could be down in the dungeon having fun and earning a living out of it! So I gave it all up and became a dominatrix full-time. I was very happy there for about three years, then decided I wanted to go back to school for whatever convoluted reasons I had at the time! I did a course in English Literature, but then decided that school wasn't going to make me happy either. That's when the opportunity of opening the shop came up.

It's the 'theatre of the mind' that I'm interested in really, so that covers all kinds of role-play scenarios. I like to play kidnapper, boss, auntie, over bearing sister. Anything that I can basically get my teeth into, I thoroughly enjoy. Gang land 'boss lady' is a particular favourite of mine. I also love cock and ball torture, discipline and a bit of rope bondage. I like fairly heavy torture, though not to the point of drawing blood or getting terribly messy. The best bit is getting into somebody else's mind; to be able to know what makes them tick, find out all their secrets, and then use it against them! No, I'm not wicked really, just mean sometimes! How can us women be so beautiful and so mean at the same time? There's many facets to my personality, and domination is only a part of me. I'm also a budding thespian. I suppose what I'm interested in is the idea of altering consciousness through meditation, and I do think there are ways to do it through the S&M scene. There's definitely a bit of a hippie in me, as well as a stern, frosty faced mistress!

Seriously though, you can feel with some people when you're in the flow, and you're understanding each other and the transaction that's going on energy-wise. It makes it all very exciting. You don't often get it though, and certainly not in the first session. An S&M relationship is like any other, and it needs to be built over time. But there some good submissives out there, and I've got some lovely slaves that I've known now for a good few years. It's a thing that can develop all the time; depending on the scenario, of course. If they're simply looking for a constantly overbearing mistress, that's fine. But, generally, you'll find by that stage their ideas are constantly changing and, as long as no one's boundaries are being stretched beyond what they're comfortable with, then it all goes very well. Of course, their idea of being comfortable is being stretched beyond the boundaries!

I've always loved plastic and shiny clothes and the texture of rubber ever since I was a little girl, apparently. I do feel it is an empowering thing. When I'm dressed in my PVC, I automatically feel empowered through association, as well as what I'm wearing. In other words, you've got to look the part to feel the part! I've heard it called 'high drama sex', and I can understand what they're getting at there because you've got to entertain more than just your physical senses. There's other bits you can get to as well.

Nowadays, most of the people who come to see me have fairly demanding jobs and, perhaps, demanding families as well. They're in the role of having to tell people what to do constantly. I think everybody's got a little submissive side to them and, if you're constantly having to play that role, on the other side of the coin it's probably going to be good for you to let it out in order to get your balance back. I've probably got a little submissive side in me too, but I've never found anyone who I'd want to submit to. It would have to be somebody who inspired that in me, because I'm so used to being dominant now. It would also have to be something fairly unbelievable! That would be a hell of a scene! Submission is an impressive gift to give anyone, so they're going to have to be a very worthy character indeed! Imagine the power of a mistress submitting! I attract submissive men all the time in my personal life. Maybe it's because when they find out what I do, it becomes a natural progression for them to submit.

There's no solid rules in this world, but certainly on the corporal punishment side, an awful lot of it is linked to experiences at school or parental experiments when they've paddled you with a hair brush or what not. If it happens around about puberty then there's going to be some sort of associated link between sexuality and corporal punishment. I think that's how it a lot of it goes, anyway. With foot fetishism, for example, I would think that is something that goes directly back to a person's babyhood; to a time when you were on the floor and people would rub your tummy with their foot. Their foot is so big that it would reach both your tummy and your genitals. Remember, you were born a sexual being. 'Looking up skirts' is another one that probably goes back to a very young age, when you're crawling around on the floor.

I have been asked to do some quite bizarre scenarios, like nailing foreskins to bits of wood or nailing scrotums out and beating them. That's going too far, I feel. I know someone who does that, but I don't do it myself. I'm also not terribly adept at the 'baby scene'. I don't know if that's because I haven't got any myself so I haven't got any 'script' to go from. I've got one man who I call The Rubber Man. He's completely fixated with all things rubber. He's decked his own dungeon out in rubber; rubber pillows, rubber sheets, rubber hoods with pipes out of the nose for restraint of breathing. One thing I found interesting was the Rubber Mackintosh thing. He wanted the hood pulled over his head and belted, so he was completely wrapped in this thing. Then he wanted me to sit on top of him and sort of rustle around while calling him 'Anne'. That's quite a good one. Here's a man who's totally fetishised this Mac for some reason.

Generally, as long as I know the person I'm talking to is of a fairly good intelligence, I will make no bones about telling them what I do. All my friends know. In fact, I've roped half of them into helping me from time to time. I came across a negative attitude when I first told them, but within three or four sentences they realised that whatever negative reaction they had was due to their own hang-ups. They realised they were judging people and that everybody has a kink, whether they admit it to themselves or not. Most of the people I deal with are very honest in the sense that they've at least looked into their own sexuality and they've come out and said: "Look, this is what I need and I'm going to go and get it!"

Obviously, a lot of them do feel guilt about it, but maybe that's part of the kick as well! The best ones to do scenes with, I find, are the ones who have examined their sexuality, and have come out the other side and are quite comfortable with life. They're the nice ones to deal with. You're not trying to get past this instant barrier of: "I'm here, but I wish I wasn't". Drop that and you're going to start enjoying yourself!

I have many transvestite friends, as well as clients, who are lovely people. I also know one or two who are the most conceited, vain creatures that you'll ever meet in your life! They seem to need to accentuate the worst aspects of what they perceive as 'girly-ness'. Real women just don't behave like that! But, then again, if you spend that much time looking into a mirror, you are inevitably going to become self obsessed. That's what I find annoying about them. To be honest, I don't have the patience for a full-time dressing service. Dressing up in a domination scenario is fine, but I couldn't do a full transformation. I get bored when I have to praise people, especially when they should be praising me!

I used to do a lovely scene with a guy who had a complete obsession with ladies underwear! I mean this was taken to the point whereby every single female he met during the course of his day he would get into detailed fantasy about what sort of underwear she might be wearing. The first time he came to see me, I told him he had to guess what underwear I would be wearing and wear the same stuff himself. He would be unerringly accurate right down to the last detail! He was supposed to be coming to see me in a 'doctor capacity'. The idea was that I was supposed to be helping him to stop wearing women's underwear with aversion therapy and various other techniques. For months he'd come round every second week, and we'd have a little session.

I grew fond of him because he was a lovely guy, and he really did want to stop doing this in case his wife ever found out. He was convinced it would end in divorce and he would lose his kids. In the end, he reckoned I'd cured him which, of course, is absolute rubbish. He'll stop doing it for a while, and then start again when he feels his head is going to explode. He'll be back, I've absolutely no doubt! It's always the way. They go through phases where they'll stop for a while, but if it's there they will always return to it at some point in time.

I had another lovely scene once with one of my regular guys where he wanted to be dressed up as a young fashion model who'd been sent to London to do a photo shoot. I was supposed to be his/her protector and chaperone. What I was really supposed to do was abuse his trust and talk him into doing pervy photos and generally get him to submit to me! Then there was a fabulous guy who was totally into the whole Venus in Furs thing. He had a big fur coat that I'd wear for him and he was into the scenario of grovelling about, being called a worthless worm and pretty much being kicked around. He was so totally believable as this pathetic little specimen that I took great delight in telling him that was what he was. It's great when a submissive gets so heavily into a particular scene like that, it enables the mistress to do the same.

My oldest slave is eighty four and is great fun. He's got a little T-shirt with 'naughty school boy' printed on it, and he wears a little leather thong to save any 'embarrassment'. I've never known anyone who can take a caning like this man can. He puts a tape recorder under the chair to record the whole session, complete with his little ooh's and aah's in various places. He's got a complete ritual that goes with this as well. Basically, I've got to have a stop-watch and time the strokes at fifteen second intervals. He always wants me dressed in everyday clothes and, whatever cane I'm using, he wants red lipstick on it so the stripes are really noticeable!

I can never hit him hard enough. In fact, it's always the older ones who can take the most unbelievable punishment. Maybe they have the nerve endings in their bottoms fried after so many years of taking it, I don't know. He's so little and frail, you'd think he'd break but he takes everything I can dish out. He's also very polite, one of the old school of gentlemen. He just wants to get his arse caned and that's it, really. At the end of the session, he will very politely ask if he can put just one hand on my buttock. If I'm in a good enough mood I will allow him and that makes him a very happy man indeed!

I'd like to find more submissive girls. I do have one girl who's coming round for an interview. She used to be a 'working girl', but she says she's tired of that and wants me to train her up as a mistress. She's basically submissive though and, to be honest, I could make more use of her as a submissive. The pecking order would be: me, the submissive girl and then the male slave. I must say she seems thrilled at the prospect of taking orders from me and being generally bossed around!

As far as women in the dungeon are concerned, I've only had a few experiences and the last one put me off the idea hugely. It was a couple where she was submissive and he would sit and watch. She would type out a scenario of what her punishments would be and all that. Part of it would be things like I'd have to blow her nose and stuff. I said: "What? Well, we'll give that one a go and see what happens". But, basically, these instructions were ridiculous, like caning someone on their fanny. I wouldn't even want to do it. She would be in floods of tears and sobbing her heart out just at the thought of it. And this guy's saying that she can take it, it's okay. In the end I told him that I was in charge around here and he could fuck off!

I even asked her once what it was she getting out of this. She said that she hated it when it was happening, but when she got home it was all fine. I picked up from that, that she didn't actually enjoy it, but he was making her. Presumably, when they got home she would be venerated for doing as she was told. I really didn't like it, and I eventually told them I wasn't interested in doing this kind of scenario and off they went. Ultimately, I suppose she wouldn't have been doing it unless there was a part of her that enjoyed it. But it's not my bag. I don't want sobbing women in my dungeon. I'm afraid that does absolutely nothing for me at all. I found it all quite distressing, really. Apparently, she's left him now or so I've heard. Great, I thought, he deserved to be binned. She's now shacked up with some guy twenty years her junior and having a ball! She was such a lovely lady and he was such an absolute bastard!

I haven't really come across that many women in my traipse through the S&M world. There was a mad German once, whose husband was a complete voyeur. She was into everything and anything. Then there was a most amazing looking American woman who was fifty, but looked about thirty. She was buying into anything she could get her hands on. She was married to this rich American guy, and he thought he was onto a right winner with the most 'up for it' woman he'd ever met in his life! He must have thought it was his birthday when he first met her, but it turned out she just out ran him in the end. He realised there was no stopping this woman and no controlling her. I think he passed out in the end.

With these kind of women though, I find it's just not balanced. It seems to come from somewhere very dark inside them. My attitude is that if you're already a victim when you come here, I'm certainly not going to facilitate your fantasy into 'victim mode' even more. I'm here for people who are aware of their needs and are quite happy to fulfil this side of themselves. But if you've got an out and out victim mentality, then you're asking for trouble!

What I'm doing in a session is affecting the individual to the extent that they'll come here in one mode, they'll have a transforming experience that will allow them to leave in a completely different and uplifted mode and, ultimately, they are going to affect everyone they touch with their new and improved mode of the day! That's why I like doing this. This and, perhaps, teaching are the few things that I feel are genuine jobs. Most of the jobs out there involve just pushing bits of paper around or doing things for people that they're perfectly capable of doing for themselves, but they just can't be bothered. I like to feel I'm doing something that people can't do for themselves. This is a real service I provide.

I've never had any really bad experiences. I had a guy who went for me in the dungeon once. It was actually his way of trying to provoke me into giving him a genuinely outraged beating! But it's all got to be controlled, as I'm not into just giving someone a good kick-in. This is theatre and there are rituals to be performed. Of course, the whole sub-dom scene is an illusion anyway. The submissive has all the power and the final say. He has power to stop the scene and start it again with something he feels comfortable with, which is fair enough. But, as long as the illusion of power stays in my control, I'm happy!

I intend putting on 'couples nights' in my new dungeon for open minded adults who want to play with other people, or just want to be around other people who are playing. I'll have a maid in there looking after the guests. It will be mainly on the fetish side, but these things do tend to take on their own shape, which I won't restrict as strictly as I would if I was just down there by myself. I'm also setting up my own live one-to-one telephone domination. I've found when I'm just amusing myself in the evening by flouncing about on the Internet and generally bossing people around in chat rooms that very quickly you've got men asking for phone numbers. As there's no way I'm going to sit around talking to slaves for nothing, I'll get a special phone line put in to deal with them.

Another thing I love doing is writing about my experiences and putting them up on my web-site, so that slaves can find out more about both me and the whole fem-dom scene. I'm getting more and more interested in magic and the whole pagan and wicca thing these days, too. I think we've gone way off track regarding sexuality. Christianity has made sexuality more or less taboo. I believe people can pretty much regulate themselves. They might fuck up a bit now and again, but with controls on them they're just going to overdo it anyway. It just doesn't work. But then, I don't run the world yet! Give us a chance!

My ideal would be to build up the business so I could sell off franchises. Then I could spend one year working as a dominatrix, and one year off working for the peace of the world and helping people worse off than me. Basically, it would be a year of being a filthy pervert alternated with a year of being Mother Theresa!

When this stops being fun, I stop working. If I'm not still meeting people that are interesting or strange or weird or whatever it is you want to call it, then I don't want to play anymore. I've got to the stage now where I just don't want to do the average submissive anymore. I like slaves that I can have some sort of connection with, and where our ideas match. I like the ones where I can sit down and work out a role-play scenario with them that we're both comfortable with and bounce ideas around. I like people who are keen and amazed by this whole scene in itself.

This is such an interesting and wonderful way to make your living. I would fully encourage any woman to give it a try! But, then again, not everyone could do this job. And even the ones who think they can, very often can't. I've got a friend who used to try working with me and, as much as she is lovely and bossy, there's something not quite believable about her. Too young, perhaps? Or not enough natural authority. I don't know. Maybe she's not emphatic enough. As much as she wanted to, her personality just doesn't fit the role.

I wouldn't describe myself as a lifestyle dominatrix, there are too many other facets to me. But, having said that, I could quite imagine myself in a stately home somewhere with the maids and the butlers and all the rest of it. I would thoroughly enjoy that. I'm looking forward to that phase in my life when it comes! I will be making a start in that direction by bringing in some slave workers to help me do up my new shop and dungeon. I won't be lifting any paint brushes myself, naturally!

Chapter 13: Madam Karra

Boy meets girl. Boy and girl fall in love and get married. Pretty usual stuff so far, isn't it? After all, that's what people do. However, what happens when boy also wants girl to be his mistress? In other words, what do you do when one partner is in the "scene", while the other thinks it's just all plain weird? Well, that's exactly the situation that faced slave-husband Richard and his lady love, the divine Madam Karra.

Several years ago, my husband Richard got bitten by the bug that breeds submissiveness towards the Superior Female. I'm afraid I was, in the early days, a very reluctant mistress who just didn't realise her potential. My poor husband would meticulously detail a sub-dom session on reams of paper in the hope that his 'Mistress' would follow it word-for-word. Sadly, he was mistaken and had to settle for a rushed version of his masterpiece. Admittedly, for someone like myself, who didn't really understand the reasoning behind a male wishing to be bossed about and disciplined by a female, his written compositions were quite off-putting.

In those days, a typical 'session' would begin with his preparing an outfit for me to wear, and changing into something effeminate himself. He would arrange all the instruments in a neat row, then inform me that my outfit was prepared. Then he'd wait patiently in the corner, probably going over the 'agenda' in his head. Eventually, I would appear in something completely different to what he'd so lovingly prepared! The outfits he had selected were designed to give a female a sense of 'power-dressing'. Inevitably, my version would be more like 'half-throttle' dressing! Not to be deterred though, he accepted my choice and looked forward to the meaty stuff. Topics for his sessions varied from schoolgirl to housemaid, to effeminate slave. Basically, anything which allowed him to wear women's clothes, especially lingerie. Every session involved housework, inspections of chores, discipline and lots of standing in corners!

Due to my lack of understanding, there was never any genuine anger in my commands, I'm afraid. Punishments would be rushed and meaningless; punished for no reason, so to speak. Inspections were also rushed and he was praised for good work a lot of the time. This avoided me having to punish him, so that I could carry on watching television. In short, I'd try and get the whole business over with as quickly as possible, hoping it was just a phase he was going through.

These sessions progressed for some years and up to six months apart. Frustration was an understatement for my poor slave! Over the years he managed to tone down his desire to wear women's clothes and adopted simple thongs instead. This helped a bit, as I felt more at ease with him as a 'male' slave, and things improved slightly. Then one day, after reading a story in a Fem Dom publication, he hit upon an idea or rather, an ultimatum! He decided he would risk his whole fantasy life in one last attempt to make or break the woman who was his wife! There would be no reams of paper and no dressing-up; just seven whole days of continuous 'make-it-up-as-you-go-along' mistress/slave scenarios! My only conditions were that he would do anything for me and would be punished at least once a day. Well, seven days turned into twenty one days and, by the end of it, he was begging for no punishments at all! Don't ask why or how it happened! But I am now his 'Mistress' as well as his 'Governess': Madam Karra, a Superior Female with a total commitment to dominance of the inferior male. She who must be addressed as 'Ma'am'!

The way it came about was that I had, by this stage, become so extremely irritated with my husband's demands for a 'Domination

Session', that I decided to call his bluff and, hopefully, put a stop to his perversions once and for all! It was time to take him up on his ultimatum, and a week-long session-to-end-all-sessions might be just what was needed!. I was tired of getting home from work only to find him 'demanding' to be dominated! He'd spend an absolute fortune on gear to satisfy his own fantasies, and hope to get me to wear the stuff for him! Occasionally, I would agree to carry out a session and have to work through his long and detailed transcripts of 'how it must be done'. Needless to say, I skipped the parts I didn't like and invariably rushed through the rest. Now my conditions were that I must control the entire session for the whole seven days, and there was to be no silly 'pieces of paper' with endless scripts. One hint of interference would terminate the session and disrupt any future sessions. I felt pretty confident that he wouldn't be bugging me anymore once I'd finished with him! I reckoned three or four days would be all that it would take.

I began the first day by giving him a huge list of chores to complete. This kept him occupied for most of the evening, and I soon detected that he hated doing them! I deliberately ignored him the whole evening and simply instructed him to complete every chore before reporting to me. This really annoyed him as well, because it meant he wouldn't receive any punishments at all until right at the end. As the evening went on, I sensed a weird kind of 'evilness' inside me. I knew what I was doing was totally against his own desires, as my denial was more of a 'punishment' to him than actually giving him what he wanted!

When the moment of completion finally came, I was simply going to pass every chore and praise him for being such a good boy. However, during the inspection of his first task, I suddenly decided to look very closely at his efforts. I can't really describe exactly what came over me, but I just became very 'nit-picking'. His face dropped as I began to ask for his excuses for such sloppy work. Of course, he couldn't come up with anything except: "I have failed you, Mistress. I beg your forgiveness, Mistress". Oh, how boring this pathetic phrase had become by now! I went to town on all his other tasks and really let him have it! I insisted that to be a slave of mine would require a lot more effort than what he'd put in so far!

By the time the full inspection was over, I wasn't very pleased at all! To make things worse, when I informed him that he'd have to be punished severely for his lax efforts, his little face positively lit up! Now this made me genuinely angry! In fact, my rage actually frightened him as he'd never experienced any real anger on my part during a session. I decided to tie him to the bed to receive his punishment (which was another unusual move that worried him) and informed him that he would be caned and whipped! The first salvo involved a thin, bamboo cane which snapped after several extremely hard strokes. My next selection was a riding crop which also came to pieces after an enthusiastic beating. My slave was writhing about in agony by this time, and close to tears. Another mean-streak came over me and made me ignore his welfare and really make him cry! I fetched a stranded whip that, ironically, he'd made himself and began to lash his body with it. He gritted his teeth, made muffled screams into the pillow and jerked as much as his bonds would allow. It was all to no avail though, because I'd already detected an anger in him that he was using to counteract his tears!

Because I'd succeeded in making him angry, I felt that I had defeated him; which, in turn, gave me a huge thrill! I'd never felt so good before now at someone in true pain! I was convinced that this would put him off sooner than I had thought but, at the same time, I secretly hoped I'd have the opportunity to repeat the treatment! I decided it was best to leave him tied for twenty minutes, so he could cool off. I admit I was a bit worried that he may have taken it badly and retaliated. This had been one of my main concerns in the past. Before we went to bed that night I asked how he was feeling, as I was still wondering if I had gone too far. His response was not the one I wanted to hear! He said: "That's how I've always wanted it done, Mistress". I immediately tasked him for the morning chores and made him write out a list of jobs that were to be completed once he had returned from work!

The next couple of days went much the same as the first. In

fact, it was soon turning into something of a routine. Around the middle of that week I realised I was beginning to enjoy the situation. I was getting home from work to discover that everything was done and a meal would be ready for me! Simple little things that a woman could normally not expect. Usually, of course, it's the wife who has to cook, clean and run about after her man. I was very quick to realise that I could live a life of luxury as far as housekeeping was concerned!

Interest soon got the better of me and I decided to experiment further. A short list of rules were drawn up to test exactly what power I had. Things such as having him massage my feet as soon as I had come home, warming up the toilet seat before I sat on it, cleaning me after I had been to the toilet, having him make me a coffee at one snap of my fingers and generally running around fetching things for me. All these were factors that slowly drew me into the world of Female Domination. Each day passed with surprising ease and I could sense that I was becoming more and more dependent upon the services of my 'slave'. He showed no signs of giving in to the harsh chastisements I was inflicting on him each day. In fact, I noticed him that adopting an even more obedient attitude as he grew tired of the beatings.

Near the end of the seven-day period, I increased his workload substantially. By this stage, he was doing absolutely everything about the house and running about for all my personal needs. This was becoming sheer bliss for me, as you can imagine. My stress-levels were falling and I found myself becoming happier, both at work and at home. Being pampered and waited on was an experience I wanted to last forever. Not only was I enjoying the experience of having a personal servant, I was also beginning to enjoy inflicting pain. For some reason, which I can't explain to this day, I started to feel great delight in chastising his vulnerable flesh! If I ever felt some tension, or had been annoyed by something during the day, I'd instantly make it an excuse to punish my husband. He provided the punch-bag upon which all my tension could be taken out! He never once complained, retaliated or walked away. It was my own power of dominance that kept him there, and I could see that he accepted it totally and without question.

My thoughts soon turned to prolonging this situation, indefinitely! I still wasn't happy with the fact that most of the week had been conforming, in the main, with his ideas of Female Dominance, rather than mine! Sure, I had introduced some of my own ideas and he'd been quite happy to carry them out, but I still needed to condition him to my way of thinking and my way of doing things. During his last evening of slavery, I drafted out some of my own ideas and methods. While doing this, I realised that I was actually composing a list of ideas that would demand absolute perfection in order to be achieved! Well, if perfection requires a strict set of rules which must be intricately detailed, then so it shall be! Before that evening was over I had dictated a huge list of rules and regulations to my slave. I instructed him to learn these off by heart, and to abide by them from now on. He dared to raise the question that a set of such detailed rules was a bit late to enforce at this stage of the session. My response provoked a mixed reaction from him. I simply informed him: "I may wish to extend the session!"

One of the first major changes was my title and form of address. I'd become so engrossed with the situation that I decided to adopt the Female Dominant title of Madam Karra. I'd once read a book which characterised a female executive called Karra. She was ruthless and insisted on perfection from her male underlings. The form of address had to change as well because, personally, I don't like to be referred to as a 'Mistress'. Seeing as I was a Madam, I thought that 'Ma'am' sounded more appropriate, and instructed Richard accordingly. The ground work had now been laid for my total control over his life.

Surpassing the seven-day deal saw a change in me that made me realise that dominating the male of the species is what I should have done years ago. It's the only thing I've experienced that has made me content and confident as a woman. My life was very routine and average before, but now I feel I have a real vocation in life. As each day progressed, I became aware of new ideas that would

groom my husband into an obedient and well-disciplined personal
servant. I had to change his way of thinking, of course, so that all his
actions would conform to my ideals. His workload increased, too,
as I became even more demanding; but he soon began to carry out
tasks as if it were second nature. I must stress at this point that I had
introduced a severe punishment policy. Any mistake, sign of disobedience or lax discipline, no matter how trivial, was met with harsh
chastisement. I felt that the only way to prevent him from deliberately making mistakes was to punish him very severely in the first
place. A second offence would merit automatic doubling of a previous punishment. A third offence would triple it, and so on. By this
stage he was working as I wanted him to. He'd learned his lessons
the hard way and was aware of the consequences in the future. I had
converted my husband into an obedient, well-disciplined personal
servant who worked hard in order to avoid the wrath of my punishments. I became increasingly aware of my endless power over him
and was determined to take him to the utmost limits of obedience!

One day, while we were out shopping, I got the urge to make
him display his subservience then and there. Knowing that such dis-
plays in public are limited, I got the idea of having him kneel at my
feet, but in a way that would seem quite normal. Instructing him to
re-tie the laces on my boots provoked a surprised look from him. So
I gave him one of my angry stares, snapped my fingers, then pointed
to the ground and said: "Boots! Laces! Now!" No further prompt-
ing was needed as he dropped onto both knees and re-tied my laces
to perfection. I actually enjoyed the feeling of power as other men
passed by and stared. The moment they realised that I was watching
them they averted their eyes and scurried away. It felt wonderful to
watch the so-called 'macho' sex squirming with embarrassment. As
soon as we'd got back home, I gave him such a severe caning that
he has never again refused or questioned one of my commands in
public!

I felt that I'd now created a new lifestyle for us both. He's now
actually doing what he'd merely fantasised about before, except for
the fact that he has to do it my way and not his! And I'm begin-

ning to enjoy the advantages of having my own personal servant. You could say that he treats me like royalty; serving, obeying and protecting me. Another thing I drastically changed was his time off. With both of us working in full-time employment, we find it hard to get compatible days off. Before, I'd have to get up and go to work while he still lay around in bed. This had to stop, of course! I decided to enforce a routine where he would have to get up early and prepare my breakfast. On his days off, he'd also attend to my morning shower and prepare everything I would normally do myself. When it came to my days off, and he was working, I would waive the breakfast chore. Compatible days off were best of all. I would instruct him to get up early as usual and give him a list of chores to complete. This ensured that he maintained his routine and left me to enjoy a longer sleep. Because a lot of his chores would have been completed early in the day, it left more time for me to have some fun with him!

These periods of fun now occur on a regular basis and involve physical exercise/endurance, obedience re-training and humiliation. His exercises consist of either static repetitions or a run. Obedience re-training involves his abilities to control himself and, as far as humiliation is concerned, I usually 'transform' him. Physical exercises which can be conducted in-house are usually press-ups, sit-ups, squat-thrusts, 'burpees', and the like. I'll make him sweat for at least an hour. Running is a completely different ball-game. I will designate a particular place he must run to and return in a specific time. Failure means a repeat of the run and embarrassment for him. Why embarrassment? Simply because the designated point is a particular shop which I know stocks its own brand of goods or has preprinted price labels and receipts. This ensures that no cheating is possible. Returning to the shop for the second or third time for one item will baffle the staff and cause him some embarrassment as he tries to explain away his reasons.

One thing that I capitalise on whenever he is carrying out physical exercise is the fact that he sweats profusely; this is one thing that really turns me on sexually and I take full advantage of his tongue! I've discovered that a woman can gain ultimate sexual pleasure without having to indulge in full sexual intercourse. Whenever I detect that my slave is becoming frustrated at not being able to relieve himself sexually, I usually make him repeat the whole process all over again! As this arrangement has developed, I've become more aware of my feelings towards his denial of pleasure. It sends a mean streak through me and makes me very happy indeed!

Although denial of his sexual pleasure pleases me, I know it can be dangerous to leave it too long. My solution to this is simply to allow him a controlled and supervised period of relief. I will designate either a specific amount of time for masturbation, or a number of 'pulls' on his cock. For every second or pull below my figure, he receives one stroke of the cane. For each second or pull over, he'll get two strokes and so on. This is, of course, in addition to my compulsory punishment for allowing him such a privilege in the first place. One has to maintain strict discipline at all times.

Any humiliation of my husband makes me laugh no end. Most of the time, I'll make him dress as a baby and treat him with the same kind of love and affection that any 'mother' would. And he hates every minute of it! I'll make him carry his teddy-bear everywhere and he must crawl at all times. He's never allowed to speak, and always has a 'pacifier' in his mouth. Obedience re-training involves exercises of self control and discipline. An example of this would be to simply have him put into a 'stress' position for an hour or two, such as sitting cross-legged, back straight and arms outstretched horizontal to the ground. To make this particular exercise harder, I'll place a book in each of his upturned palms. Every fifteen minutes he'll be given a litre of strong orange juice. The aims of this exercise is to train his posture by ensuring his back is kept straight, strengthen his arms so he will be able to carry out heavy labouring, and to train his bladder to hold a lot of fluid. The final aim is especially important, because I only allow him three toilet breaks each day!

Although I have come round to the idea that dominating males makes me very happy, content and important, I've never found the idea of personal abuse very appealing. A slave is an asset, a tool that a woman can use to make life easier. If you don't look after the tool then it will break and become ineffective. To this end, I will never do anything that would jeopardise his health or personal safety. It may be very well for a lot of other women to make their slaves eat and drink body wastes, but I don't agree with that at all! The body ejects this waste for one reason only, and that's to rid itself of toxins and unhealthy material. I actually cringe at the thought of anybody readily accepting these by-products from another person!

I don't condone the practice of burning the flesh, either. This seems well over the top to me. I punish my slave hard and will create superficial markings, but they soon disappear and, unlike burning, leave no permanent scarring. Candle wax is acceptable, however, because it merely leaves marks that will disappear quickly and without trace. I've recently discussed with my husband the subject of 'branding': the ultimate symbol of ownership! He suggested a tattoo and, once he had designed my symbol, I became very excited at the prospect that my obedient husband actually wanted a mark of ownership on his body. Needless to say, he will be getting it etched very soon!

Though my compassionate side sometimes comes out, I'm still introducing Richard to even tougher regimes! One way in which I constantly remind him of his place is during mealtimes. He must prepare a meal for two, as normal, but then prepares his own a stage further. First of all, he blends his entire plateful together. Then the resulting pulp is transferred into his dogbowl and placed on a plastic mat at my feet. This is how all of his meals are taken at home now, and I get enormous satisfaction watching him struggling to eat them. Again, I can't explain why I like to see him eating in this way, I just find it so amusing, that's all. Another reminder for him of his place in my life, is the wearing of his collar and personal restraint. This also serves to increase my own awareness of the power I hold over him!

The regime I now run is based entirely upon my own ideas (some of which I've read about and adapted) of exactly how I wish my slave to conduct himself. For example, his own fantasies had never touched upon the complexities of domestic subservience which I've now successfully groomed him to. Basically, his ideas all involved dressing up, getting beaten and finishing a few hours later. He wasn't too keen on losing his dominant-male status for too long. But I soon made him realise exactly who the dominant status really belonged to! One thing that has made this all too clear to him is the control of his finances. He gets nothing unless he works for it and has to pay for his mistakes. Losing control of his financial affairs is something he hates because he likes to spend money. Now that he has to earn his 'pocket-money', he's become much more aware of the value of cash. I won't hesitate in 'fining' him for misdemeanours either, as well as chastising him. This has become a double incentive for him to behave and work harder, because he knows I will charge him for every stroke I have to give! The way I explained this to him was that I had to ensure that he remained obedient in order to retain his privileges. If I had reason to punish him, then he must feel the true cost of his disobedience. A chastisement soon wears off and is forgotten about, but actual loss of earnings creates a long term period of guilt that ensures he thinks twice in the future! It's human nature to prefer a loss of face rather than a loss of cash, and even more so with the inferior male species!.

That initial week-long session has now lasted over twelve months and is showing no signs of change. I've become so used to my new role as a Dominant Female that I really can't see me ever reverting back to the way I was. My slave-husband is now trained to an acceptable standard to serve me for the rest of my life. I need only refresh his memory occasionally! Of course, being an inferior male he isn't perfect and does make mistakes, but I find great pleasure in rectifying his lapses in concentration! So enjoyable have been my experiences, in fact, that I feel I now want more. My aim in the future is to provide a service that will train bachelors to become 'instinctively' domesticated. I'd also like to train couples in their responsibilities; that is, for females to adopt a strict regime of dominance, and for males to accept that their place in society is to obey, work hard for, keep contented and to protect the females who are far more superior than they are!

My husband now has a weekly routine that must be strictly

adhered to. He has compulsory chores which are carried out every day. In addition to these, he gets tasked with a list of jobs and chores whenever 'Madam' thinks of anything else to keep him busy! It must be stressed that his list of chores is realistically set for a normal household where the male is in full-time employment. Inspections are absolutely dreaded by him these days. I carry them out every day and will search every square inch of the house for dirt! One mistake means severe disciplinary action, a repeat of the chore and possible loss of any hard-earned privileges as well. A daily report is made in order to access performance. It all leads to viable excuses for punishment. Richard is never punished unless there is a genuine reason, by the way. His life is now totally regulated by the desires and wishes of his Governess. The situation is such that I now decide everything that happens, when it happens and for how long it happens!. My husband is now, in effect, 'on duty' for the rest of his life. Marriage is the ultimate in ownership!

Unfortunately, his shift work can play havoc with my requirements of him, so he's encouraged to always try harder. In addition to physical chastisement, I will at any time remove or restrict any hard earned privileges he has been granted, such as pocket money and credit cards. As you can imagine, this is highly embarrassing at work when his mates find out that a husband's allowance has been stopped by his wife!

A stringent set of rules has now been devised and must be constantly added to. For example, meals must be prepared to high standards of nutritional and caloric values, presentation and without use of predetermined menus or recipes. Clothing is to be cleaned, ironed and neatly put in its correct place. The house must be kept at a comfortable temperature and extreme care taken to avoid draughts. It's also the slave's responsibility to keep fit and healthy at all times, as this will ensure a positive and efficient approach to hard work.

Due respect will be given to any woman, no matter what her looks, age or attitude. Admission of misdemeanours are to be given every day; better a slave admits rather than his Governess finds out! The word 'sorry' will not be used at all. After all, a punishable motive or excuse can easily be hidden by an insolent or insincere apology! Compulsory chastisement will be given every day, at no fixed time, in the form of a caning. Additional tasks will be given as and when required. A collar will be worn at all times unless told otherwise. Only I may command the removal of subservience devices. All meals for the slave will be served in , and eaten out of, a dog bowl. Only in exceptional circumstances will a plate and utensils be permitted. I will be attended to at all times. Upon summoning, the slave is to be at my feet in less than five seconds. Sluggishness constitutes gross disobedience and will be severely punished.

My level of commitment to the Fem-Dom lifestyle is growing with each day. So far, I've enjoyed the powers I've developed immensely. Although my activities still remain strictly private, I have, as I said earlier, got the urge to command other submissive males into my presence in order to test my skills by training a complete stranger. Although I hate to admit it, my slave-husband is now showing a certain degree of efficiency in some areas of work! Mind you, when he feels I can't find fault he does have a tendency to get a bit cocky. The perfect excuse for some concentrated lessons on his behaviour and conduct!

All in all, my husband now finds himself serving a self-made dominatrix who demands a great deal. I believe it is in every woman's interest to commit herself to a deserved life of luxury. For it is women who do the real work and deserve the best things in life. Ideally, and it is slowly becoming fact, females should dominate every position of power and supervision in all areas of life. Men have ruined this planet and need so desperately to be supervised and disciplined by the Superiority of the Dominant Female Powers. May Female Dominance prevail!

Chapter 14: Mistress Mai-Ling

A Chinese psychiatric nurse from Singapore, turned professional dominatrix, Mai-Ling retired from the scene a year after this interview took place and is now running her own highly successful property development company in the midlands.

I first got into the scene by accident, really. I used to work in the field of psychiatric medicine. I had a friend of a friend who owned a studio. I was very dissatisfied with my job in the medical profession. I knew I wasn't going to get anywhere. I was looking for a way out when this fellow suggested I get into the S&M scene. I said: "What's that? What are you talking about?"

He offered to bring round a few magazines to show me. He also asked me if I wanted to go to a party that Saturday. Remember, I didn't know anything at this point. I didn't even have any clothes. I had to borrow some from the Mistress of the House where the party was being held. I decided not to think about anything. I thought I'd just leave my mind a blank and go with a completely open mind about things.

I was introduced to the people there as a 'Mistress in the Making', and I'd reply that I was thinking about it. I spoke to a transsexual mistress called Sadie and she was really nice. She told me to stick by her throughout the evening and I'd learn a thing or two. She showed me how to use the whip and all of that. Though, to be honest, watching all these people walking around half naked, I was secretly thinking: "Oh, no. This isn't my scene at all!"

At one point, as I was sitting down, someone said to me: "Mistress, can I be your footstool?" So, I said, rather casually: "Okay, yeah." He lifts my feet up and lays them across his naked back. I had really high heels on and I didn't want to hurt him. I didn't even realise at this point that, that was what he wanted more than anything in the world. But he said: "It's alright, Mistress, dig them in a little deeper." Well, if that's what he wants, I thought, okay. But I was also bursting to go to the toilet and I was wondering: "What do I do now?" The drink was beginning to go to my head, so I just kicked him and said: "Out of my way, I'm going for a pee". And he said: "Oh, Mistress, may I accompany you to the toilet?" I didn't have a clue to what to say to that, so I simply shouted: "How dare you!"

Later, the man who took me to the party asked me how I was getting on and I told him about the fellow and what had happened. And he just fell about laughing and said: "Why didn't you just piss on him and make him drink it?" I said: "What! Why should I?" Well, according to him that's what you should do. I didn't know! Anyway, that party was my introduction to the world of Fem-Dom. I soon got the hang of it, though. In fact, the very next day, the same guy phoned me up and asked me to go round to his house the next weekend and try my hand as a mistress. I said: "I don't think so, it's too much for me. I can't whip people like that."

Look at it from my point of view. I was very straight. I'd never dressed up, never done anything like that. I didn't know anything at all. But he was very insistent that I should go and see this other mistress and watch how she worked. So I went along when she had one of her regular slaves with her. Remember, this is the time I'd ever walked into a dungeon. I said: "What's this, for heavens sake?" He replied, very matter-of-factly: "This is a dungeon and this is a slave. And these are the weights you put on his balls."

He went on like this, talking about all the things they use. Then the mistress took over and told me to watch her whip the slave's backside, saying that I could take over later. When I took over, I hit him a few times and the slave started complaining, saying: "Mistress,

I don't think she's doing it hard enough." The mistress told me I had to really give it to him. So, I thought to myself: "Okay, I will!" I really started whacking him harder after that! But still not too hard because the blood put me right off, you know.

Afterwards, I asked the mistress if that was it? Was there anything else I needed to know? She said: "A lot. You've got to learn everything about this business. The best thing to do is to come and work with me now and again to get the hang of things." I didn't want to disappoint her, so I said alright. Later, I thought to myself: "Oh God, I've committed myself to something here! I don't know what I'm letting myself in for." Now and again I went down to see her and that's how I started to learn. But all the while, I was thinking: "I really can't do this. It's too harsh for me". Then my friend said: "I think you're looking at it from the wrong angle. There are other aspects to it. It's a big field that ranges from whipping to water sports". It was at the next party that I really started getting into domination. But it still took me another two years to build up enough courage to become a full-time mistress.

It was when I was on holiday in Italy that I thought to myself: "I think I'm going to go into that". When I came home I literally threw myself into it. I didn't think about anything else. I immediately made inquiries about taking a dungeon. By that time I'd seen a lot of videos and read a lot of books on the subject and felt ready. I gave a months notice at work and left. I knew this was something I wanted to do.

I still remember my very first client. He wanted a really good beating. I thought: "What shall I do? I'll just clear my mind and give it to him". And, amazingly enough, he came back for more! In fact, he ended up being one of my long term regular clients. It just started from nothing. That was six years ago now. Obviously, I've progressed a lot since then and got better and better. Each mistress develops her own style and individual techniques as time goes on.

Above all, to be a good mistress, you have to be confident. As soon as a slave walks through the door you have to take over. What happens is that when they arrive, after making an appointment first, of course, my maid lets them in and shows them around the dungeon. They never see me at this point. When I come in I am dressed in ordinary clothes and I'll tell you why. We'll spend about ten minutes discussing exactly what they want out of the session. Some might just want to be a naughty boy and stand in the corner. Others might want to be a real slave. We'll both sit down, but I always make sure I'm sitting higher than they are. I've got a list of about a dozen rules written down which they must read so they'll know exactly how to behave in my presence. They are also given a choice of what they want me to wear. Remember, the session is their fantasy, not mine. So I try to make it real for them. I ask them what they like. Leather, rubber, PVC? High heels, thigh boots? Whatever they like, I try and get it for them. By the time they see me again in the dungeon, I am dressed for their fantasy. Now the session starts.

First of all, I will humiliate them. Not in a big way, but in a small way. However, I make sure they know who is the mistress and who is the slave. I look down on them, see? It doesn't matter if it's only a couple of inches. But they always have to raise their eyes to look up at me. Once I'm dressed and the session starts, I don't stop for anything. That's the whole idea of sitting them down at the beginning, so that later I can just run smoothly with them. They understand that once I walk in dressed in full uniform it doesn't stop until the time is up. They're already acquainted with my rules, so they know what to expect of me. If they forget, then I have to forcibly remind them.

But it is more than just the physical side. Take humiliation as an example. The real humiliation comes from the mouth. It's in what I say and the way I say it. Although I'm doing what they want, I'm making them do it my way. For instance, if they want to worship my body, I tell them where to worship and for how long. If they want to lick my boots, I make sure they do a really good job and lick all the dirt off. They must only touch me where we have agreed beforehand they can touch. Absolutely nowhere else. If I tell them they may kiss my bottom and they start holding me there with their hands, I let them know that it is wrong! And I make sure they won't do it again, believe me!

The kind of punishments I meter out varies from one slave to another. Not everyone likes heavy punishment. But the point is to find out what they like and what they don't like first. My kind of punishment is to give them a little of what they don't like! They won't do it again! The kind of situation where I would give out what I call 'real' punishment would be, for example, when they are not supposed to touch me unless I tell them to. Even if they just brush against me without permission they will be punished. If they tell me they don't like to be marked, then I will mark them. But only for a short period, though. By the time they leave the marks will be gone. But it will be enough to make my point. It's the fright you put into them that counts. Not all of my slaves can afford to go home with marks on them for their wives to see. Another slave may have told me he doesn't like his nipples played with. So what do I do if they're naughty? I'll tie them up and yank their nipples a little bit. Of course, you gag them first so they don't scream. And, again, you don't do it too long. Just long enough to let them know that they should never disobey. If they do, they'll know what they'll get! And the next time it will be harder. Above all, never let them know when the punishment is coming. Most of the time they will learn to like it.

I never work on the basis that I know what a slave wants, because I don't. They have to tell me and then I carry it out. For instance, some slaves like to take Amyl Nitrate. Personally, I don't like the stuff. But, if that's what they want, then they have it. Also, although they tell you want they want, they expect you to fill in the gaps between. It's difficult to explain what that means, really. For example, they might give me a piece of paper. Maybe three or four sheets. I can scan through it, but there's usually no way I can carry all this stuff out in an hour or an hour and a half. The theory that's in their heads doesn't translate into reality. So I say to them: "Well, we'll do most of the things you want and I'll fill in the gaps". Others don't actually know what they want, so again I have to fill in the gaps and make it last. Just because I'm a mistress the slave thinks I know everything, but I don't.

Even when trained slaves come to me, who may have served another mistress for years, I still say to them: "You must forget your old mistress completely and go my way". And that's how we do it. I tell them I'm going to break them body and soul. I tell them: "You're new to me and I'm new to you. I don't even want to know what you've been through before". I don't mess around with them. It's the only way to do it, really.

There are some so-called mistresses who haven't a clue what they're doing and that's the truth. I have rules and regulations that all my slaves understand so they know how to treat me Once I'm dressed up and in the working room I will break them into my rules, but within the constraints of what they want. At the end of the day you have to remember it's the man who's coming to you and you're the one who's got to please him. You can see I'm being very frank with you. I'm not cutting out anything.

When I come to the end of the session and want to end it, I give them permission to dress and see them to the door. At that point we're back to normal. If they're new ones I will ask them if they are happy or if they have any complaints. So far I haven't had any complaints. Sometimes with the new ones, if I have the time, I will sit down with them and explain why I did this or that during the session. If they're the sort who have come with unrealistic scenarios, I'll tell them to go away and think about what they really want and to read some books on the subject. That way we can progress in the next session.

As a mistress you have to be a good actress. You've also got to be able to read people's minds which, fortunately, I can due to my training as a psychiatric nurse. Above all, you've got to be in command throughout the whole session. Never relax. Never let them know if you don't know or unsure. You, as a Mistress, must surround them, in a sense. They're watching you all the time, so you've got to be on top from the first minute to the last. If they talk without permission, tell them to shut up. And when you punish them, smile at them. And they will smile back at you and say: "Thank you".

I always use hand contact between whippings to relax them

and bring them to attention. Any mistress or master will tell you that. You can't just hit someone anywhere and anyhow. That's not domination. That's just beating someone black and blue. Domination is an art and the person doing it is an artist. What I do is very classy. I combine hard and soft techniques. I have lots of little brushes and other equipment as well as my fingers to relax them. So you've got to be an artist, you've got to be able to read their minds and you've got to be dominant without being forceful. But, most of all, you've got to be natural.

I never swear at them. Well, I don't know how to swear to be honest with you. I'll call them names, but I don't like ugly words. I'll call them 'cabbage-brains' or something like that. The beauty of it is that they respect me and I respect them and we have a relationship. They phone up say: "Hello, Mai-Ling. How are you?" I don't like to be called 'mistress' when I'm not actually working. I don't think it's on. I keep the dungeon separate from normal life. It's beautiful. I love my work.

In the course of a day, I may cover all sorts of things. Torture scenes and interrogations. I have to treat them as terrorists or prisoners or whatever. For this I'll put them in the cage or tie them up and blindfold them. Then I treat them rough. I mean very, very rough because they love it. I do a lot of threatening and I put a lot of panic and fear into them. It's like acting in a film. You have to treat them like dirt. Grab their hair and all sorts. Whatever it takes. It's hard sometimes because some of them hold on for an hour or more before I can get information out of them. A favourite one for them is to pretend they're in Changie prison in Singapore. Other times I am a customs officer. But I always give some leeway. That is, I give with one hand and take back with the other. The trick is never to let them know when you are going to give it to them and when you are going to take away.

I also have a room set aside for TV's and Adult Babies, too. When I do something I like to do it properly. In there they've got the wigs, the dresses, the shoes, everything. Sometimes at parties I will dominate other women. But it doesn't really do anything for me. I can do any male. Young, old or in between. Most of the men I see are between twenty and sixty five. Not younger or older. But they've got to be strong physically and not ailing. I won't see anyone who is ailing at all. I mean there is the risk that they might drop down dead. And I'm not joking! The other thing is that I won't put people at unnecessary risk. Nothing has happened so far, but I won't put people's lives in danger. It's a game and I keep it as a safe game. I don't do degradation or shitting on people. Definitely not, under any circumstances. If anyone phones me for that, I'll say no. If they call again, I'll just put the phone down. There are lots of other mistresses who will do it. But I've got limits to what I'll do. The clients I see are more than happy with me and I am happy with them. Once they know what I do and don't do, that's okay.

I'm not looking for people who don't respect themselves. And I don't want someone who is just coming here for one day to get a kick out of it. I want someone who has a genuine interest. Someone who says: "Mistress, I'm in your hands. Do what you want with me". Within reason, obviously. Someone who wants me to teach them how to be a proper slave and who sincerely wants to learn how to worship a mistress. Once they tell you that you know they will keep coming back. These are the sort of clients I want.

I like to tie people up and tease them silly in lots of different positions. These people are not into the heavy S&M thing. That's what they want and that's what they get. No marks, no nothing. I never go over the top with anyone. If they say that's all they can take I respect their limits. Unless they're doing something they shouldn't. That's a different matter. Then, obviously, I do what I want with them because I'm the mistress and they have to take it whether they like it or not.

They never know what I'm going to do next. I'm very unpredictable. Everytime they come it's a different thing altogether. Never do the same thing over and over again. It's boring and I lose interest very quickly. So I tell them that next time they come we'll do what they've set out, but then they're going to learn. I'll introduce new things for them. But I'll always give them what they want first. A bit of body worship, whatever. And then introduce something else. There's so much you can do with them. It can go on and on and on. But never give to them all in one go; prolong it.

I have been occasionally asked to be submissive, of course. But I can't do it because I'm naturally dominant. Sometimes I'll get a call from someone asking me to be submissive for them. This is very, very rare. When it happens I'll ask them where they got that information? So they read out my ad over the phone and I say: "Where does it say about being submissive? It doesn't. You'd better find someone else". If I'm in a bad mood, I'll just slam the phone down. I give and they take. That's the whole idea of them being here and there's no in-between. But the genuine people don't waste my time because they're wasting their own time, too. If you're genuinely dominant, then you can't be submissive. These people are worms, they can't read. All they see is a phone number. If they're here in the room and they ask for that then I really give it to them hard because they're stupid.

What I plan for the future is to take in overnight stays and weekend visits on a one to one basis. They will have to write me a formal letter of introduction for this service as I am only interested in very genuine scene players. I'm having a booklet printed which will be sent to each applicant. So they will know what they're letting themselves in for. At the same time they must explain exactly what they want. I don't know anyone else who is providing this service. I think there is a call for it. I'm really looking forward to starting.

I'm often asked about the funniest or weirdest requests I've ever had. It would be impossible to list them all because there have been so many! When I first started I was very shocked by some of the requests I got, but I never showed it. I pretended I knew what I was talking about, even though I didn't! But I'm doing this five days a week for six years now, so I think I've heard it all! I don't let anything shock me now. Why should I? There's nothing to be shocked about. Sometimes I might wonder where he gets his ideas from? I look at the client and the paper he has written. I look back at him again and tell him that I don't think I can carry this out, not to this extent. I mean some of the ideas clients have are just too fantastical. There's nothing you can do with them.

Yet it's like you're in a glass house. You're being watched all the time. You've got to be competent, confident and in total control. If you take on something you can't do, you've lost it. They're not coming back to you. Best to be honest with them. I don't cheat clients with their time or their money. That's why I always sit and discuss everything with them before hand. And if I can't do what they want. I tell them straight I can't do it. It's just not applicable. But we can do this and this.

You can see by now that being a true dominatrix is very hard work. I've got so many role-plays and so many screen-plays. Sometimes they will come to me and want us to pretend we're at a party. Do to me what you'd do at an S&M party, they'll say. He's never been to an S&M party in his life, never even been to a fetish club. And he's asking me to take him there in my workroom in fantasy! Now what do I do with him? Do you see how hard it is? He doesn't have the chance to go in real life. He'd love to go. His fantasy is that he's on stage at a party. It's so hard to put on that sort of thing. But whatever they want, I can't smile or laugh. I have to be serious. Obviously, if it's something funny we'll have a good laugh about it afterward. But I can't laugh in the workroom.

I had one slave in particular I must tell you about. He had a wife he loved, but she didn't love him. The arrangement between them was that he was her slave, but she could take any man she fancied. So, she brought this new man home and introduced her husband as her 'slave', and told him he had to serve both of them. This new man was very dominant and started taking over. Pretty soon his wife is dressing him up in a maids uniform and sending him over to me for further training, because she couldn't even be bothered to train him herself anymore. Not now that she had her 'dream lover', as she called her boyfriend.

Meanwhile, the poor chap is having to call the boyfriend 'Master'. He used to force my slave to come into the bedroom and watch him make love to his wife. This went on for four months. Then the boyfriend decides to move some of his stuff into the house and stay over most nights. At this point, I said to the slave: "Do you think you can handle this?" He says: "Sure. No problem".

He had to do things like clean the boyfriend's car every Sunday. Outside in the road, this is. All dressed up in pink knickers and everything. But it did start to get a little bit out of hand when some of the boyfriend's mates were brought back and he had to serve them drinks and wait on them and curtsey like a maid and everything while they all got drunk and took turns having sex with his wife.

He started getting really unnerved about that. He wasn't getting anything, you see. No sex, nothing. Meanwhile, she's going out dressed really teasingly with short, tight skirts. When she comes back she would take off her knickers and let him smell them and then she'd tell him about all the men who had spunked over them that night. This was the nearest he was allowed to get to sex with his own wife now. He wasn't even allowed to touch her. Then the boyfriend banned him from even sniffing his own wife's knickers. Instead, they got him a blow-up doll and he was allowed to sleep with that for a couple of nights a week.

Things became really heavy for him when his wife's lover (who was a builder) decided to take him away on a six week contract. He was made to work all day for nothing. But worse than that, the boyfriend had another mate on the building site. He told everything to this chap about what went on. How he has sex with the man's wife and everything. So this mate started taking the mickey out of him. He used to say things like: "You've got a really nice wife. We're all going to come round and fuck her for you". Things like that. On top of this, he became the dogs-body to everyone on the building site. If they wanted anything from the shops, he would have to get it. For the whole six weeks they treated him really rough. Making him work from seven in the morning till seven at night.

Back home he was forced to live in the box room of his own house. No furniture, nothing. Now and again the boyfriend might allow him to watch them having sex and then punish him if he got an erection. Then the boyfriend announced that he was going to leave his own wife and move in permanently. At this point the fellow phoned me and he was not too happy. He visited me to talk about it. Yet even then he still thought he could cope with it.

Shortly afterward, the boyfriend went away on another contract and the wife started pining for him, saying how much she missed his cock. Her husband offered to fuck her in his absence and she got really angry. She said: "How dare you" and slapped his face and then proceeded to beat him very hard. Anyway, during this period she started letting another boyfriend come round to satisfy her. The two boyfriends didn't know about each other, you understand. Only the husband knew. But he still insisted he could cope with it because he loved her so much.

Finally, and I don't know exactly what happened to trigger it, but the boyfriend was making the husband call him 'Master', as usual, and forcing him to get on the floor to lick his wife's boots, as he did everyday, when he must have said something to make the husband snap. He went completely over the edge and grabbed a baseball bat and chased both the boyfriend and his wife down the street, hitting him all the time with the bat while the neighbours watched. This is while he's wearing stockings and his maids uniform, remember! So, in the end it was too much for him and he couldn't cope with it. Now he's decided he doesn't want to do the slave thing anymore. He wants to try straight forward S&M for a change.

Now you understand that I always have to keep my mind a blank in this business. I never wonder who's coming. It could be someone I've seen ten thousand times, but I still ask them what they want to be. What they want me to do with them today. He might have changed his mind from the last time. How do I know? He might have read some books and got some new ideas. Every day is a new day and every time they come I treat them like a new client. That's why they love coming to me. I don't just ask them what they want and get on with it. They'd get fed up and so would I. Then I'd get lax in my work and start getting angry. And when they come next time, I'd say: "Oh no, not you again!" See what I mean? It's got to be new all the time. They come to me to be relaxed in their own specific way and I give them exactly what they want. It's as simple as that.

To any woman who wants to become a mistress, I would say this: don't try to be mistress all the time. You need time away from it to develop new ideas and different ways of dealing with your slaves. Ensure that each session is new and exciting for both you and your slave. Always make the slave wonder what he can expect, what will be done to him today. Make it work for him and don't forget to enjoy yourself, too. Above all, give your all to each session. Give it your heart.

Chapter 15: Mistress Midori

Born in the ancient Japanese capital of Kyoto and raised in the hi-tech city of Tokyo, Midori is the daughter of a Japanese mother and German-American father. Both her parents are university professors. Following a varied and successful career in the United States Army and in commerce, she now works as a professional dominatrix in San Francisco. Incidentally, this is the only interview in the book that was conducted over the Internet, hence the rather stilted and premeditated style of the dialogue. Despite my own dislike for this particular medium, I decided to keep this one in as it seemed to me to be tantamount to a 'master-class' in how a professional American mistress presents herself to the world

I had a very unique multicultural upbringing that combined Japanese and German-American influences with feminism and a fierce devotion to individuality. It's a background that brings a distinctive edge to my play, I think. I moved to the States as a teenager, where I attended and graduated from the University of California at Berkeley, where I studied psychology with an emphasis on neurobiology. Shortly thereafter, I enlisted in the US Army. I eventually received my commission as an intelligence officer attached to Soviet Tactical Intelligence. I'm also airborne trained and an expert marksman. Since then, I've also been successful in the corporate world, but eventually turned my back on it to pursue my true passion of SM.

My current hobbies include working out as well as many outdoor sports. I'm extremely passionate about shoe shopping and enjoy vintage fashion collecting, too. I also enjoy a spirited discussion with my friends after watching good movies; everything from arthouse to fashion flicks! I love to travel and have already seen the world from St. Petersburg to Tokyo and from Canada to Mexico. And I look forward to discovering many other parts of the world. My ultimate fantasy would be to combine world travel with the elegant couture of the 19th century (steamer trunks full of exquisite gowns and with all the Sherpas and servants to carry them!) With a grand spirit of adventure; canoeing down the Amazon, trekking the Silk Road in the footsteps of Marco Polo and living among the tribesmen of some exotic rainforest!

I also like very physical sports. I guess I'm a real thrill seeker! The vibrant pleasure of living is reinforced every time I push myself in a physical or mental challenge. I'm very athletic and routinely enjoy snow-boarding, skiing, kayaking and white-water rafting. I'm even considering eco-adventure racing. I thrive on living life to the fullest, and I'm very greedy when it comes to gaining pleasure and experiences. I don't want to waste my time on the vulgar or the mundane.

Fetish for me is a visual, tactile and sensual passion. It's something that triggers my erotic desires and stirs my imagination. It pleasures my animal soul as well as stimulates my intellectual fancy. When anthropologists speak of a 'fetish', they usually mean a religious or spiritual object. Something to focus belief on. My definition is the contemporary usage of the term, as applied to clinical psychology, as well as to popular sexual reference. We're talking about two different things here, because the term has deviated substantially from its original meaning. The word 'fetish' has currently been applied to everything from Zuni amulets to fashion trends, and from sexual novelties to an enthusiast's hobby, and even to sexual dysfunction! My own personal fetishes include shoes and boots, fur, leather and corsets. Those are the things that come to mind immediately, but there are many other things that turn me on in the right situation. The 'second skin' of latex provides a sensual contact, yet denies the animal touch.

I've noticed there's a greater popularity of availability of leather in the United States. I've also found in the US that there's a greater influence from cowboys and leather-men in our fetish shops. Here, on the West Coast, we're very influenced by our Pan-Pacific heritage, of course. For me, it seems that Europe taps into fashion tradition; everything from Byzantine to the French Court. Europe also has a strong history of elegant balls and costumed festivals, which we lack on this side of the Atlantic, unfortunately. Americans, however, have a legacy of organisations, tribes and cultures from which we draw our archetypal imagery. For example, the military, ethnic costuming, motorcycle gangs and even labourer's coveralls. I think that the popular rise in fetish imagery is a by-product of urbanisation, industrialisation and commodification of human sexuality. The desire for the 'genital' has been replaced by a desire for manufactured objects.

I think my success in the fetish world is due to the fact that I am a real woman, and not just a two dimensional visual icon or an SM caricature. What I bring to all my scenes and performances is intellect, physicality, as well as my own beauty. I bridge the gap between many worlds and communities. My charm appeals to both the SM and fetish worlds, as well as the mainstream community.

Chapter 16: Miss Spiteful

As her name suggests, Miss Spiteful's interests definitely lean toward the hard-core end of the SM spectrum, including the nailing of foreskins to tables and the burning of swastika's into flesh with cigarettes. She is also a leading practitioner of the intricate art of Japanese rope bondage Despite her predilections for the more extreme forms of game-playing, she strictly adheres to the limits of safety and consensuality. Born in Newport, Wales, Miss Spiteful now lives and practices her dungeon crafts in South London.

I suppose, like a lot of people, my interests in SM developed over time. I remember, when I was a child, I saw a drawing in a Christmas annual of a man tied up and found that very exciting, but probably didn't understand why I was so attracted to it. I first began to understand SM when I read the Story of O back in the 1970's. When I met my partner in 1981, he was already heavily involved in the TV scene and a number of people on that scene were also involved in the SM scene. There was always this undercurrent image of SM in the clubs and places we used to visit, although there was never any action as such. We used to get Skin Two magazine and the images in that were unbelievable. During this period, a major turning point happened in my personal life and I began to get more heavily involved in the SM scene. A couple of friends, who were on the scene, and I had a number of sessions together and I got a real taste for it. One friend, in particular, introduced me to the club scene about 1992. To be honest, my first experience of a club was very disappointing, but I'm glad I kept going because I do think they're great fun. Compared to an SM club, ordinary clubs are too tame.

I've always been interested in the images of SM. I love the cold, dark gothic image of the dungeon and the image of the heartless and cruel dominant woman. I also enjoy the empowerment of the SM scene. When I go to the SM clubs and I know people are watching me dominate a sub, it really excites me! I like the shock factor, too. I like the look on people's faces, because some of the things I do are very, very hardcore. Things like burning a sub's penis with a cigarette or piercing their nipples with needles. I've even burned a swastika on someone's back with cigarettes and nailed men's foreskins down with a hammer. It's really very severe stuff! I'm not talking about just flicking at someone with a whip. I love knowing that people watching me are really horrified by what I'm doing!

Before I became a professional mistress in 1995, I worked as a secretary for some very high powered companies, including working as a treasurer's secretary in the City. In fact, slaves often comment on how well written my e-mails and letters are. Incidentally, I'm often horrified at the number of illiterate letters I get from men (especially young men) who can't even construct a sentence! Perhaps people should look at their standard of education.

Anyway, in those days, I was doing this just for fun in clubs and occasionally had people back for scenes in my own dungeon. I then realised I was very good at it and enjoyed it so, in effect, I turned my hobby into a profession. I think the fact that I really enjoy it myself comes across in my sessions. That's why people keep coming back. Personally, I don't regard anything I do as unusual or weird. I literally adore dominating people and hurting them. Having said that, there are certain things I won't do. For instance, I won't do 'hard sports', and I certainly won't have sex with clients. I'm not a great lover of water sports, enemas or anal penetration either. I'll do it, but I don't particularly enjoy it.

What I enjoy more than anything is people who will interact with me. I like people who are slightly impotent. I can feed off that and use it back at them. I like verbal humiliation, too. And I don't mean just shouting at people while they're standing there like a lump saying: "Yes, Mistress. No, Mistress". I like them to think and work at it. Then I can use what they say and throw it back at them. I can sound very authoritative without having to rant and rave all the time. I don't feel the need for it. In fact, you can get much more out of people that way. I like them looking at me while I'm hurting them, too. If you're just going to shout at someone for an hour or get them to lick your boots, then there really isn't much enjoyment you can get out of that. And I do like to get some pleasure out of a session, too. I don't do this just for the sake of earning money.

I think if you're a professional dominatrix, then you have to be intelligent. You also have to keep your wits about you! For instance, if you're going to act the part of a schoolmistress, it's no good asking questions you don't know the answers to yourself! You have to get inside someone's mind and use everything they say against them. As I said, domination isn't about shouting and screaming at someone for an hour, there are much more subtle ways of dominating a person. Most of the dominatrixes I know are well educated and intelligent. I know two who have university degrees. Although I had a normal 1960's education, I'm educated to A-level standard.

Depending on what we do, I'll offer someone a session lasting from one to two hours. The reason I do that is because I don't think it's fair on the person, or on me either, to tie them up in a very intricate fashion and then, after about five minutes, tell them their time is up and start untying them again. Sometimes they'll come down from a session and they won't have a clue where they are, so you have to bring them down gradually. It's very unusual if I don't offer someone a cup of tea after the session and a chance to come back down to earth. If I don't, it's because I'm glad to see the back of them! One case was a chap I had recently who walked in as if he owned the place, took a look around my dungeon and then told me he was really looking for someone younger. He was just about to leave when I said: "Before you go, I'd like you to take your trousers down". I thought he might be a newspaper reporter, you see. If it is a reporter, I thought I might have a problem. And I know they will never take their trousers down, they won't expose themselves. Anyway, he dropped his trousers and I said: "Well, actually, it's just as well because I wanted someone bigger!" I've had a few like that who come round thinking they're Jack The Lad and find, when they get in the dungeon, they just can't handle it. You can see them visibly shaking.

As a matter of fact, a lot of my sessions aren't even about thrashing people all the time. They might just like to be tied up and teased with whips or simply touched. There's a lot of sensuality and eroticism in what I do through the feeling of helplessness. Just being touched can be as torturous as being whipped, sometimes more so.

I enjoy the 'adult' schoolboy and schoolgirl scenes very much, too. There are so many subtleties involved and phobias you can touch on. And such a depth of humiliation, as well. Teachers back in the 1950's and 1960's did things to children that were absolutely unbelievable. I mean, totally sadistic. They traumatised people for the rest of their lives. It's that generation that end up coming to me for those kind of scenarios. Consequently, there's a whole area you can concentrate on with a wealth of sub plots that go on. I have one favourite who loves to act the part of a 'schoolgirl'. We've been through endless scenarios exploring this theme. He's run away from home and become a prostitute. Other times, I've sent him to Catholic school. I've sent him to the police. It always ends up the same way though, with him other the desk being thrashed!

As I said earlier, I really enjoy nailing foreskins down. I've done it in the clubs, as well as here in my dungeon. To be honest, it looks much worse than it actually is. It doesn't hurt that much, it's more the shock value. I've even done it to someone without a foreskin! I've never nailed scrotums, though. How it came about was that I had a friend who was a carpenter and was very heavily into bondage. He was also very excited by the idea of nailing. He was tied up on the whipping horse one day, and we just did it! We experimented with different ways of doing it, using varying numbers of nails and it went on from there. It frightens people at first, as I said, but it's more the shock than anything else. I've had a lot more blood from pushing a needle through someone. That's because a nail goes in faster. And we always use masonry nails made from hardened steel, because they don't rust.

I got interested in bondage in the early 1990's, but I've always found it erotic to watch and partake in. I was always fascinated by the sheer helplessness of it. I think rope bondage brings a special sensuality to the session, because it's so erotic being tied up in this manner. My partner used to be in the Merchant Navy, so he was able to show me a few simple knots to start me off. It's the same with Japanese bondage. They're very simple knots, but because of the way you tie it, it becomes almost unbreakable. It's also very decorative. In Japan, it's considered a great art. They have what they call Rope Salons there.

I became so fascinated by Japanese rope bondage, in particular, that I set out to find someone to teach me. I was at Club Whiplash one night about four years ago, and was lucky enough to meet an English rope-master, who lived in East London. He fuelled my interest even more and was kind enough to teach me some techniques. I started going over to his studio on a regular basis. Although we have tied each other up, he's in a league of his own. He is far superior to anything I could do. Now I'm totally fascinated by it. I can get so much pleasure in tying some one up and just looking at it. That might be difficult for some people to understand, but it's such an empowering feeling. And for the person tied up it's very comforting and, at the same time, they feel quite helpless and vulnerable. It's very intense and very erotic, but some people are afraid of it. You obviously have to be very careful what you do and watch to see that the person isn't getting into trouble. For instance, you have to watch their fingers to make sure they're not going numb or very bright red.

I know there's a myth that women who work as professional dominatrixes are men-haters and just do it to get revenge, but this certainly isn't true of me. I think I'm more attracted to men than to women. I can have a great deal of fun with men, as I see them as the weaker sex. I know they like to appear the stronger, but they're not.

I like their company, but I also like the company of women, too. I think, at the end of the day, it depends on the man. I see men in all shapes and sizes, and some men you're more attracted to than others. Some men have nice bodies and nice personalities, and some don't.

The SM scene has always had a bad press, because newspapers are only interested in selling newspapers, not public morals. If they think a story will sell a newspaper, then they'll print it! They're very fond of taking a righteous moral stance. They'll call anyone who dresses in leather 'perverts', and cause the people involved a lot of embarrassment and sometimes real harm! Reporters will try and infiltrate a someone's dungeon because it's an easy story. Next week, they'll expose something else. Of course, you'll always have nosy busybodies who'll want you to live to their standards; but they're going to be very disappointed with me, I'm afraid, because I live my life to suit myself!

There does appear to be a movement to make the scene more open and more acceptable to the general public, with things like the SM Pride March. Personally, I don't think this is a good thing. The SM scene has got a certain appeal because it is so underground. If it becomes too accessible and too open, then it'll lose that appeal. I don't want to walk into a club in rubber clothes and have people not take any notice! I want ordinary people to look, because it's not something they come across every day. I enjoy the shock value of the scene. If rubber clothing became fashionable, it would take away that shock value. I understand that SM Pride even has a committee. To me, that's ridiculous! Unfortunately, I think I'm in a minority of one on this!

The SM club scene has definitely become more popular over recent years, but whether that has anything to do with the fear of HIV, I don't know. I understand swingers clubs are still as popular as ever. Probably some people will explore areas like SM because of the fear of HIV, but I think there has always been a lot of men, in particular, attracted to the SM scene anyway. I'm sure there are a lot of men who like the feeling of having the power taken away from them and being humiliated in some way by a woman. And there will always be people who think this scene looks interesting and want to experiment with it by going to a couple of clubs. But I also believe those who get involved on a long term basis do so out of enjoyment, as well as a deep seated fascination for it. Personally, I don't see the point of publicising SM clubs so widely that they become packed out with tourists. Nowadays, it's quite common at clubs to see young women with riding crops, and you just know they don't have a clue what they're supposed to do with it! I'm sure in this day and age anyone who really wants to get on the scene will be able to find the information they need on the Internet or through fetish magazines.

As I said earlier, I know some women only look on domination as a way of earning money, but I thoroughly enjoy what I do and I would hope this comes across in the sessions. I get a lot of people who come back on a regular basis and I'm kept pretty busy, so I guess I'm doing something right! If you only do this for the money, people will recognise it and look elsewhere. I've heard of some so-called dominatrixes whose only 'equipment' is a chair and a whip; that sounds more like a lion-tamer to me! One chap told me he'd had a session that only lasted ten minutes! I asked him what can you do in that time? He said there were two women who put him over a chair and beat him as hard as they could, then masturbated him and kicked him out! As I already said, most of my sessions will last anywhere between an hour and two hours. If I don't think the person is responding or is responding too fast, and they're almost at a peak, I'll let them ejaculate and let them get over it. Sometimes I'll end the session myself and we'll have a cup of tea. Other times, I'll carry it on as long as I want, if the other person feels like it and doesn't have to get back to work or anything. I'm probably not coming across as some kind of Lady Macbeth saying all this, but I do feel that just because I'm spiteful and sadistic in the dungeon doesn't mean I want to rip people off.

In fact, I have four or five almost full-time slaves. My most faithful is Quilp, who's in my dungeon at the moment. I call him Quilp after the character in the lovely Charles Dickens story The Old

Curiosity Shop, who got drowned in the Thames. I met him about five or six years ago at a party. At the time, he was the plaything of a number of mistresses up the West End. He's quite well known on the scene, in fact. We got friendly and he ended up belonging to me. Not that I particularly want him, but he is nice to torture! He's also quite good as a domestic slave. And, of course, I also use him as a kind of 'living model' to practice my new rope techniques on.

One of my favourite incidents was with this chap who actually wanted a session on Christmas Eve, and ended up staying over for the whole holiday! I'd just got to my front door with all my Christmas shopping when he called. I thought surely he's not going to show up at this time. But he did! Anyway, during the session he told me he liked to eat shit. I told him I don't do scat or hard-sports, but he said that was okay because he'd brought his own in his carrier bag! I said he wasn't going to borrow one of my spoons to eat it with. But that was alright too, he said, as he'd brought his own spoon as well! He then produced this pot which contained what looked like shit, but could have been chocolate sauce for all I knew. I certainly wasn't going to taste it to find out! I must admit, it really turned my stomach to watch him munching his way through whatever it was he was eating!

Anyway, we came downstairs and he happened to mention he was going to be spending the Christmas period on his own. I told him he was welcome to come over for some lunch, if he wanted to. On the Christmas Day evening, as it happened, we had a mistress friend and a couple of gay guys come over who were heavily into CP. Well, it ended up with the five of us queuing up to beat him, and there was blood all over the walls and ceilings and everywhere!. It was an unusual way to spend Christmas, to say the least!

I see couples, occasionally. I had one couple who came to me regularly who were both into the spanking scene. Unfortunately, they've split up now. They were both subs and liked me to be their strict aunt and give them a spanking or paddling together. Another guy came up from the south coast who brought his girlfriend with him, but she didn't get involved. She just sat in the corner and watched. I find it a bit disconcerting when there's someone in the room with no interaction. Another couple phoned up a couple of days ago. They both wanted to be tied up, and then I was supposed to sexually assault her while he was watching.

I had a really strange one recently when this woman phoned up. She said she used to be a slave when she was in her teens. She said she was in her forties now, and wanted to know if I dominated women. I told her that I didn't mind. Then she asked me if I knew what the legal age was for dominating a woman? This was quite a strange thing to come out with, I thought. She then confessed that it was a young girl that she actually wanted me to dominate. It turned out the girl was under sixteen, so I really wasn't interested. Nothing came of it and, whether it was a wind-up or not, I don't know. But it was definitely a woman on the phone, and she sounded quite genuine. But you don't know what the sub-plot is in situations like that, do you?

I have had 'vanilla' relationships in the past that didn't involve the scene, but found they were just not fulfilling for me. With domination, there's always that little bit extra. Since I met my partner, I've always been involved in alternative, underground scenes. I suppose our relationship could still be termed 'normal', as he's not on the SM scene. But I don't want to be part of a 'normal' lifestyle! I couldn't bear staying at home, watching television and doing what passes as 'normality'. It just doesn't appeal to me, I'm afraid. It's as though something is missing. I want to live a bizarre lifestyle!

Chapter 17: Ms Christine Deering

Ms Deering is one of several Chapter Leaders of the Femina Society; an organisation that promotes Female Supremacy in a Matriarchal Society. The society, based (unsurprisingly enough) in the United States, is quasi-religious in its leaning toward the feminine archetypes found in such diverse belief-systems as paganism and Hinduism.

Maybe I should start by outlining the process a trainee slave must go through before being admitted into the Femina Society. During his initial period of rigorous and thorough postal training, the slave will learn one of the basic tenants of the society; that is, that a slave has no free time. Free time is for free people. A slave is not free. All his time belongs to his owner/instructress and, through her, the Femina Society itself.

Part of his training is in 'sensual servitude'. Besides the 'sensual tapes' he receives, the prospective slave candidate is constantly instructed to do erotic writing assignments that give free rein to his fantasies. Topics include giving his mistress an extremely erotic massage, worshipping her feet, serving her in the bathroom as a toilet and many other topics. He'll be given lessons in humility and taught the Femina Society's twelve positions of respect, so he'll know how to behave when he's finally given the reward of serving a lady in person.

Another aspect of the training is the serious study of Female Supremacy: why it's natural, why it's right and why it's necessary. For example, I've currently set a slave to work on his Matriarchal Studies Summer Study Project. To complete this project, he must read and report on three books, and I don't mean 'fuck books'! I'm talking about serious studies on the natural Superiority of Women, the origins of human society as a Matriarchy and how the patriarchy has unnaturally reversed the roles of the sexes and oppresses women. Another topic of study in this project is male violence in society, and against women in particular. Also included are lessons in honesty, loyalty and how to be a proper and pleasing servant; which means learning to do useful work and serve only to please the mistress, effacing one's own wants and desires. As you can see, this is serious all-encompassing education!

The would-be slave is also trained in networking to promote the growth of the Femina Society and to spread the Society's goals of Female Supremacy. In order to describe this training, I'll need to explain the nature and structure of the Femina Society. The Society is a sisterhood dedicated to re-establishing women in their rightful place in the world; that is, as Rulers of Society! Men are allowed to participate in the Society only as students, servants and workers. Women are catered to, make all the decisions and have all the rights. Males have no rights, but simply serve, obey and carry out assigned tasks. The Femina Society is definitely not a sex club, and males who only want to have their fantasies fulfilled have no place in it. Submission to Feminine Authority is a serious business and requires a serious attitude. I have a saying that applies: "If it was fun and easy, they wouldn't call it work."; and being a servant for the Femina Society is work and not always fun!

Structurally, the Society consists of a Mother Chapter, Sister Chapters and Associate Branches. Located in New England, the Mother Chapter under the leadership of the foundress Ms. C, organises all facets of Femina Society work. Education is carried out through the School for Servants and the Centre for Matriarchal Studies. Networking is carried out by communication with Sister Chapters, Associate Branches, other non-member Dominas, mailing projects and advertising. The Mother Chapter is the final authority in all matters concerning the Society, especially membership, but works closely with Sister Chapters.

Sister Chapters are established under the auspices of a Chapter leader; that is, a Domina who wishes to promote the teachings and goals of the Femina Society in her geographical area. In the Society hierarchy, a Chapter Leader is second only to Ms. C., but is considered a partner, not a subordinate. The activities of a Sister Chapter mirror those of the Mother Chapter.

This brings us to Associate Branches. A Branch exists where there's a worker or a trainee but, as yet, no Domina has stepped forward to become a Chapter Leader. It is the duty of a Branch worker to conduct networking through mailings and in person to promote the growth of the Society. Branch workers are assigned to the Mother Chapter and receive instruction and supervision from it. The goal of a Branch is to become a Sister Chapter.

Whether a person is a submissive male who wants to surrender to Feminine Authority in all aspects of his life, or if she is a woman who wants to work toward the rule of women in a Matriarchal Society (either as a Domina or as a Handmaiden who serves other women; though, it must be made absolutely clear, no woman in the Society ever serves a man in any way!), I urge you to consider the Femina Society as the place where you may fulfil yourself and advance your goals. The male will find a life of useful servitude (which should be the only reward he seeks), while the woman will find a Sisterhood that offers both a shared vision and practical support for her chosen lifestyle.

Here I can use my own case as an example of how this can be fulfilled within the Femina Society. Being both a nurse and a dominant woman, I naturally find I can blend these two aspects of myself together as a Domina. They fit together beautifully. For example, when I'm giving a slave my version of a physical examination. To start with the slave will disrobe and either remain naked or don some suitable apparel worthy of his station in life. This depends entirely on my whims and how much I want to embarrass him. Most times I like them to be totally nude. Then comes some suitable bondage. Usually this involves simple handcuffs; sometimes in front, then in back, then behind the head. This last one is a lovely position to have a slave in; standing with legs spread out, hands tucked behind his head. He is so vulnerable. I'll usually have a riding crop handy, just in case he shows any signs of moving about!

First, I'll deal with the 'vital signs'. These are assessed and recorded on an examination sheet made of rubber. Hands fastened out in front for this. Temperature is rectal, of course. Blood pressure, pulse and respiration are next. Should the slave ask what the readings are, he'll be told that they're none of his business and that curiosity can get him into a lot of trouble!

Flashing the eyes with a penlight is especially fun! This is to determine the level of alertness. Woe to the slave who is found not to be alert for his mistress! Next, to the extremities. For this I like to spread-eagle the slave, untying and re tying as seems appropriate. There is much pulling, pushing, pinching and a lot of fun for me, of course! I especially enjoy working on the toes. Then a more extensive taking of pulses at various parts of the body, both lying down and erect. I like to tease the slave mercilessly, at this point, because the pulse invariably quickens quite dramatically! The results of which you can imagine!

Perhaps the most fun is to have the slave erect with hands behind the head and legs spread as noted earlier. In this posture, I have the slave talk while monitoring his breathing and tormenting him in endless little ways. I work with particular attention to the cock and balls. Heaven help the slave who even twitches while I play my little games! It can mean the riding crop where he is most sensitive! In that sensitive area, I'll poke, prod, pinch and apply pressure to his balls. I'll even poke the end of my riding crop up his asshole, making him bend over to make it easier for me!

Then I'll have him kneeling, nose touching the floor, while I question him intensively about his diet and eating habits. Most slaves are overindulgent and have sluggish systems. It seems willpower is also a missing factor to the true submissive psyche. Of course, the remedy is a good cleansing enema. The beginner gets a small enema, but those with more experience will receive at least two quarts. The slave is instructed in breathing during the enema session.

After his enema, I always like to administer my golden fluid. This is done in various ways. Most often in one of three ways: a shower over the slave's body, in a drinking cup or down a funnel straight into the slave's mouth, so he's forced to swallow it as quickly as I produce it! After he's cleaned himself up, I'll assess the slave's skin condition and sensitivities are noted. Disciplinary implements are employed to discover reddening factors and his reactions to various types of instruments. This is essential in setting limits for the discreet slave who must remain unmarked. Next it's time to turn to the question of slave posture. The slave is taught to kneel properly, stand and walk. Also, he'll be instructed in the correct positions for discipline and submission to a mistress. The body is examined at each step for correctness of form.

Finally, the slave's psycho sexual make-up is assessed. This is accomplished through intimate questioning and observing reactions throughout. This helps the slave to better understand why he is a slave in the first place! To finish the examinations, the slave is given a herbal drink. These are individualised for each slave, and contain calming herbs, potency herbs, diuretics or cathartics. I find these examinations extremely helpful in finding out the potential of the novice slave. They're also valuable in accessing the changing conditions and attitudes of more experienced slaves. And, most importantly, they're fun for the mistress, too!

Chapter 18: Mistress Rowena

A former psychiatric nurse in her mid thirties, Based in London, Mistress Rowena graduated from being a masseuse and escort to full-time professional dominatrix, specialising in the training of transvestite maids and bi-sexual males. She has since left the profession and gone back to college to study art history.

The first person I ever saw as a dominatrix is still with me. This particular guy rang me one day, completely out of the blue, and asked if he could be my slave. At the time I didn't even know what he was going on about! I was working doing massage and escorts at the time. But he persisted—as they do—and became my first slave, and that's where it all began, really. It certainly opened up a whole new world that I hardly knew existed before. Eventually, he told me that I should be doing this full-time and drop the other stuff. I couldn't believe how busy and popular it was. It was just mad for the first few years. That was about ten years ago and there really wasn't much competition back then. There was only about three or four women doing this in my area, that I was aware of. I thought this is fantastic! Compared to what I was doing before, this was great. I could come in and do exactly what I wanted—to a degree, that is. I used to get two or three people a week who'd stay for the whole day, so I could use them as sluts with other clients. They'd love it and be back next month for more!

I don't know why I attract so many TV's and bi-sexual guys,

but I do. It seems to have become a bit of a specialisation. Maybe it's my looks, I don't know. But there's definitely a lot of cock sucking goes on around here—and it's not me doing it, I can tell you that! I think they just like being under the control of an understanding mistress while being 'forced' to do something that, actually, they've always wanted to do anyway. None of them would consider themselves gay though.

My first full time transvestite maid was called Natasha. She was also my introduction to the TV and bi-sexual scene. She rang me up and asked if I need a maid. No, not really. But she persisted, of course, so up came Natasha! To be honest, I was expecting a maid who would keep the place clean and answer the phones and everything, but Natasha was more into seeing lots and lots of clients. She was very oral and a complete little slut—bless her! It was her, in fact, who persuaded me to get a proper dungeon going with lots of equipment and all the rest of it. I was doing it already, but not to the standard I am now.

It makes me laugh when people, especially the feminist lot, automatically assume someone like me is being exploited by men. Honestly, I've had men round here licking my toilet clean with their tongues while I watched day-time television, ate the box of chocolates they brought me and got paid for the privilege of letting them do it! Looking at it that way, I don't think I'm a poor exploited female, do you? Having said that, I do honestly think there is a price to be paid as well. Not meaning to sound dramatic or religious or anything, but sometimes I do think I've made a pact with the devil. I've lost a lot of my 'normal' friends from when I worked in nursing. The ones who've since got married and become very respectable tend to distance themselves from you. It's something you also have to keep quiet from your family. My mum and dad still think I'm nursing, so I literally have to live two lives. I drive two cars, for instance. One is a sports car and the other is a clapped out old rust bucket that I use when I go home to visit my parents for the weekend, because that's what they'd expect an overworked and underpaid nurse to be driving. You have to lead this strange double life. It's completely ridiculous, really.

A friend of mine, who's also a dominatrix, told me a lovely story about her little daughter that shows just what I mean. This little girl is about seven or eight now and she's one of these kids who's too clever for their own good, if you know what I mean. Anyway, she's listening to all these 'funny' phone calls her mum is getting from clients and slowly figuring things out and putting two and two together in the way kids do. Then one day she turns round to her mother and suddenly says: "I know what your job is!" My friend is like, oh my God, what's she going to come out with? She says: "Oh yeah? And what's that then?" And the little girl announces: "You beat people up for a living, don't you, Mummy?' Imagine that! I think I'd have fallen through the floor! I mean, what do you say to that?

Then there are the people who wonder why I'm still single at thirty five when I'm apparently so attractive and sexy and intelligent and all the rest of it. But the bottom line is, who would I get involved with? The men I meet either want to exploit me (that is, become my pimp) or they want to save me as some sort of 'fallen' woman! Neither of the above is particularly appealing, to tell you the truth. I've known some mistresses whose clients have become their boyfriends. I think that's ridiculous myself, but I can understand how it happens, because that's the only people you end up meeting. You can become very isolated in this business, if you're not careful.

I'm not saying that you can't become friends with clients though. One of my regulars was in his seventies and had been doing this stuff secretly for years, but had only come out with a vengeance after his wife died. He had the most amazing stories to tell, like tying an empty baked bean can to his genitals as a sort of improvised chastity belt, and this was when he was only six years old! Unfortunately, he seems to have 'disappeared' a while back. I've got a horrible feeling his daughters, who couldn't understand what he was about, have had him put away in a home. He used to joke that his family thought he was mad because of his fetish side. Maybe they really have done it and used the 'perviness' as evidence of his madness! It's quite medieval, if you think about it. Like witch-hunts or something!

But, then again, some people are very scared of all this. I don't think people in the scene are doing themselves any favours when they call themselves 'pervs'. I know it's only meant jokingly, but it does put a lot of people off who otherwise might get into it. When they hear the word 'pervert' they immediately think of child abuse and wife beating and a whole lot of other dark and sinister stuff that has nothing to do with this lifestyle. Now if they simply replaced that with something like 'kinky', which has got a much more lighthearted and fun kind of vibe to it, they'd find they would get a totally different reaction. People aren't threatened by that word. In fact, most find it quite titillating and naughty; sort of seaside postcards and all that. And that's the way it should be.

The type of clients I get are definitely not just the public school types, that's a great misconception. Although, it's true that they're usually the ones who can afford these little indulgences. But I've also dealt with plumbers, postmen and all kinds of normal, working class and middle class people who'll religiously save up their pennies so they can visit me. Having said that, I would say that many of my clients do come from very repressive backgrounds. Apart from the single-sex boarding school types, I've seen lots of men who come cultures where women are traditionally regarded as both social inferiors and as sex-objects whose appeal has to be constantly resisted and denied. For these men, the idea of submitting to a woman is the ultimate perversion; it's blasphemous, in fact. Consequently, it's incredibly erotic for them as well, as you can imagine!

What I would add, though, is that most CP addicts are English, or at least, of Caucasian stock. I've dealt with a few Germans, and Frenchmen really appreciate any form of exotic sex, I must say! As for the Latin races, you can forget it; sado-masochism is simply not part of their macho tradition and the very idea of being punished by a woman is alien to them. Apart from their mothers, I suppose. But that's a different thing. The same is true of Asians and most Afro-Caribbean's, too. As well as the macho aspect, I think the whole thing would be a turn-off for most West Indians. Think about it historically, they've experienced chains and slavery for real, and it wasn't exactly sexy, was it? So, I'd say there are very marked cultural differences here with the white northern Europeans dominating,— or not as the case may be!

I really enjoy having the transvestites here, but only if they want to 'do' something. Unfortunately, a lot of them just want to sit around and pretend they're at a Women's Institute coffee morning or something! Just the fact of 'being' a woman for a couple of hours is enough, they don't feel the need to actually do anything! Which I can understand is great for them, but it's a bit boring for the mistress who has to sit there with them. I especially like the ones who want to be total tarts! They're lots of fun! Now my favourite was a client called Natalie. She absolutely adored being a little slut. We used to have all the guys who fancied some bi-sexual fun come here one afternoon a week. Natalie would take the afternoon off work and, for that period of time, would be 'the good time that was had by all'! She loved every minute of it, and then would change back into 'masculine mode' and go back to her normal life of husband and father. I think these clients like having a TV join in because they can still kid themselves they're having sex with a woman. Therefore, in their own minds, at least, they've not had a 'gay experience' at all, and they can reassure themselves they're totally straight. Even though the experience they've just had is not 'totally straight', and neither are they! It's a way of justifying it to themselves, I suppose.

I remember one regular client of mine who was so into transsexuals, as well as domination, that he ended up living with a pre-op mistress as husband and wife. He even helped finance her sex change operation, which was why she was doing this in the first place. Incidentally, you know a lot of the pre-op transsexuals in this business are just doing it to pay for their operation, don't you? I feel very sorry for those ones, because quite often they'll really hate the work. But what else can they do? There's no other job around where they can be themselves or be wanted for what they are, is there? They really are very marginalised in society; much more than the rest of us. Anyway, as I was saying, this guy set up home with her and everything, and eventually she had the operation. Since then, she's turned into a real 'twin set and pearls' suburban housewife who spends her time baking cakes for the church fete and doing flower arranging evening classes! She doesn't want to have anything to do with 'mistressing' either, or straight sex for that matter, so the poor sod's missing out completely! The irony is that he actually helped her to be what she is today. He paid for all this in the hopes that he was creating the mistress of his dreams! And she just doesn't want to know! These days he's having to go back to visiting professionals and paying for it again!

But getting back to what I was saying before, the demand for TV's is so great, especially among the older clients, that I've had a few working for me as maids or submissives. The most memorable was one was called Layla who I inherited from a mistress up north who was badly mistreating her. I'd got to know her over the years at scene parties and clubs and so on, and one day she phoned me up in a very agitated state because her mistress was really taking the piss and doing some pretty horrendous stuff to her. I'd rather not go into all the details about what had happened, but it was pretty bad. Let's just say that poor Layla was really exploited something terrible by this bitch. This particular mistress had found out that Layla had left his/her wife because of this lifestyle and had got into a bit of a mess with debts and so on. She was on the run, basically. The mistress was forcing her to do really hard-core stuff, horrible stuff. Anyway, I agreed to take Layla on as my maid and receptionist and told her to jump on a train down here. She showed up with one carrier bag looking like a bag-lady or a refugee from Bosnia or somewhere. She was extremely popular with the kind of guys I mentioned—especially as she was hung like a cart horse!

Even before doing this, I've always been into bizarre sex. I suppose I like things that most women wouldn't even consider. I guess that's another reason I attract the transvestites and bi-sexual men, which would be a turn off for lots of women. But I love them. It's amazing how many men have bisexual leanings. A gay male friend of mine told me a great line that the only difference between a straight guy and a bisexual one is about six pints of beer! I think there's a lot of truth in that. It doesn't take much to bring that side out in most of my clients, I can tell you that!

For instance, another one of my regular clients loves the idea of being forced to have sex with other guys. Usually it's just oral. As I don't do any kind of sex , it's great having this guy as a 'cock slave' to finish the clients off with his mouth. He loves it and the clients, to be honest, are that excited by the end of the session they don't much care if it's a man or a woman doing the sucking. Some guys are blind-folded so they don't even know it's another guy doing it. Another of my guys will only suck men off if they're blindfolded. He couldn't bring himself to do it if they were looking at him. I'll be bringing the session to a close and, of course, the client will be all tied up and in a highly excitable condition! Then this guy will tip-toe into the dungeon and go down on him. When they'd finished he'd scamper off back into the other room and I'd take their blindfolds off. They all thought I was the one who'd just given them the blow job, rather than this seventy year old filthy bugger! I must admit I find the de-ception an incredible turn-on!

You hear horror stories in this business all the time. Not all mistresses are as professional as they could be, or even as sane they should be! I know of one mistress who has her black boyfriend work-ing with her who will join in whether you like it or not! He has a real attitude problem where whites are concerned and shows it! As far as his attitude to women are concerned, it's that 'fucking the plantation owners daughter' chip on the shoulder trip. With the sub guys, it's about fucking the plantation owner himself, I suppose. I heard one story from a client, who was also a bi-transvestite, about a session where he was tied up by this mistress, and then this big black guy walks in bare-ass naked and with a big hard-on and says: "So, you want to be a woman, I'll treat you like a woman". The client was bi-sexual, but that still doesn't mean he wants to be raped, does it? The black guy then has his way with him and what's he going to do about it? He's not going to go to the police, is he? The mistress isn't going to do anything either, because this bastard is her drugs supplier, as well as her boyfriend. I wouldn't mention any names because, apart from the fact that it would be unprofessional, it would be downright dangerous, too! There are mistresses out there who are vindictive, nasty bitches. They wouldn't think twice about stitching me up to the police or the tax man.

And some of the things these women get away with, you wouldn't believe! But it shows the way some of these guys get hooked, and the extremes they'll go to in order to please their chosen object of desire. One mistress I know of had this silly old fool come over from the States. He'd worshipped this woman for years and took care of her advertising and bought her clothes. He'd even paid for her boob enlargement for her. And you know what? He'd never even met her! But he still used to sleep with her knickers Sellotaped to his forehead every night. Then he does come over to Britain to see her. In the whole two weeks he was here, she allowed him to see her just once—and that was only to take her on a shopping trip. Talk about retail bloody therapy! She took his credit card off him and literally drained his bank account. When he got home, he discovered she'd taken him for every cent he had, which was something like twenty thousand dollars! And he still worships the ground she walks on! That's the kind of mistress who gives the rest of us mistresses a bad name. In this world, it's not about protecting society from the so-called 'perverts', it's more about protecting some of these idiots from themselves! It's absolutely criminal, but what can you do with someone like that old guy? Not much, really. They really are obsessed some of them. And it's nearly always old men, probably not a lot else going on in their lives, I guess. One old chap phones up regularly, and you really wouldn't believe the extent he goes through the contact magazines. He knows all the telephone codes too, so he knows exactly what area of the country a girls based. It's rather spooky, really.

I don't tend to deal with submissive women, unless they come here as part of a couple. I can tell you that, in my experience, submissive women are a damn sight weirder than any of the submissive men I deal with. One professional submissive girl I knew was really into big time. God, the risks that girl took in pursuit of what she called her 'perfect master' were quite unbelievable. I was telling a mistress friend of mine once that I wouldn't be surprised if she didn't end up floating down the River Thames one day!

Don't get me wrong, it's not the fetish scene I'm having a go at here. The scene in this country is great and the vast majority of people involved in it are fantastic. Even girls on their own are totally safe in a fetish club. I mean, could you imagine a young girl wandering around an ordinary nightclub, stark naked with a dog lead on and a collar that said 'slave' and being left in peace, of course not. It's just these lone loony ladies like that girl I'm talking about; answering ads and getting picked up by God knows who. She freely admitted to me that straight sex meant nothing to her and that she could only orgasm through being whipped. And we're talking blood on the ceiling here! Quite frankly, I think some of them have got their emotional wires crossed. As far as I'm concerned, these girls don't need a master, they need a therapist! I may be a dominatrix, but I'm not an evil bitch. Call me old fashioned but, at the end of the day, I'd rather give these girls a motherly hug instead of a whipping. But they wouldn't thank you for it, would they?

Frankly, I don't like that whole male dominant and female submissive side of the scene, anyway. It's a whole different ball game to what I do in female domination. It's much darker and, quite frankly gives me the creeps. With fem-dom, you can actually have a laugh with your clients and, most of the time it is fun. It's fantasy, pure and simple. And afterwards I'll sit down with my clients and have a cup of tea before they go. We step out of our respective roles then. And, believe me, the clients I get are not submissive at all in real life. In fact, anything but. A lot are quite high powered businessmen and people who have to give orders and make decisions all day. All those old clichés about kinky high court judges and bank managers are true! I think that's not difficult for even non-pervs to understand, though. If you're in that stressful kind of position then it's a like a mini-holiday to come here, swap your pin-stripe suit for a French maids outfit and pretend to be Fifi the Maid or whatever for an hour or two. But it's not like that when it's the other way around. At least, not as far as I can see. Some masters are fine, but many are just really horrible guys who just want to beat the shit out of a young girl. They've got a real attitude problem where women are concerned. But, then again, so have the women. After all, there's plenty of willing victims out there.

Like all the other women you've probably spoken to, I've had my fair share of weirdness. I do find other peoples sexual fantasies and fetishes endlessly amusing and fascinating, so maybe I unconsciously encourage the extremists, I don't know. Possibly the weirdest I had was this guy who said he'd been a librarian in the French Foreign Legion, for Christ's sake! He also claimed he'd fucked three thousand women including Princess Diana, Jackie Onassis and Bridget Bardot. It was when he got to Cleopatra and Mary Queen of Scots, that I began to suspect I was dealing with someone a little less than the full picnic hamper! And by the time he added Marie Antoinette and Mary Magdalene to his list, I realised he was the full raving article! His main obsession was wanting to drink young girls pee! He even had this idea of advertising in the contact mags offering to pay young single mums to sell him their daughter's urine by the pint!

I can tell you a few stories about vicars, too. That's another cliché that holds true! I've had one as a client, and he was straight round here after evensong to suck off my TV. He'd come straight from the church, still in his dog collar! On another occasion I saw this vicar at fetish event once. He was leading a slave boy around by a lead. The boy looked like one of those junkies that hang around Kings Cross. I thought, at first, that this clergyman gear was some sort of fetish costume, till I saw him get his cheque book out to buy some bondage gear and realised he actually was 'The Very Reverend'!

One of my favourites is my Dildo Man. He'll show up here with a suitcase full of the things and likes nothing more than putting on a sort of live 'dildo-show' for me and whoever else is here and fancies watching! I have literally witnessed this guy shove at least three bananas up his bottom, and then produce this bloody dildo-thing. It must have been, I swear to god, at least nineteen inches long! When the bananas were nicely mashed up his bottom, he'd shove it all the way up himself. He got it in so far I could see his stomach coming out at the front! It was like John Hurt in that film Alien. I expected it to burst open at any moment! He did confess that he was a bit worried his girlfriend was going off him a bit, because he used to shove bananas up himself at home as well. It's one thing to come to someone like me and do that stuff, but to do it in front of your sweet and innocent girlfriend is quite another! No wonder she'd gone off him! All he wanted to do was talk about bottoms and anal stuff!

Which reminds me of another one of mine who was absolutely obsessed with shit. He'd come for an over-night stay and bring all these videos for me to watch in the hopes I'd get turned on by them, I suppose. There were these videos of women rolling around in these huge tanks filled with cow dung, and he was raving about it! He thought it was all fantastic. We'd watch these bloody films all night long and all he wanted to do was talk about shit. Licking it, smelling it, eating it and smearing it all over himself. He was hoping I'd 'perform' for him in the morning. I did it, but I didn't enjoy it. In fact, I was a bit disturbed by that one, I have to admit.

Oh, and there was another one who was really scary! This guy wanted to be buried alive. So we took him out to some waste ground near here and buried under a pile of rubble one night. That was pretty bizarre. We stuck a sort of snorkel made of old hose pipe down for him to breath through, and then we'd go to the pub for an hour and leave him there! Another strange thing about him was that he also wanted me to keep all the used condoms I'd accumulated from other clients. He'd ring up in the morning and tell me he was coming over in the afternoon and would I keep all these dirty condoms for him. He'd be dressed up in women's clothes and I'd pin the condoms all over him. Then I'd have to tell him what a dirty piece of shit he was, and that he was only fit to drink piss and things like that. He was very controlling and manipulative too, which you come across from time to time with submissives. For instance, he'd bring this card, with all this stuff written down, which I'd have to read out loud to him, and it was almost like I was saying I was the one who was a piece of shit! And then I realised that, with all these condoms pinned to him, it was almost like a reminder of what I'd done that day! Do you understand? I didn't get it at the time. I suppose I was till a bit young and naïve back then. You certainly grow up fast in this business.

But I didn't like him at all, very creepy. In fact, the first time he came here was to see my TV. And she didn't like him either. She came into me and asked if I'd stay in the room with her, which she doesn't ordinarily do. But there was such a weird atmosphere about him. It was like you felt he was getting a kick out of scaring people. I know for a fact that he goes round all the massage parlours. They call him The Dog, apparently. He used to like to pretend to be a dog on occasion. Woof-woof and all that. He used to like being put into a cage and fed real dog food. But I'm sure that's nothing you haven't heard before.

You do get some real 'spooky' types from time to time. But not too often, thank God. Another one of the weirdest was a young guy who was completely obsessed with all things Nazi. He had a very peculiar thing about concentration camps, which was a bit disconcerting, to say the least. His ultimate sexual fantasy was to be a holocaust victim! He had all the SS uniforms for me to wear and what he wanted, above everything else, was to be tortured to death by some blonde Aryan super-goddess in one of those clinical experiments they used to do! Weird or what? I could well imagine that one going out and murdering someone one day!

Those types are few and far between, though. Most are just fun loving little perverts that you can have a good laugh with—or at! My most favourite slave has to be someone who I've named Jelly. You can do absolutely anything to him! I've often ordered him to go and get some stinging nettle from the woods round the back of my place—stark naked, of course! I'll then torture him something rotten with them because he's so much fun! I'll have him here all day for no fees just to entertain other customers. I've made him eat a chili sandwich and all sorts. And these were raw Chinese chillies, and they were absolutely awful! They'd been sitting in the cupboard for months and I was just about to throw them out. You couldn't eat them—but Jelly did! It was great fun forcing them down his throat. He was crying his eyes out, poor sod. But he knew that, unless he did it, he wouldn't be allowed any relief. He's eaten a raw onion for me as well, but that was rather mild by comparison.

One of my main 'cock suckers' was this regular client who's now retired. He used to call himself The Sex God. He wasn't really into the pain side or being submissive but, if anyone wanted their cock sucked, all I'd have to do was give him a ring. His famous line was: "I'll be there in twenty minutes". No matter what he was doing, he'd be there. He'd have been brilliant in the Roman times, because his favourite scenario was orgies. Many a cock sucking orgy have we had with him, I can tell you! We used to see him every week. He did have an outstanding libido. But, as I say, he's retired now and gone to live in Spain. He did come back for a holiday recently, and I was the first person he rang from the airport! He was straight round here sucking cocks before he'd even booked into his hotel! He's invited me down to see him in Spain, but family commitments always get in the way.

Some of the mistresses I have a lot of respect for, others I wouldn't give the time of day to. Don't ask me to mention any names, because I don't want any trouble. As I said before, they will stitch you up. They'd do it just out of spite or jealousy or some other reason that was either real or imagined, which is why you can't trust anyone in this business. Unlike a lot of mistresses, I never employ a 'real girl' as my maid for the same sort of reasons that I'm dubious about getting too involved with some of the mistresses in this business. If you can find a good maid, then you're very, very lucky. Most maids work on a commission basis anyway, so they're not worried about who comes through that door. As I said, you do get the nutters, especially the girls who advertise in the phone boxes. One mistress I know quit because she found out that this guy who she'd seen herself on a few occasions had murdered a working girl. She reckoned the only reason it hadn't been her was because she was dominant. Working girls are a lot more vulnerable than us, I think. Still, it shook her up a bit, as you can imagine. She had to quit altogether, in fact, and couldn't face the job for a few years. I think she's back working now, but in a totally different area. So we're not as hard as we make out, are we? You get as scared as anyone else. The most frightening one I heard about was this mistress in Canada who ended up being the slave of her own slave! How it happened was that he was slowing drugging her over a long period of time. In the end she didn't know what was happening, and he proceeded to rob her blind! He took her for everything she had, and she ended up having a complete mental breakdown.

Because I do the phones myself at the moment, I get to judge who I invite in for the sessions anyway. In my experience, maids will invariably gossip and bitch about you behind your back. They're the ones who get you in trouble. They get paid a wage by the mistress and get commission on top, so they're earning almost as much as the girls. And they don't want to do anything for it, most of them. They're no good on the phone, either. Horrible, fat middle-aged women. If you get the younger ones, they'll have half an eye out to start up on their own. I had one girl working for me who thought nothing of waltzing off for a couple of hours to see her own clients! Yet, she still expected to be paid for her time here on top! And she couldn't see why I was making a fuss! Apart from anything else, I could have been murdered by some nutter during the time she was gone, but she couldn't see that at all. Increasingly, you'll find the girls today don't bother with a maid anymore. They might use a transvestite as I've done in the past, because at least you'll have some sort of male presence under the make-up to look out for your safety, or they'll just work on their own like me.

I go through very ambivalent attitudes and mood swings about this business. Sometimes, I can't wait to get here in the morning and get whacking and walloping! At other times, I find myself craving some kind of normality in my life. I mean this isn't exactly a normal way of life, is it? By anyone's stretch of the imagination being cooped up in a basement dungeon for eight hours a day, five days a week is a ridiculous way to earn a living! You know, I actually find myself envying the people I pass on the street in the morning. They're off to work in an office or whatever, and I'm coming here to torture people!

You can have too much of it. I think it's called 'fetish-fatigue'. I know girls who get out after a couple of years, sell their equipment and everything. But, they come back. They miss the money. Where else can a girl earn the kind of income I make doing this? Having said that, it's not as much as people on the outside imagine. And a lot of the women in this business are bullshitters about what they make anyway. You'll always find some dominatrix who'll tell you about some rich client California or Hong Kong who paid for them to jet out to them to their mansions for one evening, and then came home with thousands of pounds stuffed into their handbags! It's rubbish. The trouble is some of them begin to believe their own hype and really imagine that they are sex goddesses!

You know there's a joke in this business that goes: how does a dominatrix commit suicide? Answer: she jumps off her own ego! There's a lot of truth in that, I'm afraid. The trouble is, as I said, they start believing their own hype, and that's dangerous for your mental health! It's a bit like a drug pusher who gets hooked on his own gear, you know what I mean? Some of them are so far up their own bum-holes, that you only see the soles of their boots! I can understand how that can happen, though. When you've got all these silly men telling you how wonderful you are every day of your life, it's bound to affect some of them, isn't it? You see it all the time at the clubs where some silly cow will be standing there expecting someone to open the door for them like its her divine right or she's bloody royalty or something, and then treating all and sundry with utter contempt! That's not being a mistress, that's more an 'attitude' problem, if you ask me! If you're a naturally dominant personality, you don't have to keep proving it all the time, and you certainly don't have to shout about in order to assert yourself or get respect. You can if you want, but it's not really necessary. Personally I don't feel the need to shout, just to make myself feel better. The girls that have to do that have got an inadequacy; it's a character flaw, as far as I'm concerned. In fact, a lot of the girls in this business are actually quite submissive themselves away from it! Did you know that? I can think of at least a couple who ended up being complete slaves to their own clients.

Mind you, in both cases the clients were pretty rich, so you sort of understand the motive.

The whole thing is fantasy, really. I know that's a pretty obvious thing to say, because it's supposed to be about exploring fantasies. But you do find yourself craving something a bit more real once in a while. You can have too much of everyone pretending to be something they're not. I mean, the dominants aren't really dominant most of the time, and the submissives certainly aren't very submissive away from this. It always makes me laugh the way the guys write their adverts in the contact magazines. Like they're always saying how they worship the superior female and believe in fem-dom as a way of life but, when it comes down to it, they're only interested in being a slave to someone who's under twenty five, has got blonde hair and big tits! I wonder how many of them have helped a little old lady home with her shopping? Not many, I shouldn't wonder!

I certainly don't mean to sound like a feminist, because I'm not, but you can't avoid the double standard, or whatever you'd call it, of this business. One the one hand, you have these guys saying: "I want to be your slave. Do with me what you will", and all that old crumble. Yet, on the other hand, they'll say they only like to be submissive in such and such a way, and only in rubber and only with a 'goddess' who's got the big tits and the big hair. It's still about women doing what men want, and pandering to their desires at the end of the day, isn't it? God, I'm beginning to sound very politically correct here, aren't I?!

I also think a lot of the girls in this business get very cynical about men. After all, we see them at their most vulnerable; grovelling around on the floor, licking our boots and our bottoms and all that stuff. If the girl isn't into the scene herself and understand the mindset behind it they loose all respect for the male of the species. Even after all these years I still find myself having these weird thoughts coming into my head, wondering if my own father isn't seeing a dominatrix himself. You never know, do you? Just imagine if my own dad booked an appointment and showed up for a session! God, that would really put a weird twist on incest, wouldn't it? It hardly bears thinking about. But that wouldn't happen anyway because I work in a totally different area to where he lives. Just as well, really!

I really can't see myself doing anything else. When it comes down to it, I still love the job despite some of the negatives things I've said. It's the same with any job you've done for a long time. You'll have your good days and your bad, like any other job. And it is just a job for me now. Well, most of the time. I do still have my moments, though! But it's not as much of a life style for me as it was in the early days. It keeps you hooked, though. Like they say in the fetish world: fulfilment lasts only a moment, denial is forever!

Chapter 19: Goddess Venus

Goddess Venus is, in actual fact, a rather striking 27 year old of Italian parentage who provides, in addition to her private one-to-one sessions in her London-based dungeon, a fully comprehensive postal training academy for dedicated male submissives who wish to explore the world of female domination, but at a safe distance!

I am a Life-Style Dominatrix as well as a professional one, as I do have several slaves who are part of my life. Although, I hasten to add, I do have an existence as a human being as well, rather than just as a 'dominant android'. Because that's what it's about, isn't it? It can be very one-dimensional and 'unhuman', which is why it's a fetish and must be kept there really. Maintaining this as a full life-style, especially for the submissive, is quite a difficult role. It's very tiring and there isn't much left for the true slave. I've had slaves in the past who have been so totally servile it's unbelievable! Just unquestioning obedience and so utterly in awe of me and the whole scene that they're not really in need of much training at all. Obviously, they've got another life as well, in that they've got to earn a living, but other than that they're my property and they have to keep themselves available for me.

I'm actually still looking for that one special slave who can keep my interest totally. I tend to find that over time I become very bored. For me, what would be most interesting would be to try and integrate the dual roles of slave and partner into one, and that's something I've aimed to do in the past. Perhaps there's still hope out there, but I'm not sure. It's something that's very difficult to find. A lot of them want to try it, but I'm looking for someone who is very strong. By that I mean strong within themselves, but not dominant. There is a difference. I think that kind of inner strength and intelligence is what I'm looking for. But it's actually very difficult to find that without getting that sort of aggression from the male, which I really can't stand. That sort of blind lashing out is really abhorrent to me. On the other hand, someone who is too grovelling really makes me want to be sick as well. It makes me want to put the boot in for real! The strong silent type is probably the best for a slave/partner. It isn't anything to do with doing as they're told necessarily, although that helps, of course! It's about a man honouring the female. Now that's my private fantasy, and we're not just talking about shiny bits of plastic! Perhaps that's why I find a lot of medieval imagery so interesting.

I'm not looking for just a domestic slave, because I expect all my slaves to muck in anyway when it comes to cleaning, cooking, showing clients in and dealing with the videos and music and being 'minder'. That last role is especially important, as I never ever work alone. I know some mistresses do because it's much cheaper than if you have to pay a minder, but you do need someone with you, really. I have one submissive who works with me on a regular basis here who's a transvestite, although he's so big and muscular that I prefer to keep him as a slave. Whereas there is another little one, who actually lives in Dorset, who serves me on a personal level and does jobs for me at home, as well as here in my dungeon. He's perfect as a transvestite maid. It really does depend on the guy as to what I want to do with them. If they're not paying me, then I will totally dictate what role they play in my life. I'm not going to have their stuff pushed on to me!

With my clients, what I do is try to provide a mixture of what they want and what I want. I think that's the best way if you're going to form an on going relationship with them, which is what I like to do, obviously. They'll chat to me about their past history, and I'll find that a lot of times they're not really sure, when they first come here, what it is that they're into at all! They only know what they've done. So I try and take them on a journey of self discovery, which is what this is all about anyway. As far as my own preferences are concerned, I refuse to get involved in any toilet stuff, because I find that really abhorrent and I'm not going to go there! That's the only thing that really turns me off! I don't work with any other mistresses either, because I like to run my own show.

Regarding my work with correspondence slaves, that's something totally different and very involved. The kind of submissives who are attracted to the postal course are very different to those who actually visit. In some cases, they may be even more dedicated to me. But I think there's a lot of 'wimpery' there as well, and they don't really want to come. It could be finance, because it's obviously much cheaper to not do it for real. And, in a lot of cases, I think they're really very, very deranged people! I mean you have to be, don't you? It's still an interesting idea to develop, all the same. I'm hoping in the future it will be more computer based and I can do it by e-mail. It'll save time for everyone. Although, in some ways, pen and ink actually makes you sit there and consider what you're doing. That aspect might be lost with the computer age, I'm not sure. We'll have to see how it goes.

As I said before, what I'm interested in doing really is attracting to myself someone who would help me forward. At times, I think it might be good to work with another mistress in terms of the scene, but it would have to be someone I felt very bonded to. I would like to find out. I have been thinking of possibly advertising for that, but it's got to be someone (and I know this might sound pretentious) very spiritually and emotionally aware that I can really trust. I'm not interested in it just being about business, because really I'm also someone who needs close, bonded relationships. For me, with anything I get involved in, it's never just about money or just about business. I need someone very self aware, certainly. And it would have to be someone thirty five plus. That's what I've got in my head, anyway.

I do have very young boys, around eighteen or nineteen years old, who come to see me, and I like them very much. I know other mistresses never see clients that young, but maybe it's because I'm quite young myself. It's surprising how much they're into this. Maybe they haven't pursued it, but it's definitely there in their heads. That kind of innocence is very attractive to me. Over all, my clients range from eighteen to about seventy years old.

More than anything, I enjoy people who are as outlandish as I am, and who can totally get into it! People who are completely absorbed in the scene and are totally uninhibited. It doesn't happen very often, though. I suppose it's nerves for a lot of them. But when you do get one of those, it's a real pleasure. A lot of people (not just in this scene, but generally) are very dull, let's face it. So, obviously, that makes for dull scenes in the dungeon, too. The fantasies inside their heads probably aren't dull (certainly not to them, anyway) but it's more to do with how they respond to me with shyness. Although I understand it, I don't particularly enjoy it. I like people who are totally absorbed in this!

I would love to meet someone who was theatrical. Probably someone who is quite heavily involved in this industry themselves, because I think they would understand what I'm all about. And money, of course, is important. Not because I want someone to support me, I don't need that. But I certainly don't want to support anyone else. Romance without finance is a load of crap! It's a joke! We don't want to sit at home and eat baked beans on toast, do we?

I think that most women who are involved in the scene non-professionally (and this is just my opinion) are perhaps desperately looking for something. And it's not really about sex for them, either. It's much more about wanting be a part of this unique club. A lot of it is about exhibitionism with the gear and the fact that it's something unusual and different. I think that's why fetishism is becoming so fashionable now, because it's glamorous and a bit naughty. It's becoming more and more main stream all the time. The images you see in advertising nowadays have got lots of fetish in them. As it becomes more acceptable, perhaps the people who are really involved in it will have to either take it one step further and become even more socially unacceptable or go and do something else! I mean, what's its future and does it even have one?

When I was growing up as a young teenager, I always saw it as street-walker gear. You know, standing on street corners. I think I've come to understand a lot of it now and where it comes from. There are still certain sorts of fetishes and perversions that I find very difficult to understand, though I do try! I actually am very interested in understanding what it is and where it comes from and why. For instance, I was thinking of getting involved in medical stuff but, having gone a little way down that road, I find it's so totally removed from anything erotic or sexual that I've decided not to go there. I'll leave that to the experts or the so-called experts! Honestly, I've seen some absolutely dreadful cases of injury on submissives. They've come to me after having medical scenes done to them, and they've got huge bruises on their bodies where it's been done wrong. There could be infections and all sorts of things! I mean, how can you (unless you're a trained medic, which they're not) possibly know what you're doing?

I come from an artistic background myself, and have been drawn towards kinky clothing for a long time now. I designed rubber wear and got involved in that side of things, but there wasn't really much money in it. Not anywhere near as much as there is in this, anyway! So I decided to do this, instead. But I don't intend doing this work past the point where it's no longer glamorous. As soon as I get past it, that's it! I don't want to end up like one of these old bags, you know what I mean. I'm speaking only about being a professional in terms of seeing clients now. As a life-style, I think it's something that can be carried on forever. But, as a professional mistress, if you're not careful and unless you can raise your profile and actually take pride in what you've created, you can become like some of those women you see in the contact magazines who look as if they've been washed out by the whole thing.

And it is very wearing. This is a very difficult job, and I don't think people appreciate that. You're engaging your mind all of the time. Plus you get paid half what you would if you were catering for a 'straight' market, so you have to have dedication and you have to have a brain. You've got to create scenarios for people all the time. For instance, I don't have any 'set' scenarios, none at all. Nothing's scripted and nothing's repeated. If I'm not feeling my best and able to give my all, then I won't work that day, it's as simple as that.

I suppose I want to become, I don't know, Queen of the Entire Universe! And I don't think that's too much to ask, do you? I know it's crazy and I realise it's completely demented, but then this is a demented scene, isn't it?. Everyone involved in this world is completely mad! You've got to be to be able to keep a straight face. I think it's interesting the way people in this scene, and especially guys, will say that they'd hate other people to find out about them because it would be seen as very deviant, and all the rest of it. But I think a lot of straight people actually just find this stuff very amusing!

Kidnapping is a huge fantasy for a lot of people. Certainly, things like abductions by witches and goblins and having spells put on them and that kind of stuff. Oh God, yes. I don't really understand that one myself, even though I am very interested in spirituality in the whole of my life anyway. I've been reading tarot cards since I was about fifteen. And I think that kind of spirituality comes over in the domination I practice; which is very traditional, but very, very intense at the same time. It's very much 'mind centred'. I mean, I use hypnosis for instance, which I'm trained to do. For me, it was simply a natural progression, really. If you think about all the 'bits and pieces' involved in this; you know, the leather straps, the ropes and the chains and this, that and the other, then you can see that it's just a way of restraining the body so that the mind is free.

Then you can really get in there, right into the mind, and you can unlock stuff in there. Sometimes I'll do it in combination with bondage, using the two together is good. In fact, some submissives come to me purely for the hypnosis side. That's their whole fantasy. This may sound quite evil, but you can actually implant messages with hypnosis. You can also remove stuff over time, like irritating and negative character traits. I don't think it does them any favours to have those traits, so they won't mind if they lose them, will they? I can then replace that stuff with something more positive. It's really all about mind control. I remember back to the first time I was ever hypnotised; I fought it totally! It's the same with meditation. I spent a long time, and a lot of money, learning transcendental meditation. And I don't even use it! Of course, I know I should. But I actually find it quite scary because you can go quite deep sometimes. And, ultimately, I don't like losing control in any way, shape or form!

My whole upbringing has been based around spirituality. I would like to use it more in my work, and it's great when I get people who are in tune with me. Unfortunately, that doesn't happen very often. And that, in my opinion, has absolutely nothing to do with age whatsoever. I've met people in their forties and fifties, especially men, who are not aware in the slightest, even of themselves! They have no self knowledge or awareness at all!. And that is the worst thing, when you get someone and you try and try and try to get them to open up and they don't. Eventually I just get bored, whether it be in this way or in general. I will attempt to help them by bringing them out of themselves, but you can only go so far. If it doesn't change, it doesn't change. That's their journey and their problem!

I had a very privileged public school upbringing, but rebelled terribly and got thrown out. I didn't really settle with any one thing. My whole family is very artistic and my own interests are very diverse. Even though I'm a Capricorn, I've got a Gemini moon and so, for someone like me, the grass is always greener and something more exciting might be happening over there! Although, I must say that I've become less and less like that as I get older. When I first started out in this business, I wanted to make vast amounts of money from it, but I don't think there are huge amounts of money to be made. It's a good living and that's it. So it really is about life-style and vocation for me. What I want to do is get involved much more in the scene, generally; whether it be in magazines, videos or whatever. I'd also love to hostess my own club one day, but it would have to be something that caters for real scene people and, obviously, is as glamorous and outrageous as I am!

Chapter 20: Mistress Xena

Champion body builder, female wrestler and film stunt-lady, Xena was also one of the first female night club bouncers in Great Britain.

My mum thinks this is the safest job I've ever done; especially compared to when I was a bodyguard and was attacked on several occasions! She's quite happy with me doing this. As soon as I become jaded, I'll stop working. I have to enjoy it to do the job well. People will know if you're just putting it on.

I always insist on a detailed consultation to establish the areas a client's interested in; plus a medical check, as well. If they've got any problems like epilepsy or diabetes, for example, I need to know. I had a session just the other day where the gentleman passed out. I got him down into the recovery position and when I got him back he said: "Oh, I always do that". Now why didn't he tell me that before and I'd know how to structure the session and know what positions to avoid? Some mistresses are very conscientious, but unfortunately, some aren't. It's unbelievable the situations some people get themselves into knowing full well that the mistress isn't capable!

There are some very good mistresses in London. But, for people who don't know that much, they don't realise the difference. They might go and see some girl who's got absolutely no idea about safety whatsoever. They're just not trained up. I've heard of some horrible experiences from clients. I wouldn't even call some of them 'mistresses', because basically they're prostitutes with whips. I always tell the guys that the best way to find out if the girl is a real mistress is to ask her if she does sex. If they say no then they're a professional mistress and they're relying on their skills as a mistress. If they do provide sex then, in my eyes at least, they're not a professional mistress.

Talking about 'horrible experiences', I've known clients who've actually been blackmailed by mistresses! They threaten them with photographs, you see. I may take Polaroid's once in a while, but that's for the client if he wants a souvenir. But it will always be with discretion, it has to be. I've got one client who lives round the corner from my mum!

I know some mistresses who 'switch'; that is, they can be submissive as well as dominant. But for me that's never been a question. I've always been a dominant person in everything I've ever done. I've also known mistresses who've been slave-girls themselves. A lot if people think you can't be a dominant without also being a submissive, but I think you are either one or the other. Your mental capacity is for either being dominant or submissive, not both. Having said that, if it works for you then do it. But, for myself, I'm naturally dominant and that's it! I've always worked and competed on an equal level with men and very successfully, too! I've always been very good at every thing I do, and it's always been along with a more dominant role anyway. I was one of the first women night club bouncers in this country, as well as one of the first female body guards!

I've always been quite physical and I'm very confident in myself; especially with body guarding and door work. It's all about control. You're very aware of what you can do, if you have to. You'd much rather not, of course. You'd rather hold back and talk your way out a situation or deal with it in some other way. I think that's why I enjoy this work so much. It's fun! Or it should be fun. Some people take it so seriously, though. I've got a regular who comes to me once or twice a week just to do my house work and the gardening and so on. I'll put him into bondage and it's just fun. He's a nice person to have around. And he's got this incredible history of seeing mistresses for over thirty years; that's longer than I've been alive! To me, that's fascinating.

I've got 'domestic-slaves' who come here, too. They'll normally wear a boiler suit while they're working out in my garden, but they'll have always have ladies lingerie or something on underneath! If anyone sees them, it just looks like I've got a contractor working out there. They'll get a session at the beginning and another at the end, and they get the opportunity of long-term submission as well. I get a lot of businessmen who are used to being the boss themselves. I'll put them in a apron and a collar and order them around the day and they love it! It's because they don't have to think about anything. That way I always have my house clean, and I hate house work, anyway! Of course, if they misbehave, they're punished. That way, everyone's happy! If someone has a skill that they can offer that I need, I may consider them for service. At the moment, I've got plumbers, electricians and everything!

I only do about three sessions a day, and I'll spend about an hour and a half with each client. I prefer quality over quantity. And, besides, I do need some time to be able to sit down and relax between scenes. Because I do a lot of role play and I do wrestling as well, it can be very physically and mentally exhausting, so I need that time to myself. You find that you've just got a particular session working well and you've tuned into someone completely, and now you've got someone who is totally different! You can't keep that level of intensity up throughout.

I get so many clients from my web site these days. I spent such a long time setting it up and now it's just gone mad. I had a guy from Turkey with me yesterday. A lot of Americans, too. They come to see me from Heathrow Airport, which is only fifteen minutes away. They might only be in the country for a few hours, but they'll still come round, have a shower and a session between flights..

Every other person who comes to see me seems to be in computers these days, and they've all got access to web sites. I see so many different kinds of people; not just the high court judges, as people seem think. Everyone from corporate lawyers to postmen, in fact; that's why this has to be accessible to everyone who wants it. Lots of accountants, too. I remember joking with one of the clients that I should advertise in Accounting Weekly (if there is such a pub-lication), because I had one week where I saw about five account-ants! I think it's because their jobs are so logical, and they can just go in and do it. Their brains just go off into this vivid imagination. And the same with postmen, because their jobs are quite boring as well, I think.

Remember, for a lot of people this will be the first time they've ever sat down and actually talked about these things! That's why I keep a lot of magazines like Domina around, because it's good to introduce people to things they've never thought about before. I've got a young carpenter who comes round and he always says he loves coming round to this house, just for the magazines! It's the fact that he can just sit down and read this stuff that is so great for him. I like to talk to people anyway (if they're nice, that is), so it's a lot of fun for me when they haven't seen something before; just to watch them discover something new is great! That's why I particularly love the sessions I do with beginners because everything is new to them. Sometimes it might not be what they're into, but then you move onto something else. There's always going to be something that will trig-ger them off. They've got no preconceived ideas about anything. I'm afraid you get some of the old guys, and they'll say: "I want this and I don't want to be tied like that". There's no element of surprise, there's just control right the way through the session. And I'm wondering, just who is the 'Top' here?

Obviously, because there is so much that can be done, I like to talk to them to find out what does interest them and what they do like and if there are any big 'no-no's'. If you do something in a scene like water sports, say, or electric's or something else that they really don't like, it can stop a scene stone-dead! So I need to know in a con-sultation what they're into. And that's why I give them a safe word, too. Fortunately, I'm very good at 'reading' people through working in security for so long. All of them are polite and respectful, though. One of my bugbears is uncleanliness. Long toe nails, too. I think it's disrespectful to the mistress, because a session can get very intense.

There are a lot of things I simply won't do. I don't cater for sex, for example; which actually really surprises a lot of people. They think sex is all part of it. But, as I said before, sex isn't something a 'genuine' mistress ever offers. I do allow leg and breast worship, but I don't allow oral service. It's just not hygienic. I don't do any cutting of the skin, either. But I will do 'safe' electric's. I enjoy 'enforced feminisation' combined with role play scenarios. Like, for instance, I'll catch a guy going through my clothes and I'll make him dress up in them! Making a man go around in four-inch heels is very funny because the tilt of the pelvis is so different. It looks quite uncomplimentary, too. So that's fun to do.

Then you've got the 'serial' callers. These are the ones who'll phone up and book an appointment with no intention of turning up. It's only through experience you learn these things. I've got a very good memory for voices. Everyone's got set key phrases or something that you remember. This should be treated like an appointment you make anywhere else but, unfortunately, they don't see it that way. Remember, I've put an hour or an hour and a half aside for these people, and I might have turned down two other genuine clients! One of the main pit-falls of being a mistress is that, because you're so involved in people's fantasy worlds, you're inevitably going to get a lot of people who write to you or phone you just to talk about it without any intention of showing up. It's just in their heads. That's why phone-lines are so popular; people can get their jollies without having to do anything about it.

Then you get the 'transit' ones who just go around from one mistress to the next. I've got regulars who will see me once a month or once every six months. I understand that it is a lot of money to some people. But it's more special to them, too. And I appreciate that and show it in the session by giving them my time and attention. For others, it's nothing. They can afford to come to me three or four times a week.

Different clients might like a different kind of girl. Some like skinny girls, some like bigger ones. In some cases, I'm not old enough for some clients. We all have our individual styles. Though I get a lot of regular clients, I might even see someone from another mistress as well. There are a lot of stunning older women working, too. You don't have to be young and pretty-pretty. To be honest, some of the younger girls are just too young. They don't have the maturity. And it's maturity that you need in this business, because it's about trust. You don't want some silly, giggly little 'girly'; it just doesn't work. It's all about suspending disbelief, really.

Because I'm a trained actress, I particularly enjoy the role-play. I've got an American police woman's uniform, that I'll wear for my Captain Hardass character. And I just love 'arresting' people! I've got one old gentleman who comes once a month and I always catch him trying to steal the television set! Actually, he couldn't even pick it up! As I'm a Black Belt and an ex-body building champion as well as a body guard, I try to show people different characters and let them know that there's more things that can be done in role-play apart from just the dungeon side. And when people realise that they think: "Oh, I think I'd like to try that next time".

One of my favourites is the 'kidnap' scenario; where we go out and pick up someone at an agreed point. I've got a couple of body guard friends who are ex-marines that I use as drivers. Sometimes I'll come in with a gun. If it's done somewhere quite public then I'll just come up dressed and take them off somewhere. What I do is I make them come here first and we'll talk it through, plus they need to sign a waiver just in case something goes wrong and the police become involved. We also take Polaroid's to make sure we've got the right person. In fact, I had a friend who was training and they had to do a kidnap off the street and they picked up the wrong guy, simply because he had the same hat on and the same jacket and he's pleading: "no, no, you're making a mistake!" They kept the poor man locked up for two hours before they realised! It seems ridiculous, I know, but it does happen unless you set it up properly.

I'm not interested in things like Chat Shows. The problem with Chat Shows is that they're only interested in the shock value. They're not interested in the life-style or the safety aspect or how nice the people in it are. There's a lot of humour involved, but they only want the sensational aspects. For me, this work brings together all the elements I've been trained for as an actress, as well as body builder and wrestler. I've even done a lot of fencing, which is perfect for crop work. I can use all these things to great effect. I never know what role I'm going to be called on to be next.

In fact, my first introduction to the scene was through being a night club bouncer. I was working for this one security company and they asked me to do this club night, and it turned out to be the Sex Maniacs Ball. And it was really lovely! The people were great and it was such a mad scene! Visually it was stunning. And I was being paid to walk around and watch it all happening! It was great! I can honestly say that, of all the places I worked in security, I found the fetish crowd were the best. There was none of the drug abuse or the selfishness or macho element you'd find in a normal night-club. People were just getting off on what they were doing. What impressed me too, was the etiquette and the respect they have for each other. They would approach each other politely and ask: "May I play?" Those people who love to group everybody in as 'just a pervert' would find that amazing! In fact, other friends of mine that I brought in to do door-work with me, because I thought they'd be suitable, just loved it because the people were so nice and there was such a nice atmosphere. After that, I started doing more and more fetish clubs and met different people and went on from there.

Nowadays, I will occasionally take clients along with me to clubs if I feel they're suitable and I feel comfortable with them. People just don't realise what's available for them. Also, it's very difficult for people to get into the scene if they don't know where to go. It is coming out a bit now though. And there are the good clubs and the bad clubs. Some clubs are very big and, yes, you've got the play areas, but it is still a bit of a freak show for the 'other' people who are coming in. They may have the clothes, but not the attitude; and they know absolutely nothing about the scene. Then you've got the smaller, quality clubs where everyone's playing and everyone understands what's going on, which I much prefer.

At the end of the day, though, you need a life outside of this. I'm lucky in that I've got friends who keep me grounded. I'm still involved in body building and martial arts training, so I've got friends from that. If I say to them: "Go and get me a drink"; they'll say: "I'm not your fucking slave". I'll say: "That's because you can't afford to be!" They purposefully won't do something I ask; where as, before I did this job, they wouldn't have thought twice about it! You need to take time out of it just to chill out and relax.

THE END

If you enjoyed this book, you may also like to read the following sample chapters of other Magnolia Books

www.magnolia-books.com

'Sexual Skydivers' Sample: Clarissa

Age: 41, Marketing Director, living in Parsons Green, London, UK

Frustration was the key reason I slid into playing the submissive. Sexual frustration was the driving force behind turning that want and need into a real living experience. But how does one find the intro? How does one find the right kind of partner, or partners? Less difficult if you're male. There are numerous girls you can visit to experience an hour or so of slavery, bondage, humiliation and servitude. Almost impossible if you're female. My first real kick was as a teenager seeing the film, 'Nine and half weeks', which was slammed by the some for portraying females as being submissive to violent and controlling men. I'd read the damning articles and, as a result, became even more eager to see the movie!

My boyfriend at the time, who was incapable of ever displaying dominant tendencies, had the dubious pleasure of escorting me to see the film. Actually, it was his idea, strangely enough! Anyway, I found myself sitting in the cinema, mouth wide open and with an aching, desperate need inside I knew only too well as a deep, strong sexual urge. The urge would not abate and, as I've already explained, my boyfriend was not the one to fulfil it. He was dumped very soon after this, unsurprisingly enough.

This was best for both of us, in retrospect. I now recognised that, while being submissive or masochistic does not make you cruel and heartless (we leave that to the dominants and sadists!), it does make you more demanding and exacting of your partners. Ironically, a submissive woman will only let herself be dominated by someone she deems worthy of the prize. Suddenly, when sizing up a suitable partner, your 'shopping list' of qualities that you'd look for alters completely. Looks, sensible job, associated good stable income take second place to natural dominance and the ability to wield a whip! Can he get turned on by putting me into bondage or spanking me? Ultimately, is he sexually adventurous? Once all those answers are ticked, then a relationship can commence.

Women become submissive or desire playing the submissive role in their sex lives for a wide range of reasons. Sexual psychotherapists argue that the desire to be dominated stems from feelings of self worth, or a history of child sexual abuse, or low self confidence. This may be so in some cases, I cannot comment. I can only say that, as a professional, university educated, middle class woman who is highly successful in her career, I certainly don't feel I fit into the pigeon hole of typically abused, no-hoper!

In fact, it was very probably my own success that created that need to be controlled after work. Taking the lead in the office, ordering people around and having so much responsibility and, I suppose, power, sparked off this desire to hand over the reigns to someone else in my private life. Really, I felt no different from those executives who go to visit a dominatrix. Except that I was a woman and needed that kind of ritualised abuse from a man which, I've come to understand, raises a whole hornets nest of feminist arguments.

In those first few months, after ditching the boyfriend, I went through a strange variety of men. Usually older, not exactly handsome, and sometimes downright unpleasant. They all had to be tried and tested in my desperate search for that elusive 'dominant' character. The trouble was that the more submissive I became (and by submissive, I mean sexually submissive only, I am definitely not submissive in any other aspect of my life), the more demanding of my lovers I became.

My fantasies became, correspondingly, more severe and extreme. I remember one potential lover literally gave up the struggle.

He ended up, poor soul, with his head in his hands, sitting on the edge of my bed, almost sobbing as he admitted he couldn't hurt me. I tried to explain that I didn't want him to permanently hurt me. I just wanted him to make me scream and beg for forgiveness. It was no good. My requests left him completely mystified. Another lover dumped! From then on, and for the next few months I would go out of my way to find the kind of men I would never meet in my ordinary, well-ordered, middle class life. I picked up men through contact mags in rough pubs, even on the street. Anyone who seemed dominant or came across like a brute would be enough to fire my lust and my hopes.

After a succession of very short-lived relationships (if they can even be called that!), Which I can only describe as empty and totally unsatisfactory, I found myself close to despair. The problem was that, the more dissatisfied I became after each attempt to find love and servitude in one lover, the higher and more insanely unrealistic my expectations became. I knew I was spiralling out of control, hooked on my ideal notion of the perfect submissive 'fuck' with, it seemed to me, ever diminishing chances of realising it.

Yes, sex was very much part of the equation for me. I know many people in the fetish scene feel that the full sex act has no place in the art of domination, but I disagreed. I wanted to be tied to the bed and made accessible from all directions and angles. I needed to be forced to suck cock and to beg for more. I wanted to act the complete slut (which, of course, I never was or, at least, would never admit to being). I fantasised about being tortured, spanked and whipped. All these thoughts went through my mind endlessly. And the more I failed to realise them, the more intense they would become.

I started buying literature and props and bondage equipment for myself. I would put myself in bondage, even whip myself to get the high I craved. I kept all my paraphernalia tucked away in the wardrobe, as guilty as anyone else who has a terrible secret. That's the way I felt, anyway. I would masturbate myself every night, listening to the voice of my imaginary, idealised, lover in my head, as he ordered me to do it this way and that; in front of mirrors, in front of his friends, even live on stage at some seedy sex club. In my imagination, he would take me to expensive restaurants where I would be dressed very provocatively. At the end of the meal I would be forced to lay down on the table and be used by all the waiters as a means of paying the bill.

My imagination knew no boundaries. Sometimes I was a servant girl abused by the master of the house, other times I was a sex slave to a cruel horse trader in the desert, or a curious and rare white slave to a big black prince in some unknown African state. My genitals and nipples would be pierced and adorned with elaborate and exquisite jewels. Condoms and any notion of 'safe sex' were dismissed by my primitive masters, as chief after chief took me at his will. My body knew no limits as I was subjected to repeated beatings and punishments; each becoming increasingly more painful and arduous. Though I enjoyed all these scenarios in my imagination, I had still had sense enough to leave them there.

Being 'forced' to do all these things somehow removed the guilt. I was always helpless to protest in these situations and, indeed, when I did on occasion meet someone suitable in real life with whom to enact these fantasies, the subsequent orgasm would come more easily and more powerfully, gaining more mental release, the tighter the restraints of the mental bonds became. Free from guilt and safe in my ropes.

Real life experiences were, of course, played out with code words and within the bounds of safety and sanity! I dabbled with the fetish club scene for a while, and met some so-called 'masters' at parties and events. While many were very pleasant men, I found the whole thing ultimately a bit disappointing. I came to the conclusion that most were no more than fantasists themselves who were really quite weak in their own lives, and whose dominant natures went about as deep as their leather costumes. Either that, or they were quite horrible men who had some sort of chip on their shoulders, and were obvious women haters who just wanted to get their own back against the female sex for whatever reason, by beating the hell out of a girl. And I'm not that much of a masochist! As I said earlier they really have to deserve the prize and frankly they didn't.

I think the fetish scene works best on the Fem-Dom side which, unfortunately, is not where I'm coming from. I think the women look great and it's wonderful that they, and their subs, can express themselves through such creative role-play. But, at the end of the day, I was seeking something a lot more than dressing up and play acting. In the end, I gave up on the fetish scene altogether, as far as my own needs went. As I am quite an assertive person in my own right, I have my own home and career and all the rest of it, I'm very independent. A real product of Mrs Thatcher's generation of go-for-it women, I suppose. I certainly don't need a man in my life as husband and provider. I can do all that perfectly well myself, thank you very much. What I needed was someone who could put me under their thumb in a purely sexual sense.

The closest I've come to my ideal (who is also my current playmate) is someone I would never have dreamed of meeting if I'd not undertaken this adventure in my life. For a start, he's black and lives a life-style that is, quite frankly, on a different planet to my own world of dealing with big blue-chip clients in a marketing company. But then, that's what I wanted.

I met Omar at a club in South London where I'd gone with one date. This particular guy had a big thing about seeing me with other men, which was the reason he'd taken me to this club. His sexual fantasies invariably revolved around scenarios of me with big black 'monster' cocks, you know that whole 'cuckold' thing. Secretly, I think he was a bit 'bi' and actually wanted to be the one being fucked by a black cock. We never got that far in our relationship to find out, because the first club he took me to his fantasies came true, unfortunately without him along to enjoy the view!

I must admit I'd fantasised about black men, but had never had the opportunity to meet any socially in the circles I moved. I found it fascinating. The club was purely black. Though there were a lot of white women females in the club, there were no white guys, apart from this guy who'd brought me. Though I had already written off my date as unsuitable material for my needs, I suppose it was quite brave of him to venture into this place at all.

It wasn't long at all before I got approached for a dance by one of the black guys. What impressed me was how bold they all were in asking, as if a refusal had never crossed their minds. I have to say I found this quite new and, yes, exciting. Later, I understood the reason for their confidence. All of the white women who came to the club were interested only in black lovers. The women were, for the most part, thirty and forty some things, middle class, career women like myself. Teachers, social workers, feminists. The kind of modern, independent, politically correct women who would have been out-raged if a white man displayed the sort of chauvinist behaviour I saw going on all around me. Yet, these same women not only tolerated it, they positively lapped it up from a black man! It was an eye-opener to a whole new world that I never knew existed, and I was fascinated.

Before the evening was over the date I'd arrived with had been rudely dismissed and I was with my new black lover. The danger of that first night will stay with me forever. Omar's world was one of drugs and prostitutes and gangsters. I was completely out of my depth, but loved every minute of it. As long as I knew that, at the end of the experience, I could retreat to my safe, middle class coziness. Most exciting of all was that I knew I was going to be fucked that night; that my opinion on the matter was almost inconsequential. In fact, that first time, he didn't even wait to take me home to bed, but fucked me in the men's toilets at the club. Once back at his he revealed his 'kinkier' side. Without hardly a word he tied me up on his bed on my front and thrashed me with a tawse, before blindfold-ing me and taking me very slowly up my well-lashed arse. He didn't need any encouragement he just 'took' me as if it were his absolute right to do so, that was really cool.

Having someone as dominant and protective as Omar made me feel very safe and, as a result, very bold. I found myself behav-ing in ways I would never have imagined myself doing before. For instance, whenever we go out to clubs, I will always dress very, very provocatively and stick my bum out as much as I can when dancing for all the men to ogle. Occasionally, I will go back across the dance floor to where my master is standing and kiss him, just to show them all who I am with. I know I am turning them all on with my cock-teasing performance but, with the exception of one very polite and brave guy who actually dared to ask Omar's permission to dance with me, none of the others had the balls to try it on while my man was standing there looking so wonderfully mean and moody. It's like I have a sign round my neck letting the world know I am his property.

I've never felt that way with any white man I've ever met. Incidentally, Omar was so surprised and impressed by the guys gall that he let him dance with me the rest of the evening. He does admire guts, it's a real warrior thing with him.

Usually, anyone who dares come near me will be dealt with very severely. Everyone knows I am Omar's 'bitch' and wouldn't dare trying it on. I remember once, for example, another black guy who tried chatting me up in a pub while Omar was at the bar conducting some of his 'dodgy' business dealings that I really don't know about and don't want to know about. Anyway, when he saw what was happening, Omar came over and didn't even say a word. It was so cool. He just took the man's coat which was draped over the back of his chair and walked to the door and threw it out onto the street. The man didn't have any choice but to go out of the pub and retrieve it from the gutter. By the time he got back the moment had gone, and he looked pretty silly anyway so there was not much he could do about it. Omar had made his point without saying a word or striking a blow!

At clubs, where he is invariably known and welcomed, I am encouraged to dance very provocatively for the benefit of all the guys standing around. On one occasion a guy I knew was a 'somebody' was at the club, he—like a lot of other guys—had been ogling me on the dancefloor all night. I'd seen him before, but what I didn't realise until this particular night was that he was someone whom Omar was in 'business' with and their relationship had become a little 'strained', shall we say, for reasons that Omar wasn't going to share with me—though intrigued I knew there were some things best left unsaid between us. Fact is this guy looked like he was brute and even Omar admitted that he didn't want to mess with him—he wanted me to instead!

Whatever it was between them, it turned out that he was willing to call it quits with Omar, if he could see me 'privately' for a while before he left. Omar said a blow-job would probably be enough, but it was my choice should it go further, no pressure. Though I knew I was being pimped out like a hooker, in this context, I was a willing participant, found him attractive and was already feeling very horny anyway. I told Omar to tell him I was willing to be his slut for half an hour. Omar seemed mildly bemused that I so quickly acquiesced, but I could see that he was sort of relieved too.

About twenty minutes later Omar took me into a room that I guess served as an office for the club, I figured it probably wasn't the first time it had been used in this way either, probably by Omar himself, for that matter. After he left, within a couple minutes sure enough, in walks this guy who close-up looked bigger and more intimidating than I'd realised. A tingle hit me between the legs and up into my stomach. He said nothing, just presented me with his already erect cock and nodded down. We fucked hard on the desk in the end—after a little oral-sex! Afterwards he just said, "maybe I'll see you again?" leaving me his card. I just smiled and said, "We'll see". It was the situation that made it sexy at that particular moment in time and also the relative anonymity, it could never have quite the same 'rush' the second time around. Needless to say I didn't call him, but saw him a few weeks later with a younger blonde 'trophy' girl—the sort footballers go for, you know fake everything!

I know too many white women in my position who are walked all over. The guy will show up at their place for a fuck and even bring his mates, expecting the same. Never have any money. Thankfully, Omar isn't like that. In a way, the relationship is one of mutual abuse. He uses me but, at the same time, I am using him. Even though I like being used as a sexual plaything occasionally, it's completely at my discretion, some girls get the wires all crossed and end up being totally abused—but not on their own terms. Having said that though, if that's what a girl actually 'wants', then that's quite a different matter. For my part however, being in control and maintaining it, is the key to my own submissive behaviour—if that doesn't sound too contradictory!

You see, after six months together, he still doesn't know where I live, and he never asks. He has no interest in my world or my friends or what I do. He is content to let me call him every few weeks, when my 'need' arises. Likewise, what he does or who he fucks between times is no concern of mine. This arrangement suits us both. It lets me explore other 'playmates', for example, because though Omar is always an exhilarating lover, and will indulge and really enjoys some of my kinkier masochistic desires, I know his limitations now.

I've recently met this guy who has his own dungeon, and isn't one of those fake 'scene' creeps like I mentioned earlier. He's older, Peruvian and has this mystical, almost 'Zen' type vibe about him. He exudes a natural dominance that is without any noticeable trace of ego—an unusual combination making him quite unlike anyone I've ever met, and I'm expecting—when I've figured if I can really trust him, something like—and may be I am being overly optimistic—some kind of trans-formative, quasi-religious experience! To give over that much power though, I've learned it has to be done very carefully, but my instinct tells me he's good, and worthy of the 'prize'.

'Sexual Skydivers: Submissive women tell us their stories'
Edited by Roya Lamont at Amazon from Magnolia Books.

'The Submissives' Sample: Cynthia

I was always attracted to the demi-monde and through my private English education, came to know many independently wealthy people—either through familial connections, or my work in a lawyer's practice before becoming a hostess in a private members club on the Rue Rabelais. It was here that I came to experience a world where the prevailing sexual atmosphere was of an altogether darker hue. I, as a willing participant in this world, found myself profoundly attracted by many of the patrons—writers, aristocrats, diplomats, intellectuals, famous actors and actresses from all over the world, 'the jet-set', as the newspapers now called them. Intuitively I knew I needed to be helped and nurtured in surrendering myself to my 'true' nature. My sweet innocent lover Luc, of course, knew nothing of these innermost of desires—I didn't think he'd understand, that inside I longed to be taken advantage of in ways that were completely at odds with the outwardly 'ladylike' persona, he'd fallen in love with—or indeed, that some of my previous lovers had been women.

A formidable lady I had gotten to know through a chance meeting at a Japanese diplomats party, was introduced to me as the Comtesse De Condorcet. She was a thoroughbred aristocrat with a natural strict formality about her, visually stunning, lithe in figure and impeccably dressed in the latest Saint Laurent, she was more than a match for the left-wing intellectuals who teased her for her ferociously hedonistic approach to her life, an uncompromising approach that had me excited and enthralled from the moment I set eyes on her.

The next time we met, at a party of her own, we had the chance to talk in a more intimate manner than ever before…

She decided it would amuse her, and be instructional for me, if I had some training from a 'master'. I knew she had perceived in me that which I was simultaneously terrified of and attracted to—a male dominant—but she could make use of me in any which way she felt fit, such was the hold she had on me. Comtesse told me this was her challenge for me to face in my journey toward complete submission. It was she who arranged for me to have a series of 'liaisons' with a master friend of hers, a diplomat whom I'd heard mention of in the club, but never met. I did not know when or where this session would take place. I was instructed only to wait and respond. It was not until several weeks later that the call came.

I arrived home from work to receive a telegram shortly afterwards, instructing me to arrive at my new master's home, by taxi, at seven o'clock the next evening. He told me to wear the clothes of my choice and to bring a bag with nothing inside other than black, patent stilettos and seamed, sheer stockings and suspender belt. He wanted me completely available without the slightest encumbrance. He reminded me of his intolerance for tardiness. In his opinion this was sloppy behaviour indicative of a flippant mind. The training of a slave, he advised, was not a frivolous endeavour and if I aspired to be worthy of such a process then I must show him the seriousness of my intent. He called this respect. I called it subjugation.

It was evening of the appointed day. Fifteen minutes to seven. I was standing on the west side of the Avenue du Parc wearing the conservative outfit of a secretary. From my left hand hung a bag complete with the requested contents. I still didn't really believe this was actually happening, what a leap to make!

Also, I was starting to worry. Normally, taxis roam this avenue frequently. Normally, it would not matter if I were a few moments late. Tonight there were no taxis in sight. And tonight, it mattered greatly if I were to be even a few seconds late. Irritation settled upon my spirit and a wave of anger rolled through my stomach as I antic-ipated his blatant complacency at my being late. I walked to the corner deciding that, since he would most certainly interpret my lack of promptness as having dilatory intent and thus harshly discourage my so-called 'oppositional' nature, I might as well buy some cigarettes and enjoy the next few moments of comfortable laxity.

I stopped a taxi and scrambled in, spewed out my destination to the driver, and muttered a hollow "thank God" to the driver in front of me. A faint smile passed over my lips as I smugly appreciated that he would have to find something other than my arrival time to reproach. It was six minutes to seven and I was right on schedule.

I entered through the unlocked door. He appeared at the top of the stairwell. A violet velour bathrobe covered his physique. He exuded a strong, silent and supreme poise coated with sensual indifference. I shyly responded to his casual "good evening" as I climbed the stairs and approached this commanding man who introduced himself simply as 'Sir Richard'. Then something unusual happened. My spirit was brushed of its resistance and I felt a strange personification of apprehension, deference and obsequiousness. I found myself in front of him, staring at his feet, absent of any armour. In a whispered hush I uttered, "Good evening, Sir Richard."

He ordered me to undress and watched closely as I obeyed. He caressed me as he pleased. He invaded me as he wished. It was obvious from the outset that he regarded me as an inanimate object, existing solely for his use.

Many things were inflicted upon me that night; humiliation as he called me his slut and bound my body in defenceless positions where my anal and vaginal orifices were openly exposed for his pleasure; pain as he ignited my flesh with multiple sharp and cutting lashes from his collection of whips, paddles and crops; solitude as he abandoned me in a closed room while he enjoyed a candlelight dinner of chicken; pain once more as he twisted, pinched and pulled at my nipples; tenderness as he consoled me in my discomfort; pleasure as he placed me on the dining table, lined up three chairs, put each of my legs on the outside chairs, positioned himself in the middle and ate my sex as an entre'; frustration as he secured me on a cold seat, with legs spread, in front of an arousing erotic film featuring exquisite oriental lesbians, projected on the wall and the abject refusal of permission to orgasm; humiliation as he ferociously thrust deeply into my vagina and muttered what a good whore I was before completing his ejaculation over my face with no respect nor remorse; protection as he allowed me to share his bed for the night and kept me close in his arms; and worrisome apprehension as he told me that I was going on a journey the next day, alone without him, to a place where I would learn how to embrace servitude, integrate submission, abandon my covetous nature for control and experience the pride of docile subordination for my Master, Sir Richard.

I awoke the next morning to the taste of a tender kiss and the touch of fingers tenaciously stretching the opening of my vagina. He reminded me of the voyage. I told him that I was afraid to go alone. He replied that this was unimportant. Then he pleasured me with his hand until I thrashed to exhaustion. My Master then fed me and left the house to pursue solitary interests for a couple of hours. Just before leaving, he recommended that, at two o'clock, I was to be ready to leave his house with my bag packed. He told me that he presumed I would be silent and still in the lounge, naked except for the stockings and stilettos. I knew that he also expected me to be wet. I felt angry and unimportant, taken for granted and trivial; bored and nervous. However, I was grateful that he allowed me my mobility in his absence. A feeling of insurrection transiently tickled my flesh and I entertained the idea of fleeing his abode. Something warned me not to. The door slammed. He was gone.

At two o'clock sharp, Sir Richard came home. I realised that I had missed him and was longing for his touch, even if only on his terms. He seemed pleased at my obedience. In fact, so was I. The reward of subordination was becoming familiar to me and one that I had started eagerly to anticipate. I wondered if he would like to know this and was about to ask permission to speak when he shoved a finger in my vagina to inspect the degree of my obedience. He praised me and told me to turn my backside towards him. I did as he bidded.

As he kneaded my buttock cheeks, he observed that there were no marks showing from last nights play, adding that there was, therefore, all the more room for new ones today. He helped me with my coat and told me we were leaving. I know he saw the look of fearful anticipation in my eyes. Again, this was utterly unimportant. Once in the car, he ordered me to descend the front seat and lie back as much as I could. He placed a blindfold over my eyes, turned on the radio and told me not to speak, but just to enjoy the ride.

It seemed to me to be a long ride. Eventually, the car slowed, the engine stopped, and my blindfold was removed. I looked around and immediately recognised my surroundings. We were at the lovely home of the Comtesse De Condorcet on the corner of Rue La Fayette, near Versailles. Funny, this did not appease me. I had never been left alone with the Comtesse and had never experienced the sternness of her hand when the only object of concentration was me.

A memory flashed through my consciousness. I remembered having asked her for a cigarette at her last party and I had, admittedly, used a rather informal tone of voice. Even Francine, a quite coarsely spoken, but beautiful girl rebuked me for not addressing her in the correct manner and she was only serving the food! With obvious disdain she informed me that she was the Comtesse and that I must never address her improperly again. The Comtesse tossed a cigarette on the floor, just out of reach and turned her back on me. I was ashamed at my indiscretion and stunned at her severity. Would I see this stern severity again today? And if so, would the sternness flow this time from the crack of her whip?

Sir Richard rang the doorbell. In futility, I looked at him hoping that he would understand my covert plea that he stay. The door opened and we entered. Comtesse appeared from behind the door in the most sensuous splendour. Her tight, olive skin contrasted seductively with the black netted material which barely covered her groin and exposed her perfect, rounded breasts. I was distracted by her beauty and momentarily forgot my anger at him for abandoning me. In fact, the fantasy of being permitted to finally taste and smell her womanhood aroused me to the point of forgetting that I was there to be trained. Sir Richard's authoritative voice interrupted the delicacies of my imagination. He ordered me to obey every word that the

Comtesse uttered. He told me that he would be back in two hours. Comtesse instructed me to wait downstairs. I heard Sir Richard tell her that if I did not obey she knew what to do.

My skin felt clammy. I wasn't sure if it was from the cold or from vulnerability. I waited, motionless, in a basement room I had been led to. I heard Comtesse say goodbye to Sir Richard and a door close. The basement door opened. Comtesse stood poised at the top of the stairs. She looked delightful and seemed to survey me with equal admiration. But I felt ashamed and exposed.

Comtesse gently brushed the hair off my shoulders and brought a black leather hood close to my face. She whispered into my ear that I was about to experience something that I had never known before. She told me that all I had to do was let go of my apprehension and I would feel the epitome of pleasure. She told me to trust her. I was afraid. She told me not to be scared. And then there was nothing but music and darkness.

Comtesse began to wrap something warm and soft around my entire body. The warmth soothed me while the bondage disconcerted me in equal measures. I was completely immobilised and at her mercy for everything. She told me to lean back, but my body was frozen. She encouraged me to trust her. But still I hesitated. She firmly took my shoulders and ordered me to fall back. Reluctantly, I obeyed and she supported my weight to the floor. She told me that I had been brought here to be initiated into Dreamland; that I was finally ready. She told me that I should be proud to receive this honour. But instead, I felt like a fallen leaf, blowing alone in the wind, at the mercy of forces greater than myself, with nothing familiar to settle upon. She asked me if I was okay. I replied, "Yes, Mistress". She told me that I was to address her as 'Comtesse' at all times. She would call me Gabriella.

Comtesse began what she called the 'meditation'. Cutting through Wagner's 'Parsifal' playing in the background, her voice spoke to me with a hypnotic seduction. As I listened to her sensuality, I succumbed to her influence. Bit by bit, she relaxed my body and my mind. The leaf was now a feather and had softly settled on the ground in a warm spot protected by the base of an enormous tree. I felt safe. The Comtesse used her voice and the music in such a way that within a short time I had abandoned my body and was free of its usual sensations. She then entered my mind. She brought me to a place full of all my friends and family. The most important person in my life, my sweet love Luc, was also there. She suggested that I talk to everyone but she warned me that they could not see me, nor feel me, nor hear me. I wandered around the room, watching and touching everyone, feeling completely free because I knew they could not sense me. I felt that I could do anything, be anything, and no one would know. I did a somersault and landed in Luc's lap—he didn't notice. I kissed his lips—he didn't move. I fondled his groin— he never so much as flinched. Then I tried to go inside his body and feel every part of him.

When I tried to do this, I lost myself so I re-emerged into the room. Comtesse told me that Luc was deeply in love with me. As I heard these words, I realised that I did not have to protect myself from the powerful emotions I have for him. I realised that my feelings for him could never be a passing occurrence. A warm breeze touched the inside of me as I recognised the love that I have for him. For the first time this recognition did not scare me. I felt the strength of spirit to travel to the deep roots of this love and not to turn away until I had done so. I remember gasping as I realised how very deeply I loved him. It was hard for me to imagine that anyone else could feel what I was feeling.

Suddenly, Comtesse informed me that a new person had entered the room. Her name was, apparently, Cynthia. She told me to study her and to create her as I wanted her to be. She was tall with long, loose blonde hair, robed in grey leather. Her skin was soft and very smooth. I liked her. I wanted to talk to her. But I was afraid, so I stayed on Luc's lap. Comtesse announced that Sir Richard had also entered the room. All at once, I saw him. He moved very gracefully across the room like a panther. He strode confidently, but respectfully, towards Cynthia. She smiled, turned away from him and immediately bent over with her bottom high in the air. It didn't seem that she was afraid of him. Nor did it seem that she was angry. It seemed, instead, that she was there for him. He softly touched her buttocks and reached underneath her bent body to squeeze her breasts. He, too, was in leather. They stayed like that for a long time. The buzz of voices in the room continued, everyone oblivious to this strange scene. He caressed Cynthia's wet mound and spread some of her juices into her bottom.

Then he forced his finger into her backside and whispered that He was going to stretch her so that he could enter her there. Cynthia wriggled her bottom as indication of her submission. Sir Richard pushed his groin into her. Cynthia moaned.

Comtesse informed me that it was time to merge my persona with Cynthia's. She guided me over to her and prompted me to walk inside of her. I did so without the slightest hesitation. I wanted to be Cynthia. I wanted to embrace submission the way she had in my mind. I wanted to feel subservient without feeling subjugated. I wanted to serve without feeling compromised. It was suddenly clear to me that he had brought me here for this. He wanted me to experience submission in a way I never had before; in a way that would release me from inhibitions, fears and threats; in a way that would heighten his pleasure and mine; in a way that would bond us eternally. And, as I became Cynthia, I felt the emancipation. Comtesse then guided Luc towards Sir Richard and the two personas fused. Suddenly, I felt his finger in my anus, and I began to eagerly anticipate being anally penetrated, maybe even violated. I was excited to serve him. I felt capable of enduring increased pain and interpreting it as pleasure. As Cynthia, I was ready to obey, without rebellion, whenever it suited him; however it suited him. I had truly become a slave.

Comtesse asked me if I saw her in the room. At first, I hadn't. When the Comtesse pointed out her presence, however, I saw a bright yellow aura surrounding a magnificently exquisite lady. She was utterly statuesque; a reigning beauty. The aura slowly dissipated and Comtesse emerged. She was elegantly perched on a golden throne, powerful, mighty and goddess-like. I wanted to touch her. The Comtesse told me that I could approach the throne respectfully.

As I did so, her legs parted. I could see the glistening fur around her labia and my mouth craved for her taste. Comtesse advised me to keep approaching and to kneel down between her legs. I could smell the sweet scent of her wet womanhood. The Comtesse ordered me to lick. I saw myself on my knees, with my bottom in the air, and my head buried deeply in her mound. I could taste the indecent gormandise, yet, I could not taste enough. Comtesse then told me that Sir Richard was behind me, ready to enter from there. I was to keep licking while he used me for his pleasure. The last thing I remember was feeling his thick manhood in my sopping wet vagina and tasting her juices on my hungry tongue. At this point the meditation ended and I was brought back to the basement by the sound of scissors snipping the wrapping around my heated body.

Comtesse ordered me on my knees. She then informed me that I was to sample various instruments of pain and that I was to choose the ones I preferred. This way, I would be prepared for the next stage of my training with her. During the meditation Comtesse had suggested that one could control the experience of pain through the mind. Now, she wanted to see if I had learned anything. She began with the first of eight instruments. My backside felt the cracks and lashes and blows of all of them. I selected three for future use—Mona's riding crop, Comtesse De Condorcet's New York whip and the purple suede whip. Indeed, the pain had not felt as agonising as it could have. Maybe I had learned something more than how it would feel to have my head between the Comtesse' legs.

Then Comtesse left the room for a moment. When she returned, I felt something cold on my anus and inner thigh. She asked me if I knew what was in her hands. I did not. She told me that it was her ice penis and proceeded to insert it into my vagina. This was very uncomfortable but I managed to endure the painfully cold sensation. I was rewarded with the sound of a vibrator that found its way between my legs. Comtesse commanded me to lie on my back while she tied my legs open with the bar. She shoved a dildo inside me and continued to vibrate my clitoris. Simultaneously, she ordered me not to thrash in orgasm; that I could control this as well.

I felt the heat building in my vagina and started to writhe. She kept commanding, "don't thrash, don't thrash." I was losing control and felt my arms flailing. Suddenly, I peaked and rolled over on my side, aware that I had moved much less than usual. I was surprised that I had been able to obey her with something I did not think was voluntary. I wished that Sir Richard could have seen this. I wondered if he would have been pleased with my efforts at complete compliance. The Comtesse left me to rest for a few moments. Then she raised my body to hers and took me into her arms. She held me tightly and welcomed me to Dreamland.

She removed the hood as I rubbed my eyes. I saw a big pair of black shoes by my knees. I looked up and shrieked in pleasure at the sight of Sir Richard. He had, it turns out, witnessed the whole process. He got down on his knees and I fell into his arms, never wanting to leave the shelter of his embrace. As Gabriella, I wanted to tell him how I was now. As Cynthia, I wanted to show him the extent of my newly found uncompromised submission.

The profoundness of this experience is inexplicable. It continues to affect me, even weeks after. I have not seen Sir Richard for a while. And yet I know that he will provoke in me the new freedom that Comtesse creatively cultivated within me on that cold Sunday afternoon. My love for Luc has probably never been stronger. The fears of emotional involvement have not been eradicated. However, I now have a new strength with which to confront them. This strength comes in the form of a bond that was fortified in an enchanted place called Dreamland; a place where, through the most exquisite abandon, I accepted him as my master and my lover.

'The Submissives: A quartet of kinky tales set in late 50's Paris' by Prudence de Vernais

'Submissive' Sample: Janesca

Age: 36, Team Leader, living in Lincolnshire, United Kingdom

Though I am now a confirmed sexual submissive, nothing in my happy Dutch childhood, or very normal early sexual experimenting, even remotely hinted at the perverse pleasure I now take in my adoptive role. That knowledge was revealed to me in 1985 when I first came to live in Britain at the age of twenty one to do a years post graduate work. The knowledge so altered my life that I have lived, and loved, here ever since.

I appreciate that you're probably more interested in my sexual history, but that may be better understood if you know something of me as a whole person. You see, in my wider life there is absolutely nothing whatsoever submissive about me. I have always been a competitive sports person and a high academic achiever. My work environment is one of small, integrated scientific teams. My job, at present, is research work for a large international company. Incidentally, my HR manager commented that I hadn't operated at my best until I was appointed as a Team Leader. I say this not to boast, but to make people understand that in my normal life I am very assertive. Close friends, and non-sexual men friends in particular, have even criticised me in the past for being socially aggressive. Incidentally, this is something I refute as simply a cultural difference. It has nothing to do with my nature. Dutch women do not defer to males in the subtle ways most English women still seem to. All in all, nobody knowing me socially or professionally would recognise the persona I adapt to in a sexual environment. That persona is specific and limited to that particular sphere of activity.

A point I want people to understand is that my sexual behaviour is self chosen because this is what excites me. It is not because I am incapable of acting otherwise, or because of some long concealed psychological defect resulting from a childhood trauma. I like what I do, or rather, what I let others do. The thrill for me is the abnegation of self. I particularly like group sex where I become an object used without any consideration for my gratification. The first New Man who asks me what I want from a sexual experience would be very surprised and probably very hurt! I mean that I'm a very good Kick Boxer! I want to be told what to do, commanded, required to satisfy a man's needs. I like sex to be strong and raw and very potent. No pretence of gentle love. I don't want to be asked, because that involves me in taking or sharing responsibility for what happens to me. I want the selfish freedom of total obedience, of commands that give no option of choice and, as a logical extension of that, absolutely no guilt.

I want the privilege of saying to myself after a truly disgusting night, "Well, I was only obeying orders". That way one can indulge in the most debasing activity and feel totally humiliated, but wipe the slate clean of remorse afterwards with that as an excuse and motivation.

Okay, we'll start with me after six months in, well, let's just say somewhere in England. I had, by this time, got used to being chased by men in that curious amalgam of sexual crudity and courteous good humour that one only finds in this country. I attract that kind of attention a lot. I know I am exotically good looking. I am dark skinned with large brown eyes and long black hair. I am fine boned and rather small and petite. There were quite a few Indonesian imports into my family tree. The typical youthful Englishman's propensity to treat me as some exotic but, essentially, dim-witted doll was seriously counter productive and I resisted all attempts at seduction with little effort.

My studies threw me into contact with Vernon, a man in his early forties. Here was a quintessential Englishman, I thought. A tall, lean, supercilious iceberg on the outside, with a volcano hidden within. He was always polite and thoroughly correct in a work environment, but forever holding an invisible shield between himself and any real involvement. In a rare social moment I allowed him to know I might like a little less formality in our contacts. As a consequence, he kindly threw a small party for me on my birthday. I repaid him by getting slightly drunk. He had never, by word, look or gesture, indicated any interest in me as a woman. A sexual woman, I mean. This intrigued me. I wondered if he was queer. He bought a stone bottle of 'Zuidam' Jonge Genever—a particularly refined Dutch gin, especially for my benefit. The beauty of those bottles is no one notices how much one consumes. I consumed a lot and became inquisitive. I inquired why he had never made a pass at me. Didn't he fancy me?

We were sat on the stairs. He was one lower than me. Our heads were level. He admitted that, of course, he fancied me. I asked why he had never tried his luck? I can still remember his soft laugh when he explained the reason. He admitted he had, as he put it, strange tastes that would revolt me. The kind of games he played would not only revolt me, but hurt and frighten me, too. He told me that, in his games, he liked laughter at the beginning, tears in the middle and loud cries at the end. Those cries may be of satisfaction or of pain. With the kind of women he liked, there apparently isn't that much difference.

To this day I don't know why I pressed the point. I'd never had any great interest in him as a man. For a start, he was too old for me. And I certainly had never imagined any involvement in the kind of activity he hinted at. Sadomasochistic clubs are an accepted part of normal sexuality in Holland. I can't even pretend his words unleashed any secret desire. It was just what's often been described as my bloody mindedness that made me respond with a calculated challenge. "I thought you were supposed to be a scientist? You shouldn't theorise without evidence. Why don't you conduct an experiment?"

In answer, he leaned over, I thought to kiss me. I lifted my face. He asked, in a whisper, if I really wanted to? I nodded. He put his mouth to mine. His hand came up and cupped my breast. I grew a little breathless and then suddenly pain lanced through me as he bit my lip hard. I went to draw away, but he held me. His teeth slackened, and then his fingers found the nipple through the thin material of my dress. He laughed into my mouth as he felt it harden and then he began to squeeze with vice like fingers. Every girl has done that to herself, sometimes let a girlfriend do it. But this was more agonising than anything I'd experienced before. He whispered again in my ear, telling me all I had to do was ask him to stop. However, in my mind the challenge had been set, the gauntlet thrown down, and I would not ask. Instead, I let him continue till, at last, his own aching fingers gave way. Only then did I cry as the blood rushed back into the constricted knot of flesh. But I still watched him steadily through my tears.

Have you ever noticed how ice cool eyes can suddenly become hot anticipating orbs? He lifted his glass to me and jokingly punned that perhaps I was looking for Dutch Courage in my drink. I giggled and told him that it was rather Dutch Fear, in my case. None the less, I agreed to carry on the experiment and meet him in private that next afternoon.

Before I go on to describe what resulted from that gin lubricated talk, let me just add this. Many people, like me, will have had a conventional religious upbringing. This results in adding to sins attraction, but leaves one rather prone to guilt. Some of my internal disquiet was reduced a few days later by hearing a cleric mouthing in the wake of a tragic murder and rape. He was counselling calm to the bereaved relatives, but I felt he could just as easily have been talking about me and my situation.

He was asking why such things happen? Why a powerful being submits to such awfulness. Why not resist it? Stop it? I will tell you! Because nothing is so powerful as submission! How better to prove strength than by refusing to exert it? Overcome power by bowing to it. How better to exert ultimate superiority than by controlling one-self, not others? A willing submission denies the tyrant his triumph. Recall the story of the turned cheek. Who was the stronger? The striker or the struck?

I felt I had a spiritual sanction for an action I felt oddly compelled to see through. I approached that first meeting with trepidation, rather than excitement. No more than an intellectual curiosity and a childish sense of daring. Imagine my confusion to find not one man there, but two! Vernon sensed my nervousness and laughed, assuring me that, while he was peculiar, he was wasn't queer! His friend, Raymond, was someone, apparently, who shared his interests. And he meant, quite literally, shared! He informed me that what I was prepared to offer him, I should offer Raymond as well.

In my innocence I was relieved. My initial response had been that a third party might provide some restraint. It did, but not in the way I had thought. The restraint would be applied to me, but I'll come to that in due course. I also felt, I must admit, the first stirrings of excitement. Raymond was much closer to my own age. Less than thirty, very handsome, and with an engaging smile. I liked that smile. He smiled a lot that afternoon, especially when I cried. Strangely, I was made to feel that everything that was done to me was somehow justified as long as he smiled.

Vernon was very clever, and very patient. To this day I don't know if he magically imposed a new persona upon me or merely revealed one that already existed deep within me. What I do know is that I experienced, for the first time, the phenomenon of what I call 'my other self'. It was as though another being took over my body. The 'I' retreated into a quiet corner and became an observer, not a participant. An observer making rational comments that this 'other self'' had no wish to hear and, for the most part, ignored.

Initially, I was required to make the running. On the coffee table there were books and magazines dealing with flagellation. Vernon suggested I look at some and discuss them. The condition was that with each new volume I picked up I would be required to remove one piece of clothing. There was an odd, humiliating excitement gradually becoming naked in front of two fully dressed men. As concerned talking about the activities described in the magazines, I knew little and what I found was, I admit, mildly shocking. Looking back on that afternoon, I came to appreciate how fortunate I was to have such considerate mentors in the disciplinary arts. A more brutal introduction would not have inflamed me in the way it did. In fact, not until I had actually begged them to do anything, did either man attempt to really hurt me or physically control me. It all began with the mind games.

They could see what disturbed me in the magazines I flipped through and they made me talk about them. They asked me to imagine myself in the position described or pictured. They asked how I thought the girl felt. They required me to describe how I thought I would respond in her place. As I say, they were clever. Whenever that line of questioning got too much for me, I would toss that volume aside and select another, sacrificing an item of clothing in the process in order to avoid disturbing questions, so they won either way! They also made it clear that I was free to leave at any point. In fact, their cleverest ploy was to suggest several times that I do just that. Naturally, this only made me more determined to stay!

To cut a long story short, discussions soon turned to demonstrations. I was required to request each man in turn to spank me. I found it was not unduly painful, but neither did it physically excite me. In fact, I noticed another peculiarity about myself. In these kind of situations I seem to develop an incredibly high pain threshold. No, sorry, that's not quite accurate. I feel the pain, of course. I weep and cry out at it, but I don't somehow have the limits I would have in normal life. I can, and will, endure almost anything I am commanded to. What that first spanking did for me was to create an intense feeling of childish humiliation that ended up bringing me close to orgasm. My responses were more emotional than physical. I found myself seeking their approval and wanting to please. They interspersed the spanking by making me stand or kneel or crouch in various provocative and blatant poses, which I also found very exciting. They would then make me masturbate and lick my fingers one by one. Made me put my wet fingers up my arse, then lick them again. I found myself actually begging them to resume the spanking. Only when I pleaded 'nicely' enough, did they do it.

In fact, it was me who suggested to them that my introduction wouldn't be complete without experiencing the strap and the cane. However, Raymond felt that this was too advanced a step, considering my inexperience. He felt that I would not have the self control required to submit and would need to restrained. Of course, this was another clever trick on his part. Naturally, as soon he said that, I couldn't be denied, and he knew it! I found myself dissolving at the very thought of being helpless and at their mercy. The more they warned me that I wouldn't be shown any mercy, the more idiotically I insisted they should carry on. It was a very bizarre scenario! There was me pleading with them to be tied up and thrashed, while they both warned me in graphic detail of what they intended doing to me!

In actual fact, in comparison with later developments, they were fairly restrained with me. I had to choose who was to apply the strap and who was to wield the cane. I selected Vernon to strap me as my mental picture of Raymond with a cane in his hand had a 'phallic' symbolism all too perfectly understandable to that quaking, hidden rational self.

I wept a great deal. Both men used me sexually; my mouth, my arse, my hands, but never my vagina. They filled my sex organ with their fingers and tongues and various toys. A cucumber even played a part. But they never used their cocks, which further degraded me. Although I was deeply stirred, I didn't climax at all during the whole event.

Raymond drove me home that night, after about four or five hours of play, because by then I was in no state to make my own way. I invited him in for a 'coffee', leaving him in no doubt as to my ulterior motive. He ended up staying the night. He was very gentle, yet very ardent. The sex then was the best I've ever had. In fact, I was the animal, not him. I was insatiable and very noisy. I wanted the world to know how good it was. It's been like that with me ever since. I find that I rarely peak while actually playing games, but am primed for a long orgy immediately afterwards.

After that first session, it was left to me to suggest further meetings. They became quite regular, one or two a week sometimes. I was constantly bruised. They would invite one or two other men along, as well as the occasional submissive girl to join me for punishment. Some three months later, they took me to my first 'punishment party'. There were about twenty men there, as well as two other girls. It was harsh and unremitting, with the men spurring each other on and a new one taking over as soon as one flagged. I found myself being subjected to more pain than I would have imagined it possible to bear. There was also a strange feeling of sisterhood amongst us fellow female sufferers. Without any verbal agreement, we each knew when a girl had momentarily reached her limit and initiated strategies to divert attention. Sometimes we would actually claim her place at the whipping post out of 'jealousy'.

Strangely enough, there wasn't an awful lot of sex going on at these events, except for a lot of cock sucking, which I found degrading, but in an oddly delightful way. The ultimate humiliation was in being raffled, along with the other two girls, to see which man would have us as his bed mate for the rest of the night. I both resented and gloried in that. As it turned out, the man who won me was a useless lover and no help to me in my urgent need. I was still boiling when Raymond came to collect me in the morning. I made him pull off the road at the first opportunity in order to give me the good screwing I so desperately needed by this time. We fucked for an hour in some muddy field before I had calmed down enough to resume the journey home. Once at my place, we went straight to bed and stayed there for the next thirty six hours!

At the end of my years study there was no question of me going home to Holland. I found work in England and continued to see Raymond, but rather less of Vernon. It was an odd relationship, but very satisfying, in it's own way. We never socialised in the ordinary sense. I found my own circle of friends for my normal social life. As he put it, my time with him was strictly cock and cane! Amongst my fellow submissives I developed a taste for lesbian love. Naturally, outside of the disciplinary circle I became chaste. This was done both out of choice and necessity. After all, how would I ever explain to a 'straight' lover all my bruises and scars? In any case, sex without the preliminary stimulus of degradation and pain had lost its saviour. I had proved that to myself when I once persuaded Raymond to come away with me on a weekend trip. Without the element of discipline it proved highly unsatisfactory for both of us. We drove home early on the Sunday morning and never tried that silly experiment again!

As I understand it, I'm not required to give a 'blow by blow' account of my induction into the masochistic world. For this I'm grateful. Any woman who has been so regularly whipped will tell you that the experience becomes a blur. Only the observer differentiates the time, the tool used and the savagery or artistry of the user. For the receiver, there are only two points of reference. Those are the flood and ebb of the pain and the voice of the Master. It may encourage or denigrate, insult or praise, but one listens to that voice with greater attention than to the whine of the descending whip.

What outsiders fail to appreciate is that the submission game, like sex itself, although apparently a bodily function, is in reality a shadow play in the mind. What happens on the skin only serves to supplement what goes on in the psyche. I have discovered that to submit is the greatest liberation of all. Restrained and 'helpless' under the whip, I have a freedom few women ever know. A conventional woman, no matter how excited, either through self interest, love or just courtesy, still considers her lover's feelings. Massage his ego, compliment his technique, admire his physique, wilt under his stamina, praise his virility. All this and yet still maintain an image in his eye that will grace his table.

As a submissive, I have no such obligation. I can be utterly, selfishly absorbed by my own feelings to the exclusion of all else. All I have to do is obey my Master's command and accept whatever he chooses to do to me. Paradoxically, as a masochist, I have no obligation to make an effort to please him. In fact, he is, quite literally, pleasing himself, and me, using my body as the vehicle. For my part, I can simply focus my energies on returning to that pain filled 'sweatiness' that is our common genesis. I can sweat and fart, scream and weep at that most fundamental level that civilisation strives so hard to deny us. There is an incredible primitive pleasure in screaming that has nothing to do with the degree of hurt. It is simply a release of, and from, everything.

For example, I have frequently been made to piss myself, either as a reactive, that is, relinquishing of control due to excessive pain, sometimes even of pleasure, or simply from being kept in restraints for a longer period than my bladder can sustain. Once I even shit myself and was cruelly whipped for it. I carry the scars to this day. But where a 'normal' woman might carry long memories of shame at such ill treatment, my shame is immediate and profoundly satisfying. It's also forgotten the moment my shackles are removed. Nothing that happens to me under duress (however secretly I permit or desire it) is really my responsibility. Basically, from my point of view, he did it and he made me do it! At the price of a little temporary pain, I'm freed of any limit to my most indulgent and primitive desires.

We females are closer to our genetic inceptions than men, both in body and in mind. The process of our monthly bleeding reminds us both of our designated function and our relationship to the animal kingdom. Men try to distance themselves from this. Only men could create a religion that denies sex its pivotal role and asks its priests to remain virginal. The ancient female religions celebrated nature by having its priestess's play the whore and give themselves to worshippers on the temple steps, thus celebrating the gift of sex in congress as close to the altar as they could get. My whippings strip the 'sophistication's' from me. I can't pretend, I can't pose, I can only be... me!

Anyway, back to my story. I was promoted at work, which meant I had to move home. I was overjoyed professionally, but desperately worried about how it would affect my 'secret life'. Raymond simply shrugged his indifference and, a week later, informed me that he had 'transferred' me to a new master in Lincolnshire who would allow him visiting rights. I don't know how to explain the strange gratification I got from the knowledge that I had been disposed of like a slave at an auction!

During the flurry of moving and the resultant hiatus, I had a brief, mad interlude of a marriage to a kind, but straight, man that lasted less than six months. We parted without bitterness. It was a mistake. I still use his name though, which is why I can reveal my maiden name. Anyway, I soon returned to my old ways of sexual servitude as Raymond had decreed. I am still with that master; actually, a duo of masters! Two brothers. Within the restricted confines of rural Lincolnshire I meet both of them quite often, both professionally and socially. By convention, our exchanges have to be limited as they are both married. As I'm still in my thirties and considered very attractive, I am naturally an object of suspicion amongst the local married women. I know there is a rumour going around in local circles that I'm supposed to be gay. I've done nothing to foster this, but neither have I gone out of my way to deny it. I find it takes the pressure off if they can pigeon hole me in some way. However, my looks still ensure that I'm frequently included on invitation lists, so I'm frequently meeting my masters outside of the disciplinary context.

There is a piquancy in maintaining a nice balance of friendliness and formality when out in public with a married man who, perhaps only a day or two before, had me hanging by my ankles while he whipped me between my legs as I sucked his cock. Him refusing to stop beating until I had sucked him dry, and me, if in a playful mood, not sucking hard at all, knowing he preferred my screams to my tongues caress. Or I may give way to the temptation to lightly bite instead of suck, and thus stimulate him to vicious revenge.

The anomalies imposed by this odd mixing of the private and public worlds can produce strains that need tempering by an understanding friendship. I am very fortunate that within a year of moving to Lincolnshire I met someone at a Whipping Party in Nottingham who I recognised as living in the same village as me! We became confidants, friends and then lovers, in a comfortably muted fashion. My friend is also a kind of submissive, but more of an observer than participant, so neither would or could stimulate me in the way

I require. Our bedding is more friendly than fervent, the only kind of lover who not only doesn't object to my bruises and cuts, but is secretly pleased and excited about them. I have to say nice things about Jan. You see, I'm dictating this. It's actually Jan who's doing the writing. Thank you, Jan, darling! No, of course, that's not his real name. It's a joke between us. We share the same name, as we share so much else. It's another way we exclude reality from our private world!

'Submissive: Candid interviews with 20 lifestyle Submissives' on Amazon from Magnolia Books.

'Marquis de Sade: The Man and His Age' Sample: Fashion

Clothing! That can make women seem more desirable by showing just slight hints of charms and arousing the passions of both sexes. That is the rôle which Marquis de Sade had Minister Saint Fond impart to fashion. Saint Fond also recommended to Juliette that she should show herself half naked in the streets to the public if she wanted to remove her last vestige of modesty.

Here, too, de Sade let reality speak. The advice of Saint Fond was actually followed. "On a quiet day of the year V of the Revolution two women paraded up and down the Champs-Elysées, completely nude and covered only with a thin gauze. Many women also showed themselves with wholly base bosoms. The sight was not unusual."

The blaséness was shown in remarkable conceits. Young men and women tried to better nature and borrowed the white hair of age. The de Goncourts excellently describe the incessant changes in fashion in their bizarre fancies, their delicate concealment and unveilment, the gigantic *friseurs* of the women, their "make-up," beauty spots and patches, etc. Fashion paid homage to the age.

The nearer one comes to the time of the Revolution the more does nudity appear in fashion. The style of gauze, the preference for gossamer becomes more apparent. The clothing of the "Goddesses of Reason" becomes ever more transparent. Clothing retreated to the centre to show its opposite semicircles, bosom and legs. Ankle bracelets and golden rings on the toes were the fashion. Terpsichore, in the Greek fashion, reigned in the public gardens. A journalist who attended the opening of the Parisian Tivoli, declared that the goddesses appeared in such light and transparent dress that nothing was left to the imagination. "The women in the audience are dressed as outrageously as possible. The indecency of their behaviour is impossible to describe. In the last great ball in the opera house Madame Tallien appeared garbed only with jewels in the necessary place." These costumes, whose wearers were called *merveilleuses*, had been introduced in Paris by Therese Cabarries, the mistress of Tallien, after she thus publicly showed herself in the Reign of Terror in Bordeaux. The male *merveilleuses* were called *incroyables* and clothed themselves according to the ideal of offensiveness. For during the Revolution the highest ideal was not beauty but power and strength of muscles. Don Juan was changed to Hercules.

The perverse sexual impulses also found expression in fashion. The wide spread paedicatio, also practiced between man and woman, brought the notable fashion of the so-called "Cul de Paris." It spread to such an extent that even the prostitutes delighted in this form of passion, since it was the "style." Under Louis XVI the seat in women's dress was so extended that they resembled "Venus Hottentote."

On the other hand, tribadism was a cause of rather strange costumes. The tribades with male inclinations had remarkably increased during the Reign of Terror. The virago on the streets was a daily incident. Her costume differed little from the man's. Since her hair was cut close and her voice was strident, it took a good look to make sure of the sex.

Bordellos and Secret Pornologic Clubs

Marquis de Sade had made his studies for his two notorious novels *Justine* and *Juliette* in Paris. Here he, himself, experienced and conceived the greater part of the contents. Parisian incidents and experiences had permanently fructified his phantasy. And the models for the descriptions of individuals in his works are easy to discover.

This will be shown in surprising fashion in the discussions of prostitution and sexual life in Paris. Even today Paris justifies the remark of Montesquieu in his *Persian Letters:* "It is the most sensual city in the world where the fanciest pleasures are invented." De Sade's description of the great bordello with its ingenious contrivances and settings refers almost entirely to Parisian bordellos. Most of his heroines are Parisian prostitutes. It is therefore fitting that we should cost consider these conditions.

In Juliette, (I, 87) the Marquis de Sade describes the bordello of Duvergier in a suburb of Paris. This madame had a bordello for both men and women. In a private house, surrounded by a pretty garden, Madame Duvergier had her own cook, delicious wine and charming maidens who received ten lounsdors for a *tête-à-tête.* The house had the requisite back entrance for safeguarding of propriety. The furniture was of the best; the boudoirs most fitting for their purposes. Duvergier, protected by the police, could celebrate more atrocities than her fellow-madames. The bordello supplied princes, nobles, and rich citizens with its wares.

When Juliette organised a house in Paris, six pimpesses (*maquerelles*) were sufficient to provide for girls from Paris and the provinces. Clairwil introduced Juliette, into the house of the "Society of the Friends of Crime," which lay in the heart of Paris but was discreetly concealed. It had splendid drawing-rooms, boudoirs, *cabinets d'aisance* and harems or, as de Sade called them, seraglios in which both sexes disported themselves in wild orgies. The girls were, for the most part, torn from their parents, under the protection of the police. Here the respectable world was assisted by hangmen, jailers, floggers and flagellants (Juliette III, 33 ff.).

Alcide Bonneau believes that the Deer Park served de Sade as a pattern for his descriptions of bordellos. Nonetheless de Sade had made a thorough study of Parisian bordellos and had found many incidents to his liking. He wrote (Juliette I, 333) that in many bordellos in Paris turkey-cocks were much esteemed for lustful purposes in zoophilia. At any rate it cannot be denied that de Sade took his descriptions of Parisian bordellos from actual experiences. Authentic reports will conclusively confirm this.

The most notorious bordellos of Paris, the secret pornologic clubs and the affairs of the prostitutes will be described in later sections.

The most famous, most sought after, most mentioned Parisian bordello in the Eighteenth Century was the House of Madame Gourdan on Rue des Deux Portes; under the reign of Louis XV and Louis XVI it served the court and nobility. This bordello was distinguished by the genteel attempt to satisfy every desire of male and female visitors. A short description of the place is appended.

1. The *"Seraglio."* This was a great salon with *"plastrons de corps-de-garde,"* i.e., twelve prostitutes who had always to be in a position such as to satisfy any whim of the visitor. There the price and details of their pleasure were agreed upon. Even the minute details were stipulated. Pidanzat de Mairobert at this description in *The English Spy* cries out: "Just imagine the horrors and infamies that took place in such a house!"

There is no doubt that de Sade expressed such a great preference for the word "seraglio" from this salon of Madame Gourdan. De Sade also discussed the understandings on the price of love in his novels and was particularly concerned with the analysis of the details for preparing an orgy.

2. The *"Piscine."* This was the bathroom of the bordello, where the girls, fresh from the provinces, were sent to the madame. There they were bathed, powdered and perfumed. Among the many essences and toilet waters was the famous *Eau de Pucelle.* This was a strong astringent with which Madame Gourdan renewed "lost beauties" and restored that "which can be lost only once." Marquis de Sade often mentioned this remarkable miracle which will be discussed later under the section: Cosmetics and Aphrodisiacs. Also in the *piscine* was the *Essence a l'usage des monstres*, which made impotent persons potent again by its strong odour and excited them to passionate cruelty. The specific of Doctor Guilbert de Préval (we shall later say more of this charlatan) was truly a magic charm. For it served at one blow as a prevention, diagnosis and cure of syphilis!

Truly a sexual panacea!

3. The *"Cabinet de Toilette."* Here the students of the Venus-seminar received their second lessons.

4. The *"Salle de Bal."* From this classroom a secret passageway led into the home of a merchant on Rue Saint Sauveur. Through his house the prelates and preachers (*gens à simarre*) as well as respectable ladies could enter the bordello. In this secret room were clothing of all kinds as well as "objects of delicacy." Here the clergy could turn into laymen, officials into soldiers, ladies into cooks. Here the respectable ladies permitted unflinchingly the powerful embraces of a coarse peasant, whom her trusty madame had chosen to satisfy her indomitable temperament. On the other hand the peasant believed her to be one of his own kind and was little embarrassed in expression and action.

5. The *"Infermerie."* This was the room for the impotent. The attendants tried to incite and arouse drooping spirits by all possible means. The light fell from above; on the walls were passionate pictures; in the corners stood similar statues; on the table lay obscene books. In the alcove was a bed of black silk; its top and sides consisted of plate-glass so that it mirrored and reflected all the objects and actions of this pretty boudoir. Perfumed thorny switches served for flagellation. *Dragées-pastilles* in all colours were offered for food; "only one was needed to make one feel like a new man." They were called *Pastilles à la Richelieu* because he had often given them to women as aphrodisiacs. Women were also taken care of in this *Infermerie*. There were present so-called *pommes d'amour*, little balls of stone, to satisfy them. Mairobert could not discover if "the chemists had analysed this stone which had a decided chemical reaction and was often made use of by the Chinese." The *consolateur* was an ingenious instrument "found in convents" as a substitute for a man. Madame Gourdan did a wholesale business with this artificial phallus. In her possession were numberless letters from abbesses and simple nuns asking her to send them a *consoler*. Great, black rings, so-called aides, served the men as artificial irritations in women. Many of these rings were covered with hard studs for increasing

the pleasure. Finally there was a whole arsenal of *redingotes d'Angle-terre*, which are today called condoms, and which, as Mairobert has it, "protect from the virus of love but dull the pleasure." Madame de Sevigné called it "protector of pain and despoiler of pleasure" in one of her letters.

6. *The "Chambre de la Question."* This was a private room in which one could see through a secret peephole all that took place. A contrivance for voyeurs.

7. *The "Salon des Vulcan."* In it was a *fauteuil* of a strange form. The moment one sat in it, one was snuck a heavy blow. The person sank backwards with outstretched legs, which were fastened to the sides. This chair was a discovery of Sire de Fronsac, son of the Duke of Richelieu, and served him as a faithful aid to seduction. The *Salon des Vulcan* was so situated that the crying and wailing could not be heard outside the room. This mechanization of vice will also be found in de Sade's writings.

Gourdan was the leading madame for the respectable world. She could satisfy all desires and was extremely wealthy. In Villiers le Bel she had a private country house in the forest to which she seldom went but often sent her sick and pregnant girls. The villa also served as a useful hiding place for especially delicate debaucheries. It was ironically called by the peasants the convent.

There were two kinds of *madames* in Paris; first, the seducers of virgins, second, purveyors of already deflowered maidens. Only the first were punished by being forced to ride backwards on an ass. Gourdan belonged to the second class and took care that her novices were officially prostituted by one of her assistants. But the head-madames had also to make regular reports of the physical health of their girls.

We shall later give such a report.

In the House of Gourdan the mistresses were educated for the respectable world. The later Countess Du Barry had to thank her resplendent career to her early stay at the bordello of Madame Gourdan. Many aristocrats also sought new pleasures here. A respectable lady, Madame d'Oppy, was discovered in 1776 by the police at Gourdan's where she was officiating as a prostitute.

On November 14, 1773, Madame Gourdan delivered a funeral oration on her deceased colleague, Justine Paris, which was printed in *The English Spy* and is so full of sadism that we append a short summary of it. The idea for this funeral oration was conceived by Prince Conti, one of the most notorious adventurers of the *ancien régime*. It was read at an orgy in Conti's home. The "Funeral Oration of the very proud and very powerful Lady, Madame Justine Paris, Grand Priestess of Cytherea, Paphos, Amathonte, etc., given November 14, 1773, by Madame Gourdan, fellow Priestess, in presence of all the nymphs of Paris" has the characteristic motto:

Syphilis, O my God!
Has put me under the sod!

On their dying-bed Justine's parents preach to her that immorality is the only redemption for the future.

"Don't count the days you haven't consecrated to pleasure!" Justine immediately transposed this advice into action, which one finds on almost every page in the novels of Marquis de Sade, and dedicated herself to the advice of her parents. She then entered a Parisian bordello, where she made great advances in the service of Venus and became famous through an affair with the Turkish ambassador.

Trips to England, Spain and Germany taught her to be phlegmatic with the Englishmen, serious with the Spaniards, and ardent (*emportée*) with the Germans. She finally came to Italy and in Rome was the "Queen of the World and the centre of *Paillardise*." She travelled through all Italy, honoured and coveted by nobles and clergy. Unfortunately she was attacked from time to time by her hereditary syphilis but that did not prevent her at her return to Paris from celebrating new orgies, winning success and great honour as the proprietor of a bordello. She ended in a hospital.

Could this funeral oration have been unknown to Marquis de Sade? It is hardly probable; it is almost certain that Madame Paris was the prototype for Juliette who was celebrated throughout all Italy, in Florence, Rome and Naples as the queen of the world and as the ideal prostitute.

Casanova, the famous confidant, whose historic trustworthiness is attested by Barthold, told in his *Confessions* of a visit in 1750 to the bordello of Paris, the so-called Hôtel du Roule, and presented a living picture of the life and action in a Parisian bordello of the eighteenth century, which may here serve as an addition to the more systematic description of the house of Gourdan.

"The Hôtel du Roule was famous in Paris, but was as yet unknown to me. The proprietress has furnished it elegantly and has from twelve to fourteen splendid girls. One finds there all the desirable comforts: good table, good beds, cleanliness; her cook was excellent, her wine splendid.

"She is called Madame Paris, undoubtedly a pseudonym that pleases all.

"Protected by the police, she was far enough from Paris to be certain that the visitors to her place were persons well above the middle-class.

"The inside was well policed by servants, and all pleasures had a fixed tariff.

"One paid six francs for breakfast with a nymph, twelve for a dinner and double that for a night."

Here we pause for a moment and declare that the above description of Casanova tallies almost word for word with the description of Duvergier's in de Sade's *Juliette*. The house of Duvergier was just like that of Justine Paris.

Casanova died in 1798; his memoirs reaching only to 1773 remained in manuscript form long after his death and were not made public until 1822. *Juliette* appeared early in 1797. The only conclusion to be drawn is that both men have described independently the same bordello. To return to the description of Casanova.

"We enter a fiacre and Zatu says to the driver: 'To Chaillot.'

"After half an hour journey he stops before a gate on which is a sign, Hôtel du Roule.

"The gate was closed. A Swiss with a great beard stepped out from a side-door and seriously sized us up with his eyes. He found us respectable, opened the gate and we walked in.

"A one-eyed woman of about fifty years, but still showing traces of former beauty, greeted us and asked if we would like to dine.

"Upon my assent she led us into a very pretty salon, in which we saw fourteen young maidens who were all pretty and dressed in muslin.

"At our entrance they arose and made a charming bow.

"All were about the same age, some blonde and some brunette.

"Every taste could be satisfied here.

"We spoke a word to all and made our choice.

"The two chosen let loose a joyous cry, embraced us with a passion that was virginal, and we went to the garden expecting that we would be called to dinner.

"This garden was extensive and so arranged that it could serve the joys of love.

"Madame Paris said: 'Go, sirs, and enjoy the fresh air and reassure yourselves; my house is a temple of peace and of health.'

'Marquis de Sade: The Man And His Age, Studies In The History Of The Culture And Morals Of The Eighteenth Century' at Amazon from Magnolia Books.

www.magnolia-books.com